"It is right on the money!! I feel we wer[e]
actors need to know when they walk in

(Princess Brid[e]
Jurassic Park, Ferris Beuller

"Peter Skagen's book is as blunt as I am! I loved it! Tells the truth about what
its like to get through the process in this biz we call show. So many actors walk
into this blank canvas and have to learn as they go and make some mistakes
that follow them throughout their career. Reading this book, you can walk on
your first set as a pro already knowing whose who, all the jargon, the curtsies,
the dos and don'ts, so you can look and act like you were born to be there. I
applaud Peter for such honesty about this very tough business."

Dori Zuckerman, CSA

"No one else could have written this book this way. It's hilarious. It's
unapologetic. It hits the actor with every tool they'll ever need so I don't have
to. I call it: How to be brilliant in the audition room, and get the gig, then be
brilliant on set and get the award hardware."

Deb Green, CSA (*Brokeback Mountain*)

"A terrific book and a must-read for actors. This is one of the most informative
and entertaining books I've read! I love it!"

Paul Weber CSA, Casting Director,
Producer, former head of casting of MGM Television Casting

"Peter Skagen has a wealth of knowledge because he is out there in the
trenches with his readers. A working actor makes the greatest teacher of all!"

Amy Lyndon, The Lyndon Technique, #1 Booking Coach in Los Angeles

"This makes SO much sense!!"

Michael Lavine, Broadway Vocal Coach and Sheet Music Expert

"Peter Skagen's book is a winner on so many levels, and should be required
reading for any student of acting."

Dr. Reid Spencer – Mount Royal University

"If you want to work in the movies as an actor, get a copy of this book right now! Even if you are just curious about how things work in the industry, you should read this book! You can avoid a lot of missteps and be ready when opportunity knocks using the information author Peter Skagen has shared. This is required reading."

Professor Ann Holt, Carnegie Mellon University

"Five stars. Indispensable advice for the screen actor with great insight for writers and those interested in a behind-the-scenes look at the film industry. Skagen's frank, no BS, approach keeps the pages turning and makes it a fun, fast-paced read about the realities of show business."

Diana Belchase - Indie book blogger

"A straightforward, no-nonsense approach to the industry and the techniques an actor needs to succeed."

Caitlin Bauer - Independent Reviewer

"It is one of the best books in this genre."

Poonam Kohli – Independent Reviewer

"What you have here is a lot of real world advice and not some theoretical thought piece."

Wildman Keith, Reviewer - Vine Voice

"A must-read for aspiring actors. I was fascinated."

Tony Riches, UK Book Blogger

"A masterfully crafted work, which simultaneously instructs and provides catalytic inspiration to readers as it divulges an expertly advised road map to a flourishing acting career.... should be considered the actor's bible because of the entirely thorough information that it provides."

Lisa Brown-Gilbert - Literary Reviewer

SCREEN ACTING TRADE SECRETS

SCREEN ACTING TRADE SECRETS

How to Succeed in Hollywood
Without Really Acting

PETER SKAGEN

Poubelle
Publishing

Published by:
Poubelle Publishing
#363 7620 Elbow Drive SW
Calgary, Alberta
Canada
T2V1K2

Visit our website at: www.peterskagen.com

Second Edition
ISBN: 978-0-9937657-3-5
Canadian Copyright Registration Number: 1112257

Cover and book design by Damonza.com
Printed in Canada

As always, for my darling daughter.
You are a constant inspiration.

Untold thanks to Mrs. Noonan, Kathy Stacy, Sidney Salkow, Dr. Ants Leps, Kim Buteau, Faye Racine, Marisa Mori, Jean Becq, Peter Strand Rumpel, Kim Rondeau, Christopher Heatherington, Raymond Massey, Anthony Dutton, Doug MacArthur, Larry Reese, Jane Jenkins, Paul Weber, Dori Zuckerman, Amy Lyndon, Andy Henry, Amy Macnow, Aadila Dosani, Caralee Hubbell, Kimberly Clackson, the great William Goldman, all my students, and the generous people who supported my campaign to write and publish this book.

Special thanks to my publishing and marketing team: Deb Green, Carrie White-Parrish, Dr. Reid Spencer for his edit and sage content advice, Dr. Duncan Koerber for his meticulous final edit, Edward Ian Cibula for his editorial and proofing work, and Benjamin Carancho and Damon Freeman for the book design, and cover.

CONTENTS

PREFACE

I have seen actors by the hundreds with chops and little else sweat bullets waiting to audition. They come in, turn into a puddle of goo on the floor and burst into tears the minute they leave the audition room. And they can't understand it. It makes no sense. "What happened to my confidence? My skill? I was top of my class! Hell, I was off-book!! What went wrong?"

So they sit outside and kick themselves because they "needed that part." They work themselves into a frenzy of anxiety, fretting about lines and motivation and breathing. Then the clouds part and it's a short leap to "oh my god what if I got the part? What then? What happens next? What if I'm in a scene with the star?! What if I mess up on set!! What was I thinking? I'm so out of my depth!!" At which point, they turn blue and pass out.

They forget why they are there, they lose the story, they make it about themselves and they can't recover. They don't have the practical tools, what to expect, how to get from A to B. Along comes the little man with the broom and into the bin they go. And thus starts their long, hard, self-imposed torture trying to be an actor.

If only there was a book out there that spelled it ALL out in equal, simple, measured doses. A step-by-step playbook that demystifies it all so they could understand what they're doing and get the success they deserve. So they'd never suck again.

This is that book. You can read it or you can turn blue and end up in the bin.

Deb Green, CDC, CSA *Casting Director*

INTRODUCTION

If you really want to be a screen actor, I can save you five years of your life.

That's the amount of time the average screen actor wastes trying to learn what the heck is really going on in *the business*, get some experience, and have a shot at success. I see it all the time. I wasted at least that many years myself.

This book is my revenge.

All the trade secrets are in here if you will only pay attention. Everything you need to know, from the moment you are called to be an actor, to the end of your first day on a movie set, awaits you. Plus, I made it funny (but substantive) and easy to read.

So, now I want to make a deal with you. Here's the deal: you pay attention and work hard, and I'll get you on your first movie set as an actor. And then you take it from there. Deal?

Second part of the deal: at the end of your first day, email me your story. I want to read it, and share it with other actors. Deal?

Say "Deal."

You can contact me and learn even more here: www.peterskagen.com.

Okay. Here's the first trade secret: talent is only about 10% of the equation. And, whatever you have, you have. Everybody hopes you have a lot, of course, but I can't teach it to you. What I can teach you is the other 90% of the job that only working actors know: the trade secrets that give them the advantage over the competition.

For example: the sixteen strategies actors usually use to break in;

the ten things *they* are looking for (*they*: producers, directors, agents, studios, etc.); the qualities that make an actor inevitable; how to give yourself a screen test to know what you are really selling as an actor; how to package and promote yourself in the 21st century; how to *get* story and screenwriting, and know when you're reading something great; how to learn lines and scenes like the pros; how to control your nerves; how to audition like the top 1% of actors; how to handle yourself around stars; how to hit your marks and thrive on set; and how to avoid all the major mistakes on your way to becoming a BFS (Big Fat Star).

Does this mean you get to skip *paying your dues* (working your way up like everybody else)? Nope. But it does mean you get to pay those dues a heck of a lot faster (in the neighborhood of five years) while knowing what is happening as it is happening. Sound good?

This second edition has a more search-friendly title, and a cool new look. Plus, I updated the book and added a new appendix: 50 Stupid Stunts on Set.

I am not a BFS. I am not Johnny Depp. People will disagree with me on some points. But if you check out the reviews, you'll see a lot of bigwigs in the biz think this book is the bomb, for which I am very grateful. I'm very experienced and informed, I'm a good teacher, and although I can be a little grumpy sometimes, I actually care about your success. Not to mention Johnny Depp is probably not going to write a how-to book anytime soon.

So, warm up your latte, and let's get started.

YOUR FIRST DAY

Whoever is born of sound mind has been naturally intended by Heaven for honest work and some kind of life. Whoever, therefore, wishes Heaven to be nice to him, will go after this work and this kind of life, and doggedly pursue it. For Heaven favors things it has itself begun. You were made by Nature for this purpose beyond anything else. What you do from your tender years on, what you talk about, mold, fit, dream, imitate, what you try very often, what you can do easily, what you are most of all good at, what you love beyond all else, what you would be unwilling to leave—this is clearly what Heaven, and the Rector of Heaven bore for you. To this extent therefore, Heaven will favor your beginnings, and will smile on your life.

—Marcilio Ficino, physician, *The Book of Life*, 1485

For the moment, think of me as Google Maps. And Merlin.

What I am going to do in this section is give you a view of screen acting from 30,000 feet. You'll be able to see everything at once, how it all relates, zoom in on certain subjects, then back out again, just like you do before you go to Disneyland. You want to see where it is, what it's like, what rides you can take, who else is there, where to stay, and where to park—or if you want to go at all.

This is incredibly important research especially when it comes to your career. So many people jump into something with no idea what it's *really* like. They buy into the hype and the hearsay. When they finally arrive, there can be heartbreak and wasted time. You will not be one of those people. You will look it over from above, zoom in, look around, zoom back out, think it over, and get a feel for it. All the while, the

Merlin side of me will be sitting on your shoulder whispering the truth in your ear.

This helps everybody. If you discover screen acting is not for you, then you can move on quickly and with a happy heart to your real vocation. All you will have lost is the price of this book. (I hope you will have also learned a thing or two about yourself and about life.)

If screen acting is your calling, then you will have a map of the terrain and a feel for how to navigate it. While everyone else is wandering around aimlessly, you'll slip in the side door, say the right things to the right people, and jump on the ride. That's the goal. If everyone were like you, then the whole process would be easier for everybody.

You are about to see what the hell *they* are really looking for. And then you are going to learn a thing or two about story.

You see, story is the real reason people go to movies and Hollywood exists. It is the foundation of everything in the business, including acting. Your job is to interpret the story, and to sell it to the audience. How can you possibly do that without knowing what story is? It constantly amazes me that actors think they can get along without understanding it. That's like a mechanic who doesn't know how cars work or what they do. It's just stupid.

I have purposefully made the screenwriting section tasty and digestible so you have no excuse. If you really want to succeed, then study story and writing as much as you study acting.

Absent will be the detailed information on how to move to LA, where to live, which classes to take, how to get headshots and work visas and so on. Stacks of other books explain these subjects. Pick them up *after* you read this book. Trust me.

Okay. If you're ready, then let's begin.

Your First Morning

It can happen anywhere of course, but it usually seems to happen in bed.

In the twilight of sleep a voice says, "Hey! You're an actor. You are of noble birth, a special breed, a member of the favored race of players meant to hold up the mirror to life."

Or something like that.

First advice: Do not panic. You are not alone; it has happened to all of us following this same journey. It's frightening. It's exciting.

Here's what you need do:

Nothing.

For a while, do nothing. Don't tell anyone. Just sit with it. Let it soak in. See how you feel about it, not what you think about it. If you've truly fallen in love, then you'll just know. And these first moments of deep knowing, inspiration, and acceptance will carry you for the rest of your career. Savor them. Protect them. Many stars recount these earliest memories in their Oscar speeches. Hold onto them. Let your heart grow four sizes. You're going to need the strength and resolve. You're about to take a hero's journey into the unknown where you will endure a road of trials to be reborn. Everything you do from here on stems from these first moments of inspiration.

Every hero needs a mentor. I'll give you your special weapons and illuminate the terrain of your quest. I can be cranky and curt, but I care.

Now, put this book down until you feel yourself ready to start your journey.

I mean it.

Put it down.

Your heart must be resolved.

I'll wait.

Okay, I'll explain.

Have you ever seen a title fight in the 12th round? It's not about boxing anymore. It's about heart. Heart is more than wanting to win. It's sacred resolve, courage, determination, faith, and a very particular kind of nobility. It lives in the breast. It says: "This is who I am, and you are not going to stop me from being it. Even if you punch my lights out today, I'll be back on my feet tomorrow, and no one is going to stop me. Period."

Heart makes a champion. That's what I want from you, the actor.

Even though it looks glamorous and easy, acting on screen is like every other job worth doing: it's a lot of work. Acting on screen might even be more work than prize fighting. God knows many more people are fighting for the Hollywood prize. We actors probably need a knuckle sandwich every time we falter, like a boxer does. We'd find out our level of commitment pretty darn fast, and those who stayed in the ring would belong there, and they'd probably be a hell of a lot more interesting to watch. Without the heart for it, you'll either peter out and waste everyone's time, or you'll get beat by the next guy who loves it more. Committing to it completely—because it's you—gives you an aura of inevitability, which compels others to open doors for you and get out of the way. Commitment makes you much more creative and resourceful about your plan of attack. It makes you work. It makes you enormously compelling to watch and be around because your own personal stakes are so high. And it keeps you on course through the constant left hooks and the odd knife in the back.

Do you absolutely need the heart of an actor to make it? As I will say often in this book, there is truth in everything. In other words, maybe not. Plenty of people work with only a half-committed heart, or less. Others seem to think acting prepares them for a career in politics. In any field, many people move into another field, or they become motivated by desires other than the pure love of the doing. This is life. I just don't wish this for you. Moreover, anything less than full commitment will seriously reduce your odds of success.

Commitment means you would continue to do it no matter what. If you were making $400 a week working in the world's least-known theater, then you would still do it, just to do it. You study all the time, you read plays, you work on accents, and you do scenes in the shower. You love it. You become an expert. You study the art and craft and history of acting, you think about it and dream about it, you read up on filmmaking and storytelling, and you're always in class looking for ways to get better to become an artist and a contender. What consumes you is finding out how good you can be not how famous you can be.

If you want to be famous, then live in a bathtub in Times Square for a month. You'll be famous. If you want to be an actor, then love the work. Soon, you'll have a career. Then one day you might wake up and discover that you are famous—the way it happens for most stars—and you'll have to deal with that. You'll probably be slightly dumbfounded, rather pleased that your work has been validated by your peers, and then fairly miffed that all the interviews are getting in the way of your work.

Which you love.

Get it?

Hopefully so.

Which leads you to the next logical question: "Am I a theater actor, or a film actor?"

Film vs. Theater Acting

This topic seems to rankle many people. They argue that acting is acting is acting. And it is true to a certain extent, just like guitar playing is guitar playing is guitar playing. What they often seem to miss is the different styles and techniques of playing the guitar. You can thrash on it or you can play Schubert. Both are guitar playing. But ask the thrasher to play the Schubert. What do you get?

You get crap.

Because he doesn't know the music and he doesn't know the technique, and probably because he also doesn't *get* Schubert. So guitar playing isn't exactly guitar playing after all.

The same goes for playing your own instrument—you—on stage and for the camera. Yes, both theater and film tell stories, entertain, and share the experience of life, but they do so in different ways and different forms, and these forms require the use of different acting techniques just like the two kinds of guitar playing.

Rather than generating an exhaustive list of the different techniques, let me offer you this example related to the subject of this book: film acting.

Suppose I am making a movie and I want a shot of lovers fighting. The best thing I can do is hide a camera across the street, use a telephoto lens, and shoot a real couple fighting through an apartment window. Thus, like voyeurs, the audience peeks in on a real-life drama from up close.

This is the thrill of the movies.

Never forget it.

All of film acting is based on this principal idea.

But if I want the couple to pause for a moment while I load more film or to move the fight into the bedroom, then I have a problem. I have to knock on the door and say: "Hi. Just making a movie here. Shooting you secretly. Would you mind awfully fighting in the bedroom for a bit? Makes it more exciting, and we get a better view."

First of all, I'd probably get a punch in the nose. But supposing the couple wanted to play along, what's going to happen?

They'll start 'acting.'

They'll fight for my benefit. They'll try to fight properly and look good while doing it. Or they'll get nervous and shrink away from exposing themselves.

The audience is no longer secretly looking in at a real-life drama. Now they're watching people pretend and pretend vainly. Because it's in a close-up, the audience can clearly see them faking it.

End of the reality. End of the fun. End of movie. End of career.

So, now what?

Well, obviously I can't use *real* people anymore. Now I have to hire *film actors*. These people are willing and able to fight for the benefit of the camera *as if the camera wasn't there*, but they can also deal with the vast technical demands of filmmaking, like stopping for a few minutes while film is loaded.

Get it?

This not-knowing-the-camera-is-there business, this ability to be *unwatched*, is the key skill of the film actor. It is the ability to make the real world disappear in favor of the story world while accommodating the impossible demands of the camera. Which you don't know is there. But which is watching you from six inches away. But which you don't know is there.

But which needs you to hit your mark.

So while most of your mind is on the job of fighting with your lover, there lurks the tiniest thread of awareness of the mark you have to hit.

Plus the following:

There will be a lot of starting and stopping; shooting bits and pieces; shooting the same thing over and over again; you may have to do the last part first and the first part last; it's going to take days or months; there will be no audience and no applause; there will be enormous pressure; there will be no rehearsals; it will be dangerous, and improvisational, but at the same time it will have to be carefully prepared; it will also be boring; you will have to do parts of the scene all by yourself; you will have to accommodate a director and editor, not to mention an entire crew; you will have to let the audience look into your eyes to see your soul, your weakness, your humanity; you will need tremendous courage; you will need tremendous faith; and you will need tremendous self-acceptance. You will need to *be* rather than to *act*. To live rather than to perform. To confess your intimate life to the world from every angle.

If all this excites you and feels right, then odds are good you're a film actor.

If, on the other hand, you revere text, Shakespeare, rehearsals, the cast as family, working closely with a director, tradition, projecting, the theater environment, the audience, applause, the pressure of live performance, the challenge of eight shows a week, the security of a long run, the pleasure of exploring a single character for months or years, *notes* from the stage manager, the opportunity to refine your performance from night to night, the joy of falling deeply into a character and story and staying there until the curtain comes down, the thrill of being back stage, brief romances, constant post-show celebrations, and the chance to do it all again, then odds are good you're a theater actor.

Of course, you can do both. Many fine actors do. I am thinking now of Christopher Plummer who has won Tony Awards (*Cyrano* and *Barrymore*), and an Oscar (*Beginners*). But in my experience, most actors are attracted strongly to one or the other, and the two groups tend to go their separate ways. If you do happen to find them in the same saloon somewhere, then those laughing and gabbing in the center of the room will be the theater actors, and the guy slumped over a Jack and Coke at the end of the bar will be the film actor.

(Let that be a warning to you.)

I think I can help you no matter which way you incline as long as you remember everything counts.

Everything Counts

Your first lesson is simple to say and often difficult to do. If you intend to accomplish your quest, then you must wake up, hold your intent out front, and pay attention to everything because *everything counts* from this day forth. One wrong step can send you careening down a mountainside. The purpose of a quest is to focus your energies. Do this by reminding yourself that everything counts.

Example: I was producing a big interactive theater event that was billed as the greatest love story ever told at a barn dance. About 20 actors were planted in the audience, which was divided into feuding families. Once a year—so the story goes—the two families are forced together at the dance, and there's always trouble. The dance saw singing and dancing, contests, a beauty pageant, gunfights, a huge feast, a country music star, and of course, somewhere along the way Rodeo Hatfield fell in love with Julie-Edwina McCoy. It was great fun watching the audience become Hatfields and McCoys, get really involved in the feud, and try to influence the outcome of the story. Even though it was fluffy dinner theater, I felt we gave something valuable to the audience. Namely: a heck of a good time. That's a job that I take seriously.

One night, my star, my Rodeo, called in saying he wasn't sick but felt like he might get the flu, and he didn't want to do the show that night. We couldn't afford to have understudies. Hmm. I told him fine, stay home and be well. While I certainly don't want anyone to get sick, several of my cast members were already sick with the flu, but like all *showbiz* folks they were coming in to do the show. I switched around all the people in the cast to cover for our star. One role simply didn't get played that night. The show came off, barely, and the audience had a good time. The next day I released the leading man from the show. Not only had he offended me, let down his cast mates, and disrespected the theater, but he had *threatened my audience*. Strike one, two, three and you're out.

Then it got worse for him. As it happens, a film agent attended the show on the night he stayed home, signing up new talent from the ranks of the cast. He missed out. We can only imagine what else he missed: small film roles, a larger role, a TV series, a movie career.

An entire wedge of his career pie vanished that night because everything counts.

Even today, if another producer mentions he might want to hire that actor and asks my opinion, then I tell what I know. I am not going to lie. As a result of staying home (not to mention the negative words spread by his cast mates), another huge pie-wedge is probably gone. You don't have to make too many mistakes to obliterate your whole pie.

Even those little things you don't think count actually do count. The fellow actor in one of your classes today may be your director tomorrow. Everyone is only a few degrees of separation away from

Kevin Bacon or someone else who can help or hurt your career. If you are a serious film actor, then it is entirely possible that one of these days virtually everyone in the world will know you. As an actor, all you have to promote and sell is yourself, so you have to manage your image—your brand—the same way a major corporation does. You have to be on it 24 hours a day and 7 days a week. If all goes well, then that's just what you'll be: a major movie corporation.

Start now by knowing it's not just about your talent.

Everything counts!

And now, foolproof instructions on how to break into Hollywood.

How to Break Into Hollywood

The failed actor told the young starlet he could have made it big too, except when he was young and coming up his mother was sick, so he had to take care of her.

The starlet replied, "When I was coming up, my mother was sick too."

"Oh," he said, "How did you make it, then?"

"I let her die."

—A Hollywood joke

I'm not suggesting you let your mother die. The joke should remind you that making it in film acting requires sacrifice. It requires *breaking in*. You're not going to just stroll in the front door and amble out again with the princess and all the loot. Nobody is going to open every door for you. No matter who you are, you're going to have to kick some doors down, sneak through the cracks, or tunnel under the walls.

You're going to need to start thinking like Danny Ocean. It'll be tough. Dangerous. It'll take time. You'll need info, a team, and a clever plan timed down to the second. Danny would tell you that this is half the fun.

The Bank of Hollywood is no different than a giant steel vault. You've got to start thinking like a safe cracker, because success in the *biz* is like cracking the greatest bank vault in the world. All kinds of amazing stuff sits in there: money, power, fame, cars, parties, oysters, the world, and a few other things.

Needless to say, the people in there at the moment are pretty happy without you; it means more stuff for *them* (the movie elite). Since *they* have all this money and power and stuff, *they* want to protect it, and *they* are capable of adding to the thickness of the virtual wall surrounding the place.

You would too.

So this vault is much more formidable than any bank because the people inside are actively planning against you, the walls are invisible, the rules keep changing, and the whole thing skulks around like something out of a *Predator* movie.

You want in. Fine. Move to LA. Good luck. Maybe you'll be on the cover of *Premiere* magazine next month, and there goes all my savvy pontificating.

But probably not. Really. You are better off buying a lotto ticket.

In the Golden Age of Hollywood, some mogul might pick you out of a crowd and say, "Baby, I'm gonna make you a star." And he would. Because he could.

Doesn't work that way anymore. Now stars make themselves, and the moguls sit around—in the vault—waiting for stars to break in. Then there's a kind of mogul feeding frenzy as *they* all grapple over the young star's profit potential.

This still leaves you, the hopeful star, with the original problem. How do you get in there in the first place?

Well, obviously, you have to assess the problem, inventory your resources, and draw up a plan. Yours will be different from anyone else's. You must understand this, accept this, embrace this, and commit to it totally. No one can really help you. Sure, we can give you some advice, but it will either be generic ("You need a plan.") or personal ("Get a boob job.") or hearsay ("I heard they're looking for Canadians!") none of which is terribly helpful. In fact, it could send you off on a five-year goose chase trying to get implants in Montreal. Do not do this. You are following someone else's (possibly false) ideas. *You have to follow your plan.* Only you know your surroundings, your determination, your assets, your talent, and the contents of your soul. It's frightening, but it is the only way to success. Be your own man, woman, or child. Captain your own ship.

Start with education. Captaining your own ship does not mean being stubborn and bull-headed. It means taking counsel first so you don't wreck on an iceberg. Read everything (especially biographies). Ask a lot of questions. Go case out the joint. Find people who've been there. Get a schematic of the vault. Your most valuable skill at this point is finding out what you need to find out. The most successful people in the world are geniuses in this department. They recognize where they have gaps in their knowledge, and they find out how to fill them in. This is not as easy as it sounds.

Next, catalog your assets and liabilities: "I'm lovely and talented and want it more than anything, but I live in Podunk, Illinois, I have no money, and Dad is a jerk." Your list should be considerably more detailed. Be cool-headed when you do this, Danny. Emotions can get you caught.

Now draw up a plan. Here, you must be a creative problem-solver extraordinaire: "I need to get out of Podunk." You could just slip out the back, Jack, and hop a freight to LA. Might be perfect for you. But probably not. Los Angeles is not the place for novices without any background or knowledge or employability. More likely, the best solution would be something like getting yourself cast in a play in Chicago. You want to be an actor, right? Bingo: you are out of Podunk, you are working, you are making money, you are creating a profile for yourself, and you are a big step closer to the vault.

Next, work the plan. That is, go to www.backstage.com and see who's casting in Chicago. Find a way to submit yourself and find a way to get to the audition, and so on. You will back up a lot and make new plans a lot. For example, to submit yourself to the theater company, you need a professional headshot (see Headshots on page 69), but maybe you can't afford to get one. This new problem must be solved first. Or does it? Maybe you can talk *them* into accepting you without one. Maybe you can get your sister to do one for you. Maybe you can trade a photographer an hour of gardening for a headshot. Who knows? Only you can figure this out. The more clever you are in your creative problem solving, the faster you will move forward. Excuses are not permitted.

I can almost hear you saying, "But how do I solve problems when I don't know what the problems are? I don't know how it all works. I don't know what I'm doing." So at this point, I'm going to repeat what

I just said: it's different for everyone. More than anything, even before you take an acting class, apply yourself most strenuously to finding out what you need to find out. Reading this book is a brilliant start. Find people who are doing what you want to do. Be assertive. Ask questions. Get informed. Solve problems in a way that works best for you. Become an expert in this process. Keep going. This one skill—creative problem solving—combined with endless determination will almost certainly lead to success, whereas all the acting classes on the planet have led to failure countless times.

Realize that *you will never run out of problems.* When you are a BFS (Big Fat Star) your problems will be similarly big and fat. It never ends. Most people think that to be a star is to be trouble free. That is a load of crap. To be a star is to have planetary problems that require cosmic creative problem solving.

Here you go complaining again, "I'll have people for that."

No, you won't.

You will have functionaries, as in agents, and managers, publicists, and yoga teachers who will give you advice and then do what you ask of them because you are the president, CEO, and product of a global enterprise called International You. You are the boss. You created the product that everyone wants: you. When you are a BFS, most of your time will be spent creatively solving the huge problem of remaining a BFS. Every now and then, you will get to go do a movie. You must embrace this, love it, and get good at it right now.

Back to the example plan: once you get the job in Chicago, take your first day off from the play to start all over again evaluating your new assets and liabilities and coolly developing a new plan.

Continue until famous.

Continue until no longer famous.

Continue until no one recognizes you anymore.

Relax.

Okay, I'll give you an example.

If you're going to rob a bank vault, then it's always a good idea to case the joint. Go see what you're up against. Forget the books and diagrams; go check the place out for yourself. The Hero doesn't usually get to check out the end of his quest before he starts, so consider yourself lucky.

You live in Podunk, but maybe you know somebody in LA. Call the person. Find out where to stay and how to get started. Call five other people. Actually, get a Skype account and spend a day calling everyone. Get referrals from one to another. Ask about classes, coaches, agents, managers, headshot photographers, demo reel producers, schools, apartments, SAG, rental cars, etc. Ask a lot of dumb questions; they will get smarter as you go along. Get online and do the same. Chart out a three-week scouting trip. Fly in. Pick up your car. Settle into the place you booked on www.airbnb.com or www.vrbo.com.

Once you're settled, book and attend a career counseling session with one of the top coaches. Then book three more. Compare notes. Most coaches will let you audit their classes (sit in the back and watch to see if you like it). Audit dozens of classes. See what you're up against, what's current, how it all works, and who is who. Take a few short workshops from the coaches you like to see how you stack up against the competition. Get notes from the coach. Take a workshop from a casting director. See what she thinks.

Network your butt off. Make friends with other actors, invite them out to lunch and then casually ask them to tell you everything they know. Assess your *marketability* and your *brand* (which you will learn about shortly). Start putting together your *package* (which you will learn about a little less shortly). Get your *headshots* done by a top LA photographer who knows what she's doing, and then get a *demo reel* done by a service that knows what it's doing. Build a website for yourself. Meet with agents and managers if you can.

Realize that you can do all of this right away—no need to wait—provided you are old enough, and have all the necessary assets and personal abilities. By doing this, you are starting your LA career. People in LA have long memories, which can work for you or against you. Everything counts, remember? You've got to be grounded, and capable, and mature, and likeable, and assertive, and impartial, and driven, and know the difference between bullfrogs and bullshit. (And keep this book under your pillow.)

If you can handle it, then this can be a very profitable plan.

Bono and the guys from the band U2 decided to be a band before they could even play instruments. Have confidence. Learn the biz. Case the joint. Get a look at it first-hand. Come back to Podunk armed with inside knowledge and the start of a professional promo package. This work will give you a big advantage over all the other local actors, and it will guide you as you take classes, grow your resume, prove your employability, polish your talent, build your technique, and make your way back to LA for good.

Yet another warning: this is an example. It's not for everyone. Don't go running off to LA saying Peter said so. I'm giving you ideas, not directives. Your plan must be *your* plan.

The advanced plan: The Lion Approach. You watched Discovery Channel and saw the lions on the hunt. Somehow, they just know when it's time. They move out together, every action perfect, harmonious, contextual, beautiful and somehow inevitable because they are completely alive in the moment. They have no desire to be a star and no thought of yesterday or tomorrow. They are nothing but vision and will, intimate with now. They survey the herd without passion and without fear—they only see and intend. Their scope is totality. They react second by second to what *is*, as their instinct merges with intent and environment. It's all one big happening. Perfection.

In sports, this is called being in the *zone*. You've seen tennis players make the most incredible shots look easy. That's because when you're in the zone, it is easy.

If you can be in the zone while navigating your career, then you will be near invincible. Again, this is not as easy as it sounds. It might take you a lifetime to work out. Or you might open your eyes and do it instantly. Either way, the truth will set you free. Just see, react, and *intend*. So-called reality will bend in your direction, and you will find yourself pulled as if in a tractor beam toward your goal, provided it is right for you. Alternately, you might find yourself dropping like a stone toward a different, perhaps better, goal. You won't mind this, because you are detached from outcomes. You are *now*.

This works every time for the lion because he is a lion, not a lion who wants to be a crocodile one day. Not a lion who wants you to see how lion-like he is. Not a lion who needs your love and attention. Not a lion who wants to be famous.

If you are the real thing and right in the zone, then people will nod and doors will open whenever you and your mane approach. Your overall progress will be rapid as long as, like the lion, you never stop to admire yourself or your work. Like the tennis player, you let go of the perfect shot and go on to the next one. Egoless.

The big secret of The Lion Approach: this is also *precisely* what it takes to be a great actor. You've heard it in all your classes and read it in your books. Be present. Listen and react. Get what you want. Know your motivation. Don't think; do. The great actors are just like the lions and tennis players. They do *now* extremely well. This means you'll have to give up your desire to be seen and loved. This is the paradox that all actors face and that the good ones overcome.

A Few Tried and True Safecracking Strategies

Whether you go with the Danny Ocean plan or the Lion Approach, a few tried and true general safecracking strategies have worked in the past. One or more of these might help you somewhere along the line. They are based on what everyone in the vault wants more of, The Four Ignoble Desires: Money, Power, Sex, and Fame.

- 1. **Already be in the vault**. Works every time. It works especially well for people named Fonda, Hanks, Douglas, Spelling, Coppola, and Baldwin. If your dad is George Lucas, then you can go ahead and put this book down. Your only problem is finding a way not to get kicked out.
- 2. **Sleep with somebody in the vault (a corollary to number one)**. At some point, the person might feel obliged to invite you inside and, even better, the person might feel that you help his or her status level somehow. Unfortunately for you, this is the oldest trick in the book, and nobody inside is going to take you very seriously. You'll probably be labeled a groupie hanger-on, and groupie hangers-on are not stars and never will be. Thus, this strategy leads to an even bigger problem than before. Also, getting a peek at the truth of what's inside the vault can be a bad idea at this point. Better to be deluded and starry-eyed. It's more motivating.
- 3. **Be famous for something else**. Everybody loves famous people, especially famous people. *They* might get to sleep with *them*. Get it? Good examples of people who got in this way are Arnold Schwarzenegger (bodybuilding), Duane Johnson (wrestling), and Jessica Simpson (music).

- 4. **Write your way in**. Writers are the only creative artists in Hollywood. Everyone else waits around for a script to *interpret* on film. If you have a truly original and well-crafted piece of material, then people will talk to you. Realize that there are many people trying this. But it does work. Examples: Stallone, Spike Lee, Matt and Ben, Vin Diesel, Nia Vardalos, Tina Fey, and any number of producers and directors. Writing your way in will also educate you about the business of storytelling, the one thing most other actors seem to know nothing about. To the filmmakers, not to mention the audience, it's all about the story. Even stars can't save a crappy script. If you can help tell that story, then you'll always be welcome on set and on screen. If you're outside the vault, but smart, driven, and not so funny, then this might be your best way in.

- 5. **Be truly funny.** No doubt the funny people have the highest fame rate in world. Everybody loves them and makes money off them. Jim Carrey, Mike Myers, Steve Martin, Steve Carell, Robin Williams, Chris Rock, Jennifer Aniston, Ricky Gervais, Tina Fey, Will Farrell, Rosie O'Donnell, and Ellen Degeneres. Most of these people are also writers, having come up through stand-up or sketch comedy. That's a double whammy of vault-breaking power.

- 6. **Have a unique skill or attribute.** If you are Jackie Chan or Jet Li, then you have a good shot at movie acting not only because you have the unique skill, but also because you can dropkick anyone who gets in your way. Elvis was not known to be a stellar actor, but he could sing like hell and had the it factor. Thirty-one movies. If you are the modern Bruce Lee, or Fred Astaire, then you have an edge. Start working it. Being tiny like Vern Troyer (Mini Me) isn't exactly a skill, but it is a unique attribute that works wonders in the casting department. Other examples: Andre the Giant, Schwarzenegger's muscles, Angelina's lips. Dot-Marie Jones recently scored a recurring role on the TV show *Glee* as a coach. Dot-Marie can sing. She's also 6-foot-4 and a 15-time world arm wrestling champion. That's what I call a combo pack of unique skills and attributes. Being unbearably, stunningly beautiful probably falls in this category too, but I think it deserves its own number.

- 7. **Be 17 years old and unbearably, stunningly beautiful (if female) or about 20 years old and handsome (if male)**. Oh yes, and have raw talent. This works a lot. In fact, this is probably the paradigm of fame. See Keira Knightley (17 in the first *Pirates*), Jodi Foster (about 14 when she did Taxi Driver), Natalie Portman (13 when she did *The Professional*), Tom Cruise (21 in *Risky Business*), Ewan McGregor (about 20 when he got his first gig), and Colin Ferrell (same). Everybody loves to look at young, beautiful people. Most of the movie characters we are interested in are similarly young and beautiful: they are young vampires in love, or young Jedis, or young superheroes discovering their power. But people are not young and beautiful long, so Hollywood is always looking for the next crop. You have to get on it while you have it. The good news (as if early fame and fortune were not enough) is that if you play your cards right, actually have some talent, and earn a following, then you might be able to extend your career beyond your youth and into the mature star category.

- 8. **Go to school in LA**. Then make friends with as many potential BFSs, producers, directors, agents, publicists and receptionists as you can. You'll all come up together. Not knowing who's going to be the famous/powerful one, you'll suck up to everyone, and everyone else will suck up to you. You'll clump together like Hollywood Herring, surfing on each other's slipstream.

- 9. **Start your own damn vault**. Just create your own mini-Hollywood somewhere, make successful films, and gain so much clout that the central vault tries to annex you. This is not as easy as it sounds, especially if you're an actor. On the other hand, many new stars are found on YouTube where they are posting funny bits or appear in ambitious web series. It's definitely worth a long look. If you're going to go this way (and I recommend it more and more), then be sure to focus on your clear talent: acting. Don't spend five years learning to produce and direct. Team up.

- 10. **Show up with money**. The vault always opens for money. Of course, if you have money, then you are either a producer of some kind or a silly rich person with a dream to be an actor, which everyone will recognize to be a dream but won't let on about until your money is gone. If you happen to have money, then list it as one of your resources when drawing up your plan. Use it to drive a cool car (always a good idea in LA), get good haircuts, and take the best classes. Otherwise, don't let on. *They* won't respect you.

- 11. **Come bearing gifts**. Rather than money, show up with connections or stuff the filmmakers need, such as a great script you got your sister to write, or the rights to a book, or a close connection to Brad Pitt. Then insist upon playing the lead. This is extortion of course, which could severely backfire on you at any time, but it has been used effectively in the past.

- 12. **Come out of Left Field**. Get the lead role in a magnificent, head-turning independent feature film made by a group of similarly undiscovered geniuses from Latvia that breaks all the records at the Cannes Film Festival and goes on to make $200 million at the box office. Again, not quite as easy as it sounds, but if you manage it, then you'll have producers, directors, agents, and paparazzi camped out on your balcony.

- 13. **Have the heart and soul of an actor**. Care. Care a lot. Study from a young age. Do great work. Do it for the love of it. Eventually, they'll find you, one hopes. Many, many of our legendary film actors come from this category, but I expect many, many, more brilliant actors never got their break. Moral of the story: have a plan anyway.

- 14. **Be a master craftsman**. Devote yourself to mastering story and the craft of screen acting. You will always be employable and welcome on set.

- 15. **Persevere**. Morgan Freeman, the great Morgan Freeman, was 52 years old when he did *Driving Miss Daisy*, his breakout role. Jack Nicholson was in 42 movies before he became a star in *Easy Rider*.

- 16. **Get lucky.** It's common knowledge that all stars got a break somewhere along the line. They got lucky. If they deny this, then they're lying. Note: they were also *ready* to get lucky. So, put yourself in a position to get that break and capitalize on it when it comes.

You could also go with the combination approach. Think Ben Stiller. He used numbers 1, 4, 5, 8, 13, and 14 (and probably a bunch of others we have no knowledge of).

There are other ways. Find yours either by making a brilliant plan, or by walking with lions.

But I live in Podunk

Ah yes, Podunk. How can you possibly make it if you live in some small town away from the limelight, some Podunk, USA?

Here's how: go back and read the vault chapter again, but this time pay attention.

With few exceptions, we all live in Podunk. Few people grow up in Los Angeles, go to UCLA, and date Margot Robbie. Getting out of your version of Podunk, and more importantly, the way you get out of Podunk, must be part of your plan. Your specific plan, tailored for you, by you.

Be reassured by all the stars who escaped their own version of Podunk before you: Russell Crowe—Australia. Karl Urban—New Zealand. Colin Ferrell—Ireland. Rachel McAdams—Canada. Catherine Zeta-Jones—Wales. Penelope Cruz—Spain. Nicole Kidman—Australia again. Ewan McGregor—Scotland. Hugh Grant—England. Jet Li—Mainland China. Chow Yun Fat—Hong Kong. Gerard Depardieu—France. Franca Potente—Germany. Djimon Hounsou—Benin.

Katie Holmes found her way out of Toledo, Ohio, forged a career, and married the biggest star in Hollywood.

If you are reading this in the USA, then you are incredibly lucky; you don't have to deal with getting to America in the first place and finding a way to live and work in the second place. Oh, and in the third place you already speak English. So, the next time you want to complain about your terribly bad luck with regard to Podunk, be suitably shamed by the people who made it in your country from other countries. Jackie Chan trained in martial arts for decades, broke into the biz in Hong Kong, became a star, learned English, and *then* broke into the biz in America. The fact that you're getting your ass kicked by people with twice the obstacles in front of them should be motivating.

Here's a short list of people who did it from Canada: Michael Cera, Seth Rogen, Malin Akerman, Ellen Page, Rachel McAdams, Mike Myers, Jim Carrey, Matthew Perry, Ryan Gosling, Neve Campbell, Ryan Reynolds, Evangeline Lilly, Elisha Cuthbert, Eric McCormack, William Shatner, Pamela Anderson, Keanu Reeves, Meg Tilly, Natasha Henstridge, Howie Mandel, and Mary Pickford, the original queen of the silent movie era.

The list from the UK would go on for days.

The moral: list Podunk under liabilities, factor it into your plan like everybody else did, and get busy.

The Beauty of Podunk

As you draw up your plan—or more accurately, as your plan evolves—keep a sharp eye out for opportunities cleverly disguised as problems. Podunk can be your launch pad.

In my particular Podunk, for instance, there are only about 500 members of the professional actors' union. Half of them are men. Only about 20 percent of those are in my age group. Perhaps 80 percent of those guys fall into the 'nice guy' category—they would be well cast as dads, neighbors, and friendly cops. What it all means is that whenever a movie does come to my Podunk, my immediate competition for roles—good guy/bad guys—is about three other people. In this market, I'm likely to land about every fourth job, which is impossible—no, ridiculous—in LA. In LA, my competition is probably thousands and thousands of guys, most of them with better looks and better resumes. Now you see that Podunk is not a bad place to be. About twelve movies shoot here per year, but with my fantastic odds working for me, I might appear in four or five. In LA, I might audition hundreds of times to book just three. So instead, I stay here quietly building an enviable resume.

You can—and perhaps should—do the same. It depends on your personal plan. But probably, most likely, you should.

Ah, but you argue that they would be better gigs in LA. Not so, Grasshopper. Major movies that came to my particular Podunk: *Unforgiven*, *Legends of the Fall*, *Open Range*, *The Assassination of Jesse James*, *Resurrecting the Champ*, and a little thing called *Brokeback Mountain*.

I auditioned for three of those and booked one. I will tell you the story of how I missed out on the other two in the chapter Your First Audition, starting on page 109.

The point is that actors in LA would do just about anything to land a role in a film like *Brokeback Mountain*. They'd slit your throat in a back alley. But you, living in Podunk feeling all sorry for your-self, get first crack.

So pick yourself up, dust yourself off, and start taking advan-tage of the opportunities around you. Shrink your world. Master that world first. Build your base and your resume in Podunk, and then start looking farther afield when you have made yourself valu-able farther afield.

That's the general advice.

Of course, if you are an *inevitable*, then you should get yourself to LA as soon as possible.

WHAT THE HELL ARE THEY LOOKING FOR?

What am I looking for? Well—very tough question! To be completely honest, with the changes in the business over the past few years—more available actors and way less work for them—a lot of what it comes down to for me is "marketability"—is this person viable in the business at this time? Is this someone that fills a hole in our client list? Sounds a bit "cold" I know, but the business of acting has become so extremely competitive that we have to look at it that way. I look for raw, natural talent. Someone who has the something special, a great energy that makes them stand out in a crowd. Someone who is confident, but not cocky. Definitely look for actors that understand the business and what it takes to succeed. Someone who takes direction well from us, who is very pro-active and understands the hard work that has to go into it—on their part and ours as their reps. With me—I know right away if I want to work with someone. I have been doing this for so long now, I just know when it's going to be a good fit! So, kind of tough to put it to words ... ugh ... did this make any sense?! I hope so!

—Amy Macnow, Los Angeles personal manager

What follows is a top ten list (plus one all-encompassing dream) of what *they're* looking for in general. Remember, *they* equals the Hollywood machine.

Here they are in brief:

That you are Inevitable — the all-encompassing dream.
That you are Marketable.
That you are In the Game.
That you are Right for the Part.
That you Get It.
That you are the Guy.
That you Give Them Confidence.
That you can Act for the Camera.
That you are a Pro.
That you can Help Make Them Money.
That they Like You.

That you are Inevitable

If you are perfect and brilliant, all sins are forgiven.

—Andy Henry, Los Angeles casting director

This will be a short chapter, a tough chapter to write and likely a tough chapter to read. Sorry about that. Unless you are an inevitable. Then: yippee.

Some people are just going to make it in the biz.

They just are. They have some combination of looks and talent and drive and opportunity and *it* and good timing and whatever else that just guarantees they're going to have a shot.

It's just how it is.

Example: some singers just open their mouths and you *have* to listen to them. True. A thousand others open their mouths, and nothing happens. But that one… It's some kind of miracle. Nobody knows why. It's something about the sound of the voice, the soul behind it, the technique, the love, the God of it, some kind of sub-space communication channel that connects all humans. They don't even have to be good singers. They don't even have to sing on key. There's just something there that we all recognize and have to be part of. We'll sit silently for hours just gladly listening. And if that voice comes along at just the right time in the history of the world, then it becomes unstoppable.

Those are inevitable singers.

There are also inevitable actors.

Don't ask me how to become one. I can describe one—coming up—but I cannot teach you to be one. No one can. Like the singer, it's just some kind of miracle. I do, however, think you can work your way into being inevitable. It'll just take a little longer.

I know it sounds confusing. That's because it is confusing. It's mysterious, but true. Let me try to clear it up by describing some of the qualities of the inevitables.

They will have *camera faces*. Just as the microphone loves certain voices, the camera loves certain faces. Not particular types of faces, necessarily. It happens or it doesn't happen on a face-by-face basis.

When you see these faces, you just want to look at them. You just want to see what they say, what they feel, and what they think. You are drawn to them amongst groups of other faces. It's a visual biz and looks matter. That's why the actor's calling card is a photograph, not a diploma. One in a thousand faces somehow lights up the screen. They make us want to watch. They look different, fascinating, and captivating. It's something about the light, the lens, the angles of the face, the light in the eye, or some kind of sub-space communication channel that connects all humans. We just don't know.

Some beautiful people look like dishrags on screen. Some absolutely ordinary people look like gods. Others look exactly like themselves. You can't know until you get up there. This is why your auditions are taped—so *they* can see what the camera thinks of your face.

No, you can't go out and buy one of these faces. No amount of plastic surgery will help. It's not just about your skin or your nose. It's about your bones, teeth, symmetry, the shape of your head and its proportion relative to your body and other bodies and faces, not to mention the twinkle in your eye. Plus some magic dust. Either you have one or you don't. It's part of being an inevitable.

Apart from having faces the camera loves, the inevitables will also tend to have unique or *dramatic faces*, faces that make a strong statement of some kind all on their own. The owner could be in a coma, but his face alone would still scare you, or inspire you to love, or make you think of mobsters or high adventure. These faces make strong statements on screen just by showing up, and perhaps more importantly they are markedly different from all the other faces in the movie. Thus, the audience knows who is who.

You have to remember that a movie is not a book. You cannot flip back a few pages to re-read a section. The movie keeps going. The audience has to get everything the first time. In part, this means no two characters will look the same. Instead, you will see unique faces, faces with impact, faces you root for or hate, faces you can't mistake even when the action moves fast.

For example, quite by accident I was having dinner at Chasen's back in the early-90s before it closed. For 60 years, Chasen's was a hangout for Hollywood luminaries. Frank Sinatra had his name on a booth there. I happened to look up from my plate to see part of a face in the dim light across the restaurant. It jolted me. It caused me to remark to myself: "Wow, who is that? The guy should be a movie star." Then the crowd cleared and I saw the rest of him. It was Kirk Douglas.

Almost the exact same thing happened in a vegetarian restaurant in Vancouver. This time it was Sydney Poitier. (If you don't know who these people are, then be ashamed.)

There are two basic types of these dramatic faces: *lead* (impossibly beautiful like Keira Knightley) faces and *character* (hit with a frying pan in an interesting way like Steve Buscemi) faces.

If you don't think you have one of these faces, don't panic. Everyone can become a working actor. There are stars of all kinds. The movies need people of all kinds. Hard work conquers just about everything. But you need to know that inevitables exist, they have a massive advantage, and it all starts with the face. It's like being tall in the National Basketball Association. It's kind of an advantage. This doesn't mean you can't make the NBA if you're 5-foot-6, it just means it's going to be a lot harder. If you care and love acting (or basketball), then it won't matter to you either way. You'll factor it all into your plan and keep going.

Next, the inevitables will tend to have a 'certain something,' which is known in Hollywood as a *certain something*, or an *inner essence*, or a *quality*. It'll be a kind of mysterious, compelling, complexity that you can feel from across the room. It'll be dramatic, or comedic, or both. They emit a certain zing, a presence. Not a cocky, egotistical zing; it's more of an inclusive zing that magnetizes. People notice them immediately and want to be around them. This quality turns into ammunition on screen. Think Brad Pitt, Jack Nicholson, Charlize Theron, and Cate Blanchett.

You will learn a great deal more about these two things—your *look* and your *feel*—including how to know if you have one of these faces, in the section titled That you are Right for the Part on page 53. For now, if you want to know what these people look like and feel like, then go to the movies and watch carefully.

Next: the *voice*. In the Golden Age of Cinema, comedians impersonated the voices of the movie stars because movie stars all had unique, fascinating—and sometimes very carefully invented—ways of speaking. You can learn a lot listening to Jack Nicolson or Christopher Walken or John Wayne. In any case, the voice has to go with the face, and it should have something compelling and unique about it.

The inevitables have *raw talent*. You hear this little phrase spoken all the time in the offices of Hollywood agents and casting directors. Amy Macnow mentioned it in her quote above. "I'm looking for raw talent." What does it mean? Well, in a very real way it means the opposite of cooked talent. It doesn't need to be processed, fortified and packaged. No preparation is required. It just is. Like a pineapple lying on the ground, it is finished and perfect.

Applied to you, the actor, raw talent means you are a natural, a pure actor. You probably laid in bed as a child praying for permission to grow up to be an actor. You deeply understand it, and you were brilliant the first time you tried it. You were always good at it and people noticed early on. You were probably baffled by how others couldn't keep up with you. You found it easy, and for that reason didn't think much of it. But if you look closely, you realize you were born to do it. It is in your DNA.

There's an old saying in sports: you don't train champions; you find them.

It's that.

Inevitables tend to get an *early start*. Many of the girl inevitables are no more than girls when they begin. Most of the boy inevitables get going when they are in their early twenties. This is because movie audiences skew toward the 18 to 25 age group, and are interested in young people discovering their powers.

And then there's *craft*, the subject of this book. The inevitables are masters—or at least on the way to being masters—of the craft of screen acting. They study it as long and hard as a physician studies brain surgery. It's about as complicated. If it were simple, then we would all be Big Fat Stars now.

Next, the inevitables are *sexy*. This sexual power is independent of their fame. They were sexy before they got famous, and then they only got sexier afterward. It's an absolute common denominator of the inevitables. Steve Buscemi is not a classic looker, but loads of women go ga-ga.

I once asked the famous Hollywood acting coach Ivana Chubbuck (*The Power of the Actor*) "What makes a movie star?" She said essentially this: they are really smart people; they are very sexy even if they're not attractive; they always seem to have a crush on somebody or something; they all seem to be much more interested in other people than in themselves; they are very confident but not cocky; they are very emotionally alive, curious about everything; they are very independent.

An agent once put it to me this way: "If an actor leaves my office and my receptionist says, 'Who was that?'then I know."

It is also rumored that the inevitables are the *smartest* people in Hollywood. They always seem to be taking a few months off from their movie careers to get a PhD at Harvard.

I told you this would be difficult.

Moreover, the inevitables *care*. They love movies, storytelling, acting, working, striving and doing. They care more than the filmmakers do. They become collaborators. They are desperate to be as good as they can be and to be a part of the major art form of the 20th and 21st centuries and the mythology of the world. They are prepared to solve all problems to this end, including working the business, being professional, calmly handling notoriety, and always learning.

There are other things.

People in the biz recognize these inevitables the way thieves recognize each other in the street. Then *they* try to get hold of them as soon as possible, before anyone else does, to capitalize on their potential, and to help tell great stories. *They* hire them, help them, train them, promote them, and hand them a lot of success.

You would too.

If you are not inevitable at this time, then accept it. Decide to read the rest of this book carefully. Apply yourself, work like hell, learn to love rejection, believe in yourself, devote yourself, dream, sweat, climb, cross your fingers, and kick doors down. Know that work can make you inevitable. Plenty of actors have become Big Fat Stars via this method. It is a noble method. You could do worse things with your life.

If you happen to be one of the inevitables, then you must accept that too. It's not always easy or pleasant. Example: Marlon Brando was a legendary inevitable who changed the face of cinema. He didn't like it much, and he was often heard to say: "It's not a dignified job for an adult." He was often heard to say: "I would quit this damn racket but I don't have the moral strength to resist the money." He was once heard to say: "Acting is the expression of a neurotic impulse. It's a bum's life. Quitting acting, that's the sign of maturity." He refused his Academy Award, he didn't work much, and he had a very conflicted relationship with his fame. He got good and fat, and yet we still watch him every time he appears on the screen.

Another example: countless other inevitables have come and gone but are still alive and well and living in LA. Imagine being an inevitable that no one wants to see anymore. You have this one God-given talent, this thing that is *you*, and nobody is buying.

Tough.

Murderous.

And so we come back to "You had better love the work." If you love it, then you'll do it no matter what your inevitable score is, and you'll keep doing it because you love it and you care.

Then again, it would also be good if you were *marketable*.

That you are Marketable

In all my research for this book, I have probably heard the *M-word*—marketable—more often than any other. It means two things.

First, it means that you are ready and not *in development*. This is why you shouldn't move to LA too soon. You don't want to be known as a good prospect who is *in development*. That doesn't really help you. *In development* means you haven't proven yourself, you don't know who you are and what you're selling, and you don't have the tools to sell what you're selling. You are not ready.

Let's turn it around and say it the other way. Agents and managers want you to be proven, employable, buzz-worthy, branded, and perfectly packaged so all *they* have to do is start selling you.

Why?

It's easier. It's faster. It's more profitable. It's better for business. That's all.

Why would *they* spend all their time developing you into a viable product when *they* could be selling the next girl who is ready? Answer: *they* won't. Well okay, maybe *they* will if you are an inevitable or a kid and *they* have only one or two of you in development at any one time. Otherwise, *they* won't. So, do not count on this.

Neither will *they* wait around for you. You get one chance. You cannot call up an agent again and say "I'm finally ready now." *They* will most likely say: "We looked at you already."

Being ready is therefore up to you, and you have got to be ready the first time. You must be fully in the game as outlined in the next section. You must be packaged: have a perfect resume, a beyond-perfect headshot, a brilliant show reel of recent work, a website, an IMDB page, and so on. You should be building your network, promoting yourself, and working the biz so that when you walk in, you are ready. In other words, you need to be succeeding on your own, first.

Provided you don't blow it in the interview, you have a chance.

Second, marketable means there is a place for you in the movie landscape at this time. Better yet, lots of places and lots of available roles suit you. Therefore, when your agent submits you, there is a good chance people are going to buy. It is no good being a great actor who just doesn't fit in anywhere.

Some reasons you don't fit: You're a dead ringer for Tom Hanks. You look exactly like the last 33 actors who walked through the door. You are gorgeous and 6-foot 8. You have a beautiful face and an 80-pound backside.

All you have to do is go to the movies or turn on the TV to see who is marketable at this time. Note that marketability varies by show and time of day and so on. You might be great for prime time drama but no good for soaps. It's tricky, so study up. Be honest and objective.

The world's most marketable actors fall into a few general categories as we have already seen. Young, contemporary, talented beauties fit in just about everywhere. Character actors who look like they've been hit repeatedly in the face with a waffle iron are always welcome to play bad guys, addicts, and 'characters.' Also marketable all of the time are very bright, talented kids, and tweens. Bright kids are easier to work with, and they might become stars. Great older actors can be marketable because they tend to be in short supply and because every movie seems to need at least one judge or senator or grandparent. Also welcome are actors with special looks, skills, qualities, and connections. Truly funny people have the highest fame rate of anyone in the world. Agents love actors who know the business well and are prepared to work their butts off to succeed. Add to that list actors who are famous, or famous for something else, and actors with resumes and reputations, and you start getting the idea of who *they* can market.

Of course, being marketable is no good if you're not *in the game.*

That You Are in the Game

People prefer to play with other players. They speak a common language. They are pre-approved. They inspire trust and confidence. They make it easy to do business and easier to make money.

Moviemaking is like going to war on Mars. The filmmakers know *they* are in for a long and bitter fight against a largely unknown enemy on a strange planet full of unexpected perils. *They* want to go out there with battle-tested warriors, not with weirdoes, dreamers, or wannabes who really want to direct one day.

And that's just for the production assistants.

When it comes to you, the actor, *they* want the same thing times a *million* because you are on screen. You are the face of the story. If things aren't working out with the gaffer, then he can be easily replaced. Once *they* have shot a few scenes with you, you cannot be replaced without enormous expense and embarrassment. If *they* are half way through the movie and you turn out to be a traitor, guess what? *They* are screwed. Sixty million dollars circles down the drain. Careers are lost and lives are ruined. You're to blame but there's nothing *they* can do about it. *They* are screwed.

Countless movies have been lost this way. It has happened to me twice; the wrong actor was hired, and the movie was *never* released. This is one reason why it is so tough to break in, and partly why you see the same actors in the same sorts of roles and the same small group of actors working all the time. They are players who give people confidence. They solve problems and do their jobs without supervision. They collaborate and cover your back. They avert disaster, winning battles and making money. They do not step on dreams.

If you had been smart and become a painter, then you'd be virtually required to express yourself with abandon. That's the nature of good painting. Painting is extreme artistic personal revelation made possible by an investment of only 20 bucks in canvas and paint. That it's almost worthless is what gives it its value. People want to buy your intimate expression done without guile or expectation of reward. Pure art, not 'the artist business.'

I am sure you know where I'm going with this. You've probably heard it before. Our art form is called *show business*—not *show hobby*—because we must do both the show and the business. As an actor, you are involved in one huge moneymaking venture, namely the movies. They make billions of dollars a year. I'm going to be grammatically awkward for emphasis and say: *this is a fact with which you must deal.* Any time you appear in a movie, it costs money. Somebody somewhere is spending thousands, millions, hundreds of millions of dollars in part so you can do your thing. I'm sorry, but *they* want that money back. Part of your job is to help get that money back. Again, to those of you who sour at the mention of return on investment, who want acting to be a pure art, I apologize, and invite you to put on a show in the garage. Send me a notice; I'll try to make it.

The rest of you, read on.

The first thing *they* want to know is that you understand all of this, and that you are one of *them.* In other words, that you are in the game and playing for keeps.

In the game means:

- You love it and are committed and want to be the best.
- Because of that, you are a student of the game, and you know its history, its rites, and its regulations.
- Because you love it, you have taken action to make your dream come true.
- Because of that, you have some experience.
- Because of that, you have learned that you are part of something

larger than yourself—that it's not about you but about telling stories and getting the job done—and you have learned how to solve problems to that end.

- Because of that, you have proven your employability to yourself and to *them.*
- Because of that, you know how the biz works and your place in it.
- Because of that you know that you are running your own little acting business.
- Because of that you have all the tools (great headshots, proper resumes, self-promotion strategies, etc.), training (classes, coaching, degrees, experience), people (agents, managers, publicists), systems (scheduling, accounting, communication), and relationships (unions, accountants, teachers, advisors, filmmakers) you need to effectively run your business.
- Because of that, you have demonstrated that you are reliable, absolutely determined, and in it for keeps.
- Because of that, you are a contender.
- Because of that, you are in the game.
- Note: being in the game won't help you if you're not *right for the part.*

That You are Right for the Part

If you're huge, bearded, tattooed, and leathered, then your outside says biker. This is what we call your *silhouette* or just your *look.* Obviously, you can't hide it.

If children and animals come running to you when you enter a room, then your insides say good and kind and Santa-like. This is what we call your *quality,* or *essence,* or just your *feel.* You can't hide it either.

Put your *look* and your *feel* together and you get a unique human being who walks around broadcasting a message, like it or not. This is what we call your *Sell,* or your *Brand,* or your *Hit,* or your *Power Zone.* In this case, you can be summarized as Biker Santa.

If *they're* making a movie that calls for Biker Santa to swoop in on his Harley and save the roast turkey, then you would be right for the part.

The first concern is not your acting, but the *message you broadcast by just being there*. You can't hide it. The camera sees it. The audience sees it. As soon as you arrive on screen, we see and feel you because your eyeballs are 8 feet tall. One of our great gifts is knowing what other people are thinking, and we have suspended our disbelief and opened our little hearts like kids, and the movie is being blasted into us point-blank.

You cannot hide.

This applies equally in the audition room. As you walk in, *they* examine you and decide if you're the guy *they're* looking for. Are you broadcasting the right message—do you have the looks and qualities the character needs? Do *they* believe you in the role?

Even more important, *they* need to know that *you know* what you are selling so *they* have confidence in you, and *they* know you're not going to try to work against yourself.

Clint Eastwood is the Stranger who is both good and bad. Morgan Freeman is God. Johnny Depp is the quirky, outsider leading man. George Clooney is the charming, cocky leading man. Jack Nicolson is the wild card. That's how it is. Before you go to a Harrison Ford movie, you know what you're going to get from him.

There are reasons: You like it when that happens. People around the world want to see more Harrison Ford movies. It helps sell and pre-sell the movie. It helps producers raise money for the movie. It creates a star around which the rest of the actors can be cast like a constellation. It focuses everyone's labors. It helps define the genre of the film. It saves time. It helps Harrison's long-term career prospects.

Clint Eastwood is one of the greatest movie stars of all time, but you will never see him sashaying around, cracking jokes, pulling off capers and kissing girls like Clooney does. Why? All together now: *because he is not right for the part*. It doesn't matter that he is a brilliant actor and a legend. The camera will not like him in the part, the story will not want him in its world, the audience will not buy him on screen, and the producers will lose their money.

Your sell or brand can be defined as the relationship between you and the audience. What do they want to buy from you? What's the best way you can deliver it? Put those things together—your look and your feel—and you have it.

Note that Clint is a major star all over the world, even when his voice is dubbed by another actor into a foreign language. It's the look plus the feel that does the job.

How do you determine your brand?

You read the later chapter on how to determine your brand.

Of course, being right for the part is no good at all if you don't *get it.*

That you Get It

As an actor, you typically think it's all about *you*. Well, I got news for you. It ain't.

Look, I'm an actor too. I grew up in dysfunctional hysteria like you probably did, and I need to be seen, loved, and admired to compensate for the injustice of my childhood just like you do. This is actually a good thing. It made us actors. It sent us deep into our imaginations where movie characters were more real than our families. It gave us riches to draw upon, and a powerful impulse to the stage. It brought us here. But I have learned a hard lesson that most of you have not.

The lesson: if you continue to make it all about you, then your career will be brief and tormented and possibly end in a drunken car wreck on the way home from a crack party at some rapper's place. Because as much as you care about you, we all care about something else.

The *story.*

We want to know if Luke is going to save the Princess. It's nice if Harrison Ford is in the movie. We like that. It's okay. But Jesus Christ! What's going to happen to the Princess and the rebels? Will Luke become a man that finds his place? They're not going to kill R2-D2 are they?

That's what it's all about.

Story is a message from God that entertains us and explains the experience of life. In other words, story is what happens when bad people try to take over your galaxy.

Story is why the audience paid their money in the millions. It's why a screenwriter spent two years crafting it out of nothing, and why a producer and director spent the next two years finding the money, and why a studio executive opened his checkbook, and why Harrison Ford wanted so much to play the part, and why "Use the Force" is part of the language and culture of the world.

Good actors know story. They know what story the filmmakers are telling, and why and how, and how they as assistant storytellers can help. It all shows up in their performance. As in, this is where Han Solo comes roaring back to the fight *because he has learned that people and love and duty are more important than money.* His function in that scene is to show us that, not to show off himself. Get it?

You'd better. Because *they* are all deeply moved by the story.

They think it's important enough to stake *their* careers on.

Story is *their* careers.

They want to know that you are one of *them.*

They want to see it in your performance.

A script is very much like a symphony. It's not like a painting that hits you all at once. Movies and music take place over time. They are temporal arts. It's the arrangement of notes, rests, keys, times, etc. that makes a script what it is.

Example: You play violin. There's an opening in your local orchestra. They send you a piece of music by Mozart to learn for the audition.

Suppose you show up at the audition not knowing the music, and you just take a stab at it. What's going to happen? You're not going to get the gig, and for good reason.

Suppose you play every other note of the music.

Fail.

Suppose you play only your selection of notes because you are an *artist.*

Fail.

Suppose you turn the end of the piece into Chicago Blues because it just *feels right.*

Fail.

The only way to be in the running for the job is to first practice the violin for about ten years so you can actually play it. Then you are going to need to read and understand the music they have given you. You need to *get it.* What's the key and time signature? How is the piece organized? Did Mozart give any other instructions or clues as to how the piece is meant to sound? What are the conventions of playing

Mozart? What is the piece about? Why did Mozart take the time to write it down? What is it meant to convey to an audience?

Then you need to practice it relentlessly until you can play it to Mozart's satisfaction.

Then you need to show up on time and follow the rules of auditioning: do not wear a bikini, do not be drunk, and do not call anyone *babe*.

Then you need to play the piece under the gun for *them*.

Then you need to leave without making any funny noises on the way out.

This is the absolute minimum.

If your performance was competent, then you will be in the running. If your performance was excellent, then you will have a chance to win the job. If your performance was marvelously musical and expressive, then you will have a chance to be *first violin*. If the timbre of your violin is exceptionally beautiful, and you are very experienced and knowledgeable, then you will have a chance to be *concertmaster*. If you are all these things plus you are somehow personally exceptional—beautiful, sexy, charming, funny, zingy, intense, fascinating—then you will have a chance to be a soloist. If you remain consistent and manage the business of your career extremely well, then you will have a chance to be a star.

It's all the same with acting.

No matter what else you do right, you will not win the job if you *don't get the music*.

As I will say elsewhere in the book, musicians are a bit luckier than actors in that all their music is written down for them—every c*rescendo*, *pianissimo* and *portamento* is typically right there in front of their eyes. But not for you. There's no room for every little thing to be indicated in a film script. Plus, screenwriters want to *leave room* for you, the actor, the expert, to bring your keen perception and talent to the role. In any well-written scene maybe only 40 percent of it is clearly directed by the text. The rest of it is in the blank spaces underneath the text—in the *sub-text*—where you have to go looking for it. Those who find it all, succeed. Those who don't, fail. In my experience, when actors fail on set or in the audition room it is mostly because they didn't take the time to read, understand, and play the all music of the story.

Theater actors may be accustomed to learning all the music in rehearsals, slowly wading into the piece, exploring, and being illuminated by each other and the director. Film actors have to do it all by themselves. No director sits with you in the bathtub while you learn your lines. Nobody will call you in advance of the audition or the shoot to talk you through it. There will be no rehearsals. In 35 movies, I've probably been directed two or three times on the set, and that's after the first take. And those were little directions like "Could you walk through the door faster?"

You need to be perfectly self-sufficient as that's why *they* hired you. You are the expert. You know exactly what you are doing. You do not need help. You show up with your violin, and you play the piece magnificently. That's it. Maybe, just maybe, the maestro gives you the tiniest direction about tempo or mood. Done. You play the piece and then go home.

The theater equivalent of this film reality would be this: they give you the script for *Death of a Salesman*, and say, "See you opening night."

You are then required to show up opening night, prepared in every single possible way after having memorized your lines, deeply understood the text, figured out all your blocking down to and including every movement of your eyes, and perform the play perfectly. You will not meet the other actors or see the set until you arrive. The audience will be in their seats.

Have fun.

That is how to think about film acting.

That is why it is so critical that you get the music of the story down to the smallest 16th note, and you can prepare on your own.

Story is what the entire movie biz is all about. That's why I spend so much time on it in upcoming pages, and that's why I wrote an entire section on story and screenwriting for you. Study it well, Luke.

Or Leia.

Or Chewie.

Of course, *getting it* is not going to help you if you're not *the guy*.

That You Are the Guy

Hollywood doesn't really want actors.

Hollywood wants t*he guy from the story* (or the girl, or the kid, or the Klingon).

Remember that the camera wants to secretly watch real people living their fabulously dramatic lives. It's the thrill of the movies, remember? The camera definitely doesn't want to secretly watch actors vainly hamming it up or stumbling along. It wants the guy, the real guy, from the story. It wants to believe that the story is real, and that this is the guy who lives that story in that world. Therefore, you must not be an actor; you must be the guy.

When *they're* sitting in an audition room and you walk in, there's a voice in *their* heads that says: "That's the guy!" or "Nope. Better luck next time." *They* have studied the story deeply, conferred with all the creative and business powers, and *they* know the guy when *they* see him.

If the response is "That's the guy!" then you must not do anything to change *their* minds.

Like 'act.'

If you 'act,' then you are no longer the guy. The guy doesn't act. He goes about his business in his usual way.

Yes, this is the acting bit.

There must be none. No acting. No pretending. No forcing. No performing. No mumbling. No planning. No guru. No method. The guy doesn't need any of that crap; he's the guy.

As you move through the world of the story, you appear to belong there completely. There is no sign that you are acting or even aware that people are watching. Every micro-second of everything you do is true and right and appropriate and believable. All of it contributes to telling the story both overtly and subtly. There is no trace of vanity or the love of being watched and admired or technique or method or schooling.

But there is every trace of you believing in your world and your goal and your relationship and your identity. You're the guy.

Do *they* care how you're able to do that?

No.

Does it matter that you spent eight years training in New York?

No.

Or that you spent just eight minutes preparing in *green room* before you did it?

No.

Nobody gives a damn. How you arrive at being the guy is totally irrelevant to *them*. It only matters that you can do it.

If you need a method to guide you, then here it is: be the guy.

Oh, and could you have a little *confidence*, please?

That You Give Them Confidence

If you're the guy, and you're right for the part, and so on, then the next thing *they* want to feel is confidence. You give *them* that by having confidence yourself. Easy confidence is even better. Relaxed, easy confidence is the best. *Alpha* dog confidence is even better than best. Most of the BFSs I have known or worked with display this kind of confidence.

To be an actor you must be free. You must be able to act any way you want at any time and to believe anything you want at any time. This requires confidence.

It's exhilarating to do. It's fascinating to watch. It's what we all wish to become: free and undomesticated. Actually, *feral* is the right word: to once have been domesticated but now returned to the wild. Not only feral, but also alpha feral. Leaders of the pack.

Ever wondered why? Sure, once you are rich and famous and a BFS, alpha dog status does kind of come with the territory. But think deeper. Be smarter. Be Danny Ocean.

Answer: the alpha dog is free. The alpha dog is at the top of the heap, therefore he is in no danger of being shamed, judged, rejected, or banished. He can do whatever ridiculous behavior he wants—like display emotion in front of a camera—and all the other dogs will still exalt him.

Imagine for a moment you are a chimpanzee. The survival of your group depends on teamwork, and your survival depends on your place in the social order. If you're the alpha male, then you make all the rules, you're guaranteed to survive and to spread your seed around like a farmer on crack, thus persisting into future generations. If you are the low chimp on the totem pole, then you are a step away from death at all times. You eat last. You are not allowed to have a girlfriend. You get bossed around, shamed, ignored, and beaten down by everybody else in the group. You have virtually no chance of improving your fate. Understandably, you can start feeling bad about yourself. To top it off, any time the others get sick of you, they can abandon you in the woods. Without the group, you will surely die a slow horrible death in the jaws of a leopard.

Now you are a human again. Acting and any kind of public performance exposes you to possible ridicule and shame in front of your troop of human primates. They could abandon you. You could get attacked by horrible creatures, followed closely by death.

Deep down, I think that is what we fear.

It is also why we spend so much time—particularly in high school— trying to fit in and be cool. We create a socially acceptable façade, and we sell it for all it's worth. We will do anything to maintain this image because it assures us survival and status in the group. Some of us spend our entire lives trying to build up our importance and service our images. We become entirely dependent on our fakeness for our livelihoods, which leads to fake relationships with fake spouses. Eventually, we mistake our fake selves for our true selves, become deeply neurotic, and live a fake life all the way to the end.

Now, if the thought of that terrifies you, then it's a good start toward becoming an actor. I hope it really terrifies you because you are going to need the motivation. If you want to be an actor—if you are completely committed—then here's what you are going to have to do: you are going to have to willingly expose yourself to ridicule and rejection by standing in front of, and outside of, the monkey troop for the rest of your life. You will have to commit to becoming a weird, scary, unpredictable, and creative type. You will commit to seeing the truth, to knowing and to feeling. You will become feral. You will get in front of the troop and hold up a giant mirror, so they can see themselves and the pickle they're in. First they will laugh. Then they will cry seeing the truth. Some will surely hate you for it. Others may begin to live better lives as a result. That is your mission should you decide to accept it.

You must also accept that some of your fellow primates are going to fear and marginalize you because you have the power to put them into a trance and feel things. You can manipulate them into thinking and feeling and maybe doing what you want them to do, which scares them.

But if you have the courage of the alpha, then all your fear is gone. All your powers are directed into your performance. You are totally alive, and totally free, and totally thrilled. Isn't this what you want? Isn't this why you were attracted to acting in the first place?

For *them*, the casting directors, directors, and producers, this means salvation. It means *they* have an actor for the part that *they* can have confidence in. An alpha has arrived, who is free and powerful and willing to take us to the limits of human endeavor and help us get this damn movie made. Thank God.

Your confidence gives *them* tremendous confidence that you can handle the job and everything that comes with it.

This makes *them* hope you will take *their* offer of work and fame.

How do you get alpha confidence? I think giving you this kind of freedom is the goal of all acting theories and classes. You can take other classes and forms of self-development work. You can meditate. You can practice. You can imitate others. You can fake it 'til you make it. You can embrace yourself. Success in other areas can be transferred. Ignoring the naysayers is paramount. Believing in yourself helps a lot. Developing confidence incrementally in all areas of your life does the trick. Natural ability cannot be underestimated. I'm a big believer in physical freedom—strength, flexibility, and fitness. Living in the moment is the absolute answer. Spiritual awareness is the absolute answer. Also helpful: clean up your room and get a nice haircut. Education is critical. Faith conquers all. Opening your heart works really well. And there's nothing like deep desire combined with the belief that you are on the right path; that you were born for it.

The other reason why you want to be an alpha is this: it is kind of a requirement in acting for the camera.

Let's go back to the monkey troop for a minute. One of the ways in which we are entirely the same as our monkey brethren is the ability to know what the other monkeys are thinking. There is enormous evolutionary advantage in knowing when to pester the dominant dude or groom the dominant chick. So, all we monkeys get very good at reading the faces and bodies and voices and minds of our troop members.

Example: You can tell when somebody is coming to kick your ass from three blocks away. You can take one look and know you're in trouble from a quarter of a mile. That's how good we are at it.

Now imagine that guy's eyeballs are 8 feet tall on a movie screen.

Pretty hard to miss now. Correct?

The camera is a huge magnifying glass. Whatever you are thinking, the audience is going to know and feel. Your thoughts, in fact everything that is going on with you, beams like a searchlight over the darkened theater. This is the very reason why the movies are so powerful. It's not because we struggle to know what's going on, but because it's blasted into us. It's because we are one with the actors. We don't try to connect, we just do. Instantly. We are like deer caught in the headlights, and we cannot escape the oncoming story until it ends.

This is a very vulnerable position to be in. We have turned off all our normal self-protection mechanisms, all our judgments, all our thoughts—in fact all consciousness of our outside lives—to live through a story. This is called *suspension of disbelief.* We know that it is a movie, that it is not real, but we force that knowledge out of our minds because we prefer to believe.

Remember when you were a kid and Dad told you a bedtime story? Same thing. You got totally lost in it. Remember when Dad screwed up the story? Pissed you off. "Dad! That's not how it goes. That doesn't make sense. That's not how the dragon sounds." You got really mad. Maybe you cried. Maybe you screamed. Dad wasn't doing it right. He was making stuff up, or rushing through it so he could go catch the game. And he wasn't caring for your little, wide-open heart lying there.

The same thing happens when you see a scared, lying, self-involved actor on a movie screen, except that you get to multiply it by 1000. Pissed off to the 5th power. Nobody, not even a monkey, wants to be shot point-blank by an egotistical, manipulative movie jerk.

You, the actor, must go alpha up there; you must honestly and courageously share your deepest self on screen. You cannot hide. The monkeys see everything and I mean everything. You must accept this totally and accept yourself. You must share. You mustn't worry about appearing vain or 'all that.' You must instead worry about being an example. You must be that which the audience wishes to fear or love or become.

I think it's that freedom and generosity of spirit, and the joy and sexiness that accompanies those things, that is *it:* that zingy energy I mentioned in the That You are Inevitable section on page 28. It can't be something you try to project; it has to be something you embody. And you can only really embody yourself. So it follows you have to switch yourself on, drop into the zone of relaxed confidence, and seek communion with others. Give everybody confidence and a little more zingy energy for themselves. Get producers to love you, get directors to desire you, get investors to throw money at your movies, and get crowds to line up for you.

Of course, once *they* throw the money, *they're* going to want to know that you can *act for the camera.*

That You Can Act for the Camera

Go take a painting class. They do not start with how to manipulate images like Picasso. They start with how to mix paint, clean your brushes, and stretch your canvas. When you're well versed in these matters your talent will start to blossom and you will have a shot at the masterpiece. But not before.

It's the same in film acting. If you desire to be a BFS one day, then you must embrace this totally. Ninety percent of your work is stretching your canvas.

If you have been lucky enough to see Sir Michael Caine's video on film acting made by the BBC back in the '80s, then you will notice that his very first lesson is how to *hit a mark.* Then he shows you how to find your *eye lines,* how to keep your eyes open, how to speak slowly, what to do in a *close up,* how to match your *continuity,* and what to do when you're not talking. He spends very little time teaching what you might think of as acting, and he spends a lot of time teaching what you might think of as technique. In other words, the nuts and bolts. Stuff that doesn't take any acting talent. You just have to learn it and do it. Stand here, look there, speak slowly.

Why did he do that?

Think about it.

Why?

Is it possible that Sir Michael was teaching film acting after all? That Sir Michael, legendary film star, does actually know a thing or two about the job and was telling you the important stuff?

I think so.

I spend most of my time teaching students how to be technically correct or technically employable, if you like. Example: I am constantly asking my actors to do scenes without any acting, just being technically correct. Just do it right for the camera. That's all. "You need to enter the scene here, connect, say some things, hold your eye lines, try not to blink, sit down after the words Thank You, say a few more things, then answer the phone."

Some actors need dozens of takes in a class just to get a scene right *with no acting*. It requires practice and concentration. It's a tough technical skill set that needs to be conscientiously developed. And it separates the actors from the auditioners.

In filmmaking, we use a camera. We shoot in certain ways. We shoot out of sequence. We have all kinds of technical limitations. We have requirements of you, the actor, that cannot be avoided. They are part of the medium. Your job is to act for the camera. And that means technique.

A bonus: technique equals performance. Or, at least, it comes damn close. If you were to watch that actor in my class take 15 tries to get it technically right, then I would show you his 15th take up on the big screen and ask you to critique his performance. Not his technique, but his performance of the scene. Guess what? Provided the actor understood the story, about 90 percent of the time you would have no complaints. No suggestions for improvement. In other words, being technically proficient is 90 percent of a performance.

That is what Sir Michael was telling us in his class.

Why is that so?

The scene itself doesn't need to be improved upon. The writer already did that.

The actor is already broadcasting the character. His brand is taking care of that.

Everything is clear and appropriate to the scene and the medium, and without distraction. His technique takes care of that.

His performance is spot on. His natural ability as a human takes care of that. It's almost impossible to do a scene like a robot. The actor naturally starts to get involved with it, take an interest in it, and his body naturally starts to play it, like a kid playing cowboys and Indians. I dare you to pull the trigger on an imaginary gun and not go "bang." Your body naturally creates the scene without any help from you, provided you understand the scene and commit to your goal.

He is not 'acting.' He is not obviously performing it for us or trying to win our love and admiration. He's just doing it. So, the 'acting' has become invisible, which is the goal of all good acting. His focus on the technique is also taking care of that.

Trust me, you can have all the talent in the world, but if you can't apply it to film—as in *acting for the camera*—you are not employable. The only way you'll work is if you are seventeen and beautiful and right for the part and without competition and willing to take classes in acting for the camera before the shoot. On the other hand, you can have very modest talent, but if you are technically proficient you are very employable and welcome everywhere. You can be a working actor.

Secondly, you must also master the technique of the audition. The only way *they* can judge your ability on set is by judging your ability in an audition or the *room*. The main way *they* do that is by setting up a series of technical audition *land mines* that the amateurs step on, but that pros step around. Example: you must not shake hands. It is not done in the room. If you did, then you gave yourself away as an amateur. You will get a big X next to your name. You will probably not book the role no matter how good your performance was. *They* are looking for pros not for talented wannabes.

You will learn all about this in the section on your first audition.

Okay. You've come a long way. Technical ability is a major accomplishment. But it would be so much better if you were also *a pro*.

That you are a Pro

If you screw up my home renovations, then I'll be mad but I'll survive to hire another plumber. If you screw up my movie, then I lose my career, my credibility, my future, and 60 million dollars.

Different.

There are certain ways I can protect myself from crappy actors, but the best way is not to hire them. If I do have to hire them, then I look for experts who know everything in this book and five times more. They don't just know the business; they also know the politics. They can sniff out danger miles away. They have the solution to every creative problem. They are diplomats, philosophers, poets, scientists, salesmen, warriors, and generals. They know how to handle the studio executive, the investor, the leading lady, the janitor, and everything in between. They can be counted on, no matter what. Period.

That's a pro.

It starts with caring. You must care as much as they do. More so. This is the primary characteristic of the pro. Caring means you go the extra, extra mile to do your job, you put the project (and especially the audience) first, you shoulder all burdens, you avert disaster, you gain 40 pounds if you have to, and you leap all hurdles to succeed. You are all in.

Filmmaking is a heroic battle against the forces of chaos. There are going to be delays, changes, challenges, and catastrophes. You laugh at them.

I am reminded of the movie *Wag the Dog* with Dustin Hoffman and Robert De Niro, written by David Mamet. The US President is in trouble, and his main man, De Niro, goes to a Hollywood producer, Hoffman, for help. They need a big, real life, fake war as a diversion until the election. Hoffman agrees to produce.

Hoffman was just fabulous in the role, especially when saying the equally fabulous recurring line given to him by Mamet: "This is nothing." Every time an impossible challenge came up Hoffman would look at it derisively and say, "This is nothing." And he would find a solution.

Even when his leading man dies half way through the fake event: "This is *nothing.*"

That's the attitude *they* want from you.

Start with grit. Be determined to learn every single thing about the business you're in, and never stop. Grit will lead to professionalism provided you learn the basic lesson of the pro: to be collaborative.

The only creative artists in Hollywood are the writers as I mentioned before. They only invent everything. Everybody else interprets the script, making them interpretive artists. To do this, they must collaborate. They have to play together like an orchestra interpreting a symphony. Finding a way to work happily together for the common good is paramount whether it is with your agent or your director. Being rigid, difficult, and right is a quick way out of the biz.

The best way to stay in the biz? *Make them money.*

That you can Help Make Them Money

It's a business, remember? It costs millions and years to make a good movie and *they* really would like to get *their* money back and put some in the bank for a rainy day. Not to mention that it helps when it comes time to make another movie.

Really, everything in this entire What the Hell are They Looking For section contributes to *them* making money. But there are a few other things you can do, including many of the things already discussed in the How to Break into Hollywood chapter on page 19.

For example: be a movie star. It works every time. It means you have proven yourself and your ability to generate wealth in the movie biz. Everybody wants to be part of that. If you happen to be Julia Roberts, then many people will be knocking on your door or flying to Paris to woo you.

Be famous for something else. That's why you constantly see wrestlers and beauty queens in reality shows, and American Idol contestants in TV movies, and former movie stars in TV series, and current movie stars in current movies. They attract customers. They make money.

It also helps to be marketable at this time so you fit into a hole in an agent's roster, a role in a TV series, or a vacancy in the current mythology of the world. Right now, for example, it helps to look like a vegetarian vampire.

It occurs to me that we do not currently have a muscleman amongst our movie stars. We always seem to have one. We had Johnny Weissmuller. We had Steve Reeves. We had Arnold. We had Stallone. For a while we had The Rock. But right now… Vin Diesel, Jason Statham? Even Hugh Jackman, maybe? Not musclemen in particular, but maybe they are just today's leaner versions? Hmmmm. Anyway, I think if you are an up-and-coming Arnold you have an opportunity.

Also… be Tom Hanks' nephew.

Be someone who will generate a fan base and possibly a spin-off TV show. This works extremely well when they are casting TV series.

Be someone who will help promote *their* movies. Half of a movie star's job is promoting the pictures they appear in. That's why they are always making appearances and doing interviews: they are promoting their upcoming movies. Producers at all levels like this a lot. (I produced an admittedly little independent film, but my starlette did not show up for the premiere. I did not like this a lot.)

Have the promise of a long successful career. This makes everything you do more valuable.

Come bearing gifts, as in your famous girlfriend, or a car *they* happen to need for the chase scene, or a rich uncle, or your pal Hugh Hefner, or a mansion in the Hills for the wrap party, or a special skill like underwater welding that will save *them* oodles in special skills stunt performers.

Be a diamond in the rough, i.e. the world's most shockingly beautiful 18 year-old goddess of screen acting. People like that sort of thing. Plus, you might get really famous later, which will help sales of the DVD.

Be the right size for the wardrobe *they* have.

And finally, be *likeable*. Please?

That They Like You

Nobody wants to work with jerks or wannabes or people that rub you the wrong way. It's just no fun, and it can cause major upheaval on the set if people bicker or have illicit affairs. It makes the battle that much more disagreeable and desperate. Many directors will *cast the cast* to minimize this problem. *They* cast the leading man, and then cast everyone else around him so that they work in story terms, and so that they also work as a harmonious group of people.

The director will pass over a particular actress because she's a raving Republican while the leading man is a well-known radical Democrat, for example. *They* have to have the right cast of characters, but if *they* can also get the right cast of people, bingo. This is why you should focus on being as professional as possible and put aside your own—usually petty—hang-ups and weaknesses. It makes you more universally castable.

This is the last thing to worry about, of course, but it can be the difference between winning and losing. All things being equal up to this point, *they* are going to work with the person *they* like the most, the one *they* most want to spend five weeks with in the trenches, or a lifetime with at the agency, or three movies with in the Bond franchise.

So if you're funny, or charming, or fascinating, or full of stories, or calm and direct, or likely to fall into bed at any moment, or a Red Sox fan, or whatever as long as it's likeable, then you have a better shot. *They* actually would like to take you out for lunch once in a while to try to stay connected with humanity. For that to happen—or for *them* to want you in their next three films—*they* need to like you.

Next, as much as you may not like it, in order not to suck at screen acting you need to know a bit about the business.

HOW TO RUN YOUR BUSINESS, BRIEFLY

How to Package Yourself

Now that you know what *they* want, you need to create your *package*. Your *package* is your promotional material. But it is more than that. It is a carefully crafted ad campaign that lets *them* know you exist, that you are employable, and that *they* would be wise to hire you.

Caution: This is one of those realities of the biz that seems to make no sense, that even seems backwards.

You: "I'm an actor. I play different roles. *They'll* put me where *they* need me."

Them: "You're in business. Tell us what you're selling, and we'll decide whether we want to buy it."

Solution: the customer is always right.

So, give *them* what *they* want. Figure out what you are selling. *Package* it. Offer it for sale to *them*. It's backwards, but it's the way it works. You need to know in advance what roles, what shows, what genres you're right for, and then you need to create a professional campaign to persuade *them* to buy you.

In the following chapters, I'll explain everything step by step. You'll learn about your sell, *headshots, resumes, demo reels*, how to get an agent and so on. But for now, let me give you the overview so you understand the concept.

Example: You are Seth Rogan. You are young, average looking, but funny, charming, and terribly likeable. You'd make a good character in a slacker comedy. Because you are charming, you might get the girl. Therefore, you can promote yourself as a slacker comedy leading man. You will accept this and be happy with this.

You will get a *headshot*—the actor's primary promotional tool— that exemplifies this in every way, that shouts, "Hey, I'm the slacker comedy leading man you've been looking for. See?"

This photograph will give the impression that you are on the set of your latest slacker comedy movie where someone just happened to take a great shot of you. It will focus on your eyes and reveal everything about you that makes you such a darn terrific slacker comedy leading man. This then becomes your logo, your own primordial image around which everything else in your story is built.

You will then get three or four more headshots emphasizing different aspects of your amazing self, i.e. super nerdy slacker comedy guy, very charming slacker comedy leading man, and emotionally complex slacker comedy leading man. Get it? Variations on your theme.

You will then generate a resume making sure it is full of movies in which you played a slacker comedy leading man. Even if you only have one such credit, then you will go with that knowing it tells the right story. Because you are serious about becoming a BFS, you might diminish or omit credits that do not support your story knowing it confuses people. If you just want to work, then you will leave everything in so *they* can see you are employable, and *they* can see who has hired you in the past.

If you have no supporting credits at all, then you will go out and get some. Nobody cares how you do this, you just have to do it. Go get them. Make your own movie. Do no-budget slacker comedies in Denmark if you have to. Just get those credits. It's best if you have at least one credit that matches each of your headshots.

You will then ensure that your resume continues your story as much as possible. It says you went to comedy school; it says you did theater where you often played a slacker comedy guy; it says you have mastered your Standard American Accent (coming up in The Accent of The Movies section on page 76) and can do other accents and voices that might be funny when playing a slacker comedy leading man; it says you have an agent who also understands what you're selling; and that you have your union status and working papers for the country in question. Elaborate as necessary, again making sure everything tells the same story.

Then you will cut together a *demo reel* of all your slacker comedy leading man roles. A *demo reel* is basically a commercial or a trailer for you and your work. It consists of a series of clips of your professional work that lasts somewhere between 60 and 90 seconds. No longer. Notice also the word *professional.* No class work, no scenes shot in a basement, no recordings of that play you were in, no recreations of your favorite scene in *Star Wars*, none of your modeling gigs, or that time you hosted a TV show, or that time you were on *The Bachelor.* Doesn't count. Professional acting is all they want to see: work you did on a TV show, a movie, an ambitious short film, a web series, or an independent film that got broad release. The focus is you, not on your stunts, or the work of other actors even if they're stars. You. That's all.

Next, do your website. If you do not already have your domain name, then get it, i.e. www.peterskagen.com. If you have a really ordinary name, like Michael Green, then you should have changed it by now to something unique. You should not have the same name as any other actor, living or dead. If you do, then change it. I myself know a terrific actor named Michael Green.

The reasons for this are simple. First, you don't want to confuse people; second, you want to get your own unique web address; and third, you *cannot* have the same name as any other actor when you join the Screen Actors Guild in Hollywood or any other actors' guild. You cannot go join SAG as Denzel Washington. Denzel is already using that. So if your name actually is Denzel Washington, then you need to change it. You can be Denzel Joshua Washington. You can be D. J. Washington. You can be D. Josh Wash. Or you can invent something totally different. But you cannot be Denzel Washington.

If in doubt, then look up your name on www.imdb.com. Is there a you out there already? Feel free to pout for a day if you like, and then change your name. Go with your mom's maiden name or your middle name or your dog's name. Does not matter. Just make sure it is unique and memorable, and that it tells the right story. If you're a Harrison Ford kind of guy, then do not change your name to Shawna PicnicBasket. That's probably not a wise move. Go with something that tells the right story. This is your chance to help define your career, so take your time and choose wisely. Do not get stuck with something you will regret.

Your name can sometimes also be *too* unique, or perhaps boringly unique, or just plain wrong for you. In other words, some people change their names anyway to stand out a bit. Think of Maggie Q. Cool, exotic and kind of tough. Perfect for her.

Real name: Margaret Denise Quigley. Not so much.

Lots and lots of actors are not who you think they are. Michael Caine is Maurice Micklewhite. Tom Cruise is Thomas Cruise Mapother IV. Jennifer Aniston is Jennifer Linn Anastassakis.

Same thing in music. Bruno Mars is Peter Gene Hernandez, Elton John is Reginald Dwight, and Jay-Z is Shawn Carter.

You do not have to change your name legally. It is your *stage* name, not your legal name. In other words, you put Maggie J. on your photos, your resume, your demo reel, all your movie credits, interviews and so on. As far as the public knows, your name is Maggie J. You are still Margaret Agnes Jones on your driving license, your passport, and your tax returns. You can change it legally if you want, but you do not have to.

So, change your name if necessary, and get the URL: www.maggiej.com.

Put your package up on your website, plus any supporting material you have: more photos, shots of you working on set or on the red carpet, interviews, awards, press clippings, your complete biography, a blog and so on. Make sure it all sells you and all tells the same story.

And since you have been dying to show *all* your fantastic movie work (rather than just your brief demo) now is the time for that. Create a little video section on your site. Cut a two-minute reel of all your funny slacker-leading-man stuff, another one of all your romantic-slacker-leading-man stuff, and another one of all your slacker-leading-man-in-space stuff. Label each of them clearly, along with their length so viewers know what they're getting. Post ten different reels if you want. This is the place for it. If one of *them* is on your site, then *they* want to see everything *they* can, even all five scenes you did in that slacker Western: *Mack and Ziri Ride a Pinto*.

Finally, spread the word about yourself across the web, on your agent's site, on Facebook, IMDB, all the casting sites, and any place else you can think of.

Update often.

You are now packaged properly.

How to Determine your Brand

Step one in all this packaging business is knowing what you are selling; define your brand. So, let us begin.

Do me a favor and cast me right now. That's me in the photo. You're doing a movie. What part do I get? The young lover? The bank teller? The kid? The cop? The waitress? Am I a good guy or a bad guy? Come on. You're doing a movie, and my uncle is your only investor. He wants me in the movie. What do you do? Can you see me in the movie some-where or do you tell my uncle that there's nothing for me? If you do see me in the movie, where? What kind of part? Look closely at the picture, look at my eyes, make a decision about what you would like to see me do. Now go a little further. Do you see me doing comedy or drama? Am I in commercials, or television or movies? If you see me in commercials, what am I selling? Beer? Viagra? Financial products? If it's TV, what kind of show am I in? Cops and robbers? Sitcom? Soaps? If it's movies, what type? Horror? Drama? Action? Sci-fi? Do I kiss the girls or punch the bad guys? What's my age range? Do you trust me or not? Do you like me or not? Do I know what I'm doing or not? Do you want me to live or die? Or do I cause the death of others? What do you expect? What do you want?

I do this little exercise in every one of my classes, and guess what? The answers are always the same. Everyone, no matter their age, or gen-der, or race or planet of origin says the exact same things every time.

You said the same things too.

Male, Caucasian, 40 to 50 years old, good guy/bad guy, mysterious, smart and in charge, white collar and/or blue collar, punches people, acts in movies, maybe TV cop shows, no commercials unless he's sell-ing hand grenades, he's a bit of a wild card, could be funny, has a code, and knows what he's doing and does what he says.

And now guess what? Those are exactly the roles I get again and again. Look at my resume. Google me. All the same thing.

Why?

It's simply because you are influenced by my presence in your brain. I'm not actually there in front of you, but I am broadcasting a message to you anyway, a message that you pick up loud and clear. It makes you *expect* certain things from me, and moreover, you want certain things from me. You *want* me to play the crazy king, or the mob boss, or the mysterious cowboy who shoots up the bad guys. You do not want to see me kissing anyone unless the kissing is closely followed by a shooting. I'm a bit Clint Eastwood and a bit Jack Nicholson (on a much smaller scale of course).

Right?

Meaning, any time there's a Clint Eastwood-y/Jack Nicholson-y part, I have a shot.

Let me give you an example. Some months ago, a TV movie came to town called *Santa Baby 2* starring Jenny McCarthy, Paul Sorvino, and Dean McDermott. *They* were looking for someone to fill the role of Worst Department Store Santa Ever. He was grumpy and possi-bly crooked. While tending his flock of kids at a mall, the real Santa (played wonderfully by Paul Sorvino) passes by. Feeling his grand pres-ence, all the kids stampede over to him. The Worst Department Store Santa Ever has a few naughty words with Santa, tells him to get lost, and eventually punches him in the nose. Later, the two of them wind up in the county jail. The movie is a light-hearted comedy. As soon as I read the *sides*, I knew the part was probably mine. Even if I screwed up the audition, *they* would still be inclined to hire me. Why? Yes, class, because I'm exactly right for it. The look, the tough, the comedy, the punching—it's all me. It's what people want from me.

Had I been living in a bigger city, there might have been 20 or 30 of us in the running, all with similar appeal. As it happened, I was the only guy in my version of Podunk who fit the description, and I knew it. I had *them* over a barrel, but I went on to show *them* that I also *got it*, could *sell it*, and was professional and fun to work with. But the truth is, two seconds after I walked into the room 90 percent of the work was done because I was right for it. It's what I'm selling and what *they're* buying. More importantly, it's what *you are* buying. You, the audience. It's what you want from me.

I booked the part and had a great time doing it.

When I was starting out in film acting, I kept trying to give *them* what I thought *they* wanted. If it was a broad comedy, then I brought in my Jim Carrey impersonation. If it was romantic, then I did Cary Grant. I am an actor right? I should be able to do anything.

Wrong. I booked nothing. Zero. Zip. Bupkis. Finally I gave up. Quit entirely.

What happens every time you do that? You get a call from your agent the very next day with an audition.

I go. I'm determined to have a grand old time kissing-off my last-ever audition. I'm going to let go completely, have a good time, and say good riddance. In my mind, I'm flipping it the bird all the way through.

Of course, I booked the job.

Why?

Because I wasn't trying to *play* something; I was *being* something, and that something was *me* in a very interesting condition. I was free and alive and spontaneous and right in my power zone.

Bingo.

Full of confidence, I booked about six jobs in succession. All the same kind of characters, but I loved that. It meant there was a place for me; it meant I got to play variations on my power zone, which was incredibly fun. Why go to work feeling terrified and bogged down in someone else's power zone character? It's much better to do your own and promote that so you get to do it some more, and so you have a shot at getting paid a lot of money to do it and see all your dreams come true.

Remember, this book is about getting you started off on the right foot in screen acting. I want you to find your power zone so you can slice your way through the competition and onto the screen, and so everyone will see you in your best light. Once you are working, you can start expanding your horizons, but for now, realize that this is your foundation in screen acting.

How do you find your *power zone*, your *sell*, your *brand*?

Two parts make up your *brand*: your silhouette (or outside, or what you look like), and your essence (or quality, or insides, or personal vibe).

Casting directors in LA call these simply your *look* and your *feel*, and they begin by assessing them as you walk in the door. First is your look. Are you a tall, 300-pound, bald, white guy? A petite and beautiful East Indian woman? It makes a difference, folks.

In film, we are above all concerned with reality. We photograph real objects and actions, and we cut them together to tell a story. Thus, as film actors, we play very close to ourselves. Casting director Andy Henry says it this way: "I'm not interested in what you can do. I'm interested in what you do."

If the story calls for an old Hungarian dude, then *they're* not going to hire you; *they're* going to hire an old Hungarian dude. If it calls for a Chinese princess, then *they* would really like to hire an actual Chinese princess but will settle for a film actress with all the looks and qualities of a Chinese princess. You might get away with playing a Chinese princess on stage, but unless you are petite, lovely, and cultivated—not to mention, Chinese—you won't on film.

Make sense?

More than that, the audience has made certain agreements with the movies over the years. For example, all people seem to know how to use an assault rifle the first time they pick one up. And there's more: 1) the hero will be good-looking but not stupidly good-looking, probably dark-haired, and if he has a cleft in his chin so much the better; 2) If anyone has scars on his face, then he's the bad guy; 3) the leading lady will have a large upper lip; 4) there is not a soccer mom in the world who has large breasts; 5) sweater plus beard equals college professor; 6) all Korean kids are math geniuses; 7) all witches have pointy chins; and 8) all billionaires smoke cigars.

So spend some time figuring out your *look* and where it fits in the movie lexicon. I don't care who you *really* are, but I care what you look like. Villain? Fairy God Mother? Girl next door? Scientist? Cop? What do people expect from someone who *looks like you?* Examine yourself. Take a good class where this is discussed. If you have a chance to talk to a casting director, perfect. Find some working actors who look like you and see what roles they are doing. Be coolly objective. This may well be the first time in your life when you have done this sort of thing, so separate yourself from your ego, erase any thought of trying or wanting to look a certain way or like a certain star, and just be objective. Ask objective friends. Examine the roles you have done and look for a pattern.

Your *feel* on the other hand is the sum total of your nature, your personality, your family life, your experiences, how much you got kicked around in high school—everything that makes you *you*. One guy walks into a room and it feels like the party just started. Another one walks in and suddenly things feel a bit heavy or even dangerous. That's their quality walking in the room. You can feel it.

Again, it is more than just your personality, or some front you put on. It is the truth of you at this time of your life. Spend time discovering your own personal *feel*. What do people expect from someone who has your vibe? How do people treat you when they first meet you? Does everyone love you instantly, or do you get stopped at the border every single time like I did? Are people intimidated by you? Do they trust you? Does everyone fall in love with you?

Here's a little trick question to help you find your *feel*, your personal, inner quality:

Write down the name of the movie actor you most admire. Do not over-think this. Write down the first name that comes to mind. Not the one you want to date but the one you *admire*. Gender doesn't matter. Make it a boy, a girl, living or dead, or even a cartoon character. Doesn't matter.

Now, underneath that name write five or six words that describe that person, such as hilarious, brooding, creepy, sexy, or charming.

Take a minute to do this right now. I'll wait for you.

Here, I'll even give you some blank lines to write on:

Star you admire: _____

Qualities: _____

_____

_____

_____

_____

Don't cheat.

Really.

Why would you cheat? I'm trying to help you here. Go back and do it. The more words you can write down about your star, the better. We are figuring out your personal quality.

Seriously. Get a pencil and write. If you cannot take ten seconds to do this little exercise, then how are you going to climb the Hollywood mountain?

The space below is me waiting for you.

Okay.

What makes this a trick question is this: the stars you admire are the stars you relate to on a deep level. They are like you, in other words. You relate to them. That's why you go see their movies; you want to see a version of you saving the princess or being the princess. That's what makes it fun and educational. So the words you wrote down will be words that describe the parts of them that resonate with you. They will describe you in other words or describe the direction you are going. Take another look and you will see I'm right. I do this little trick in all my classes and it never—okay, very rarely—fails. Those five or six words then are a clue to your inner self, your essence, your quality, your vibe, and your feel. They point you in the probable direction of your own success in movies.

Provided you didn't cheat.

Next, you need to blend these two facets of yourself together— your silhouette and essence, your look and your feel—and now ask *what do people want from the whole me?*

This is your sell, your brand, your power zone.

You could call this *typecasting*, and you'd be right. The audience— and thus the filmmakers—want to see you in the right role, and then to see the deep, real you in that role. As much as I love Ellen Degeneres, I wouldn't want to see her as Buttercup in *The Princess Bride*. There are certain roles she's right for and certain roles she would bomb in. It is the same for all film actors.

Take a look at the current crop of stars and you'll see they tend to do the same character over and over again. In many cases, they play the exact same character over and over again. Hugh Grant, anyone? Meg Ryan? Steve Carell? Jennifer Aniston?

This is not a criticism. It's the job! Find your power zone and sell it for all it's worth.

Nobody can do you as well as you can. You are the expert. That is your value. So my advice is that you pray to be typecast. It means you have found yourself and your place in the movies. Once you're famous, you can go play a quirky character in a Woody Allen film.

If you took my class, then I would put your face up on a twelve-foot screen and ask the class, "Who is this? What roles does she play? What do you expect? What do you see in her eyes? What kind of upbringing did she have? What do you definitely not want to see from her? What can she do to improve or focus her *sell*?" The class always knows. They respond the same way a huge audience would or a casting director would. And they are always right. They would have unzipped you to the soul, even against your will. Because you can't hide. I hope this lesson is clear.

Once you know who you are in movie terms, you will feel grounded in yourself and see your starting point. Only then can you use yourself to play the character and tell the story. Only then will you *really* know what you're doing.

So, get busy and figure out what you're selling. Most actors haven't a clue about this, so they flounder around for years, hoping. If they are tenacious and lucky, then they book a few things. If they are smart and objective, then at some point they look at their own resumes to see what they have booked and maybe the light goes on. "I'm getting all science geek roles. Hmmmm." And maybe then they learn the lesson and start to focus their endeavors in that direction to create a career.

Why waste all that time wandering aimlessly? Does this not make sense to you? Would you put an ad in the paper reading:

Thing for sale. No idea what it is. Ten million dollars.

That's essentially what you're doing if you are ignorant of your brand.

Do not be one of those precious actors who says, "I can do anything. I'm an actor."

That's like putting in an ad like this:

Thing for sale. Does everything. Ten million dollars.

Good luck. Really. First of all, no one is going to believe you because your claim is total crap. Second, your price is a bit high. And third, people prefer to buy things that are specialized and brilliant at doing what they do, like the world's best vacuum, or the world's finest blue, luxury cross-over. You won't find a very big market for the world's best vacuum that is also an excellent life jacket. It's just human nature.

The Producer's Point of View

I know I'm harping on this but it is crucial to your early success.

Suppose you are producing a $60-million movie, and you need a director of photography to shoot it for you. Option one is a cinematographer who went to UCLA and has since shot 35 features and just worked for Steven Spielberg. The other option is a guy who is a cinematographer/yoga teacher/part-time potter/bicycle courier who really wants to be actor. Which one are you going to hire? If you are a responsible producer, then you are going to hire the first guy because he is a specialist who will do a first-class job at cinematography, who knows every detail of the art and craft, and who will see problems coming a mile away to avert disaster. He's a world expert. You can count on him. You can stake your career on him. You can defend him to your investors and your studio. He will help you in unknown ways. He will save your ass. You want the best people on the planet in every position on your crew because there are so many careers and lives and dollars on the line.

You also want the right actor.

Along with all the other reasons mentioned thus far—it's best for the story, it's best for the audience, it's best for the box office, it's best for the actor, it's best for the financiers—hiring the right actor also helps make the movie *actor-proof.* And all of *them* love it when a movie is *actor-proof.*

See, when Clint Eastwood arrives on screen, he doesn't really need to act. His brand is selling the story. He only needs to stand there—tall, angular, fit, present, tough, determined, just, smart, dangerous—and the story works. Get it? No 'acting' required. He only needs to stand there, say the words, and punch the guy. Done. The movie works because he is the guy. Now, if Clint happens to be a terrific actor (which he is), then so much the better. He can add little details, make interesting choices, sprinkle it all with stardust. Maybe we have a hit on our hands. But if he happens to suck, then we're safe because we have the right guy in the right role. It is actor-proof.

How to Focus Your Brand

Once you've made it out of high school, you cannot change your deep self or essence. Your cookie is pretty much cooked. Yes, you can grow and evolve, but you are growing and evolving the same cookie. Perhaps one day you will reach enlightenment thereby freeing yourself of your cookie, but in the meantime, if you are chocolate chip, you are chocolate chip.

Using another Clint Eastwood example, in *Gran Torino* (2008), he is still the same commanding, threatening, and independent good-guy-bad-guy-stranger-with-a-cause that he was in *A Fist Full Of Dollars* in 1964. His look has changed because he has aged, but his quality hasn't changed in all that time.

I might consider Clint for the comedy, but only if it was a comedy about a commanding, threatening, and independent good-guy-bad-guy-stranger-with-a-cause out to put things right with his pet chimp. It's comedy based on his sell. (These were actual movies in case you didn't know. The chimp was actually an orangutan, but chimp sounded funnier.)

You can't change your inside, but you can change your outside. This is why the stars are renowned for fashion *faux pas*, salon disasters, dieting, and getting 'work' done. They are trying to create a more focused brand image or extend the lifespan of the brand they have already built. Getting really lean is the first and easiest thing to do because it tends to make you appear younger and more attractive, thus extending the duration of the career. But not necessarily. It depends on the brand you have built and the stage of your career. Sometimes, getting good and fat is better. This is yet another reason why it pays to be an expert on your own brand and drive your own career.

Monkeying with your look should be the last thing you consider after having done the deep and important work of finding your feel or quality. Most people do it the other way round, thinking it's all about the make-up and hair, because it's what they see the stars do. They are dead wrong. Find your true inner quality first.

Then, finally, ask yourself what changes could you make on the outside to focus it?

By being ignorant of your brand, you are like a fighter pilot who doesn't know how to fly. Worse, you don't even know that you don't know how to fly. You are a disaster waiting to happen. You are a dream-stepper. Do not do it. Become a specialist in your niche—*you*—know it, and deliver it consistently and well. We will all love you.

The Character Actor

Yes, there is such a thing as the brilliant character actor who is not necessarily locked into a sell, but it's probably not you. It might be best if it isn't you. Why? Because, for the most part, the audience does not want versatile actors. Al Pacino is the wounded prince; Angelina Jolie is the fatal beauty; Halle Berry is the vulnerable beauty; Meg Ryan is the adorable girl who's worth it; and Christian Bale is the brainy, dangerous and potentially unhinged outsider. That's what we want. These are the actors who drive people to the box office. The fabulous versatile actors don't.

Patrick Tucker in his wonderful book *Secrets of Screen Acting* thinks we, the audience, only allow one truly versatile actor per generation. In my generation it was—and still is—Daniel Day Lewis. Before that, maybe Dustin Hoffman. Nowadays, you could make a case for Sean Penn. These guys are stars, but there are not many of them, and they are on a different power grid than the big names.

Now, when you figure out what *you* are selling, you have to advertise it. That means: headshots and the numbers game.

The Numbers Game

When an LA casting director puts out a call for actors, he might get 2,000 submissions for each part. Two thousand, for one part. All submissions are done on-line. The submission consists of your headshot and your resume. He is definitely *not* going to see all 2000 people. He may have to cast 22 different roles for his TV cop show *this week*. At 2,000 submissions apiece, that would equal 44,000 auditions. *This week!*

So here's what he does: he scans through the 2000 submissions for the janitor role. He quickly, and by instinct, and purely subjectively, selects about 25 people that look like his vision of the janitor for this project. That's based purely on the headshot. He does not read resumes. He does not look at who is represented by whom. He does not call your agent and ask about you. None of that. It's all about the mysterious *hit* he gets from your photo compared to the vision he has in his mind based on what he knows about the project, the director, even the budget. There are many factors in play. This is the creative aspect of casting; his creative contribution is putting all the pieces together and coming up with 25 good options.

This process takes maybe fifteen minutes. He invites those people to audition. One of them will get the role.

Doing the math on this equals the following: in LA (and provided you have done everything else right), you have a 1-in-60 chance of getting an audition and a 1-in-2000 chance of booking each role that comes along.

The math also equals this: the casting director looks at each photo for maybe half a second. It's all about your headshot, and it has one half of one second to grab his interest. This is how it works. This is not going to change any time soon. Therefore, yours must be perfect.

Headshots

Casting directors are almost never looking for nice generic people, so if you get a nice generic headshot, it will never be right for anything. You will never get an audition.

Your headshot must *declare a major*; it must scream your sell, your brand, across the room like "I'm the kooky, blue-collar soccer mom!" When that casting director is looking for kooky, blue-collar soccer mom, your headshot will stand out. You will get an audition. You will have a chance. If you try to be right for everything you will get nothing. Remember: *he is not interested in what you can do. He is interested in what you do.*

Therefore, your headshot must holler what you do and only what you do. You must accept this and embrace it totally. You cannot get everything; you must focus and specialize. Do what you do. Get into your power zone. And get the headshot that advertises that.

By doing this you are eliminating 60 or 70 percent of all roles—roles you are not right for—thereby saving a lot of time and trouble and heartache. And a whole lot of rejections. You want this. You want to go out for only the stuff that's in your power zone where you have a shot.

Some lucky people have broader power zones than others. Tom Hanks is trusted and likeable. He has a broad range of characters he can play, both good guys and bad guys, dads and romantic leads and religious mystery detectives. Lucky for him. Steve Carell is zany funny. He has a narrower range. Clint Eastwood plays one basic character. Very narrow, but likewise very powerful.

You must be honest and objective about finding your power zone. You must then summarize it in your headshot so that the casting director knows what to call you in for, and so that he knows *that you know* what he should call you in for. This creates trust, and builds confidence, which is one of the things *they* are looking for.

When you're starting out, you have three main jobs: letting *them* know you exist; telling *them* where to cast you; and being ready for your break when it comes.

If you submit a bland, generic headshot thinking, "I'll let *them* decide," then *they* will decide that you are a wimpy, needy, difficult actor who doesn't know himself or the biz. And *they* won't want to see you now or ever.

Focus. Declare a major. Tell *them* where to cast you.

Having said that, some agents in the bigger markets like Los Angeles will want you to get three or four or five headshots, each declaring a different version of your major: one as the commanding business man, another as the commanding mobster, and another as the commanding dad. She will then submit the appropriate version of your brand for each different role. This creates an even more focused presentation, but you remain in your power zone.

The best headshots are exactly you and your brand summarized. They are not stiff or posed in any way. You should be relaxed, open, and real. It must give casting directors a good look at your eyes so *they* can get a feel for you. It must look exactly like you. You must not get carried away with makeup or Photoshop. If you walk in and look different from your headshot, then *they* will feel manipulated and angry. You will have no chance of getting the part. You will have no chance of getting another audition. Save the glamour shots for later when you're a star. This is not the cover of *Vanity Fair*. It's your headshot.

Confidence cannot be over-emphasized. You must not be seen to be acting in your shot. Not pushing it, or trying too hard, but also not fading into the background. Show them your easy confidence.

I suggest you don't get all dressed up. You risk looking uncomfortable in your clothes even if it is very subtle. Not good. You want it to be natural and you, and therefore wearing your own clothes, clothes you are normally seen in, is usually best. Avoid black like the plague, and white, and all patterns and logos. They tend to be distracting. Don't make it about the clothes.

It must have a *hit* that hits a casting director. I have asked several casting directors what they mean by this but most can't describe it. It just hits them in a certain way. It's interesting and confident and compelling. It fits the role.

Make sure you are looking into the camera so we can see your eyes and get a feel for your quality.

If your sell is funny girl-next-door, then be in your girl-next-door outfit, make sure your hair is not overly sexy but more girl-next-door-look fresh and clean, and smile. And be natural. And confident.

I never said this would be easy. It takes time and effort. But this is the single most important weapon in your armory. Make it perfect.

Make sure also that the background is not distracting. Most good headshots seem to be shot outside in natural light. Studio shots tend to feel posed and set up. You want *them* to think your friend (the professional photographer) just snapped a shot of you on the street corner, or even better, in a film you happened to be doing.

Don't wear hats, or big jewelry, or bring a dog, or anything else that might distract *them* from you or make you look like you're trying too hard.

Color shots are the most common nowadays, but black and white is still fine. Make sure it is in portrait, not landscape, layout.

In every major film town, a reproduction house will make copies of your headshot, put your name on the bottom, etc. They all have websites with galleries of sample shots that you can learn from. Check them out. The original one in Los Angeles is Ray the Retoucher. In Vancouver, it's RocketRepro. That should get you started.

Get a new one about every year, unless you change radically—i.e. go blonde.

So, an easy, confident, 8x10-inch, color or black-and-white shot that looks just like you looking at us, emphasizing your eyes, not hiding anything, which perfectly summarizes your brand as if it was taken right out of a movie you were in and has a mysterious, indefinable *hit* that hits without pushing it or trying too hard. Simple.

Resumes

Resumes follow a standard format; it makes it easier for everyone if resumes all look the same. Do not try to stand out by printing your resume on a tennis shoe because you're just trying to get your foot in the door. That is idiotic. *They* will keep the tennis shoe, yes, but *they'll* mount it by the water cooler so *they* can have a good laugh at you three times a day. *They* will not call you. Trust me.

Like your headshot, your resume should tell one consistent story, and that story should match your headshot and demo reel, and in fact, all your material. Therefore, you have a strong selling package. This may mean dropping certain things from your list that don't contribute to the story. If you have three big movie credits and one credit in a corporate video, then it's time to drop the corporate. It doesn't add to the story that you are a movie actor. No, it doesn't make you look more experienced; it makes you look lame and unfocused. If you have two *co-star* credits in television, then it's time to drop the five credits as an *extra*. Just having more credits of any kind doesn't necessarily help you. Remember what I said earlier: you need to let *them* know you exist, tell *them* where to cast you, and then wait for *them* to offer you the part. You want the credits to tell a consistent story, which is that you are focused and employable and ready for the next step up in your career. This is especially important if your aim is to become a BFS.

The rules:

- One page long and never more than one page long.
- Your goal is a page-long listing of lead roles and nothing else.
- Regular white paper. Please, people.
- If you want to be really pro, then cut it to 8x10 to match the head-shot.
- Three columns. Not two. Not four.
- Note how the important stuff is all in the middle column. Easy to scan.
- Titles go on the left.
- On the right, list the studio/network/producer and then the director's name, as shown.
- Basic info at the top.
- No personal phone numbers or addresses unless you want a stalker.
- Use either your agent's contact info, or your own e-mail address if you are unrepresented.
- Film first, then TV, then commercials, training and special skills. That's it.
- Don't lie. Ever.
- No explanatory paragraphs about you and your life's ambition.
- Nothing unrelated to the biz.
- No modeling, TV hosting, competitions, singing gigs, etc.
- No background performer jobs listed unless you have nothing else.
- Then only list two or three background jobs not 20.
- Be clear and truthful about your special skills, i.e. novice horseback riding, and ideally make them match your sell.

All people start. It's okay. Some directors like it better when you're new and raw.

Here's a sample resume.

As for the middle column—the size of the role you played—conventions vary. But since we are talking about how to succeed in Hollywood, following is a list of how they break down in Los Angeles.

Peter SKAGEN

Citizenship: CANADA/USA ACTRA (SAG eligible)

TELEVISION

Hell On Wheels	Supporting	AMC/Michael Nankin
Love Me	Lead	Warner/Rick Bota
Santa Baby 2	Supporting	ABC Family/Ron Underwood
Family Sins	Supporting	CBS/Graeme Clifford
Mayerthorpe	Supporting	CBC/Ken Girotti
Into the West	Supporting	Dreamworks/Robert Dornheim
Friend of the Family	Supporting	Lion's Gate/Stuart Gillard
Man in the Mirror	Supporitng	VH1 TV/Alan Moyle
Broken Trail	Co-Star	Butcher's Run/Walter Hill
Blue Smoke	Co-Star	Lifetime/ David Carson
Legend of Butch and Sundance	Co-Star	Barnholtz Ent/Sergio Mimica
Monte Walsh	Co-Star	Warner Home/Simon Wincer
The Incredible Mrs. Ritchie	Co-Star	Showtime/Paul Johansson
Wild Roses	Co-Star	CBC/Sudz Sutherland
Boot Camp	Co-Star	MGM Home/Christian Duguay
Intelligence	Co-Star	CBC/Steve Surjik
The Mountain	Co-Star	Warner/David Barrett
Distant Drumming	Co-Star	CBC/Dean Bennett
Roughing It	Co-Star	Artisan/Charles Martin Smith
Lonesome Dove	Co-Star	CBC/Randy Bradshaw

FILM

Resurrecting the Champ	Supporting	Yari Film Group/Rod Lurie
September Dawn	Supporting	Sony Pictures/Chris Cain
Snap!	Lead	RJ Ent/Peter Skagen
Unforgivable	Star	Short/Tom Carey
Million to One	Lead	Short/Dianne Winkler

THEATER

Agatha Christie's Chimneys (world premiere)	Chief Insp. Battle	Vertigo/JP Fischbach
Tony & Tina's Wedding	Donny Dolce	TNT Prod./Cara Mullen
Rodeo & Julie-Ed	Wayne B. Wayne	RJ Ent. Aiden Flynn
Disco Saturday Night	Teddy Farkas	RJ Ent./Tammy Gislason

TRAINING

Los Angeles	Ivana Chubbuck	Pro Studio Advanced
Los Angeles	Amy Lyndon	Booking
Los Angeles	Paul Weber	Audition master class
Groundling Theater	Kathy Griffin	Improvisation

Accents: Slavic, Parisian, any others on request.
Dialects: General American, South London, Educated Texas, any others on request.
Languages:Basic French.
Voice: 10 years - big lyric tenor, low f to b natural.
Sports: intermediate horseback, former tennis professional, all racket sports, boxing, stage fighting, golf, football, baseball, basketball, weight training/bodybuilding, swimming, biking, pool, and darts.
Additional: Rifles, handguns, motorcycles, bad guitar and piano, photography, acting coach, improvisation.

Los Angeles-style billing for movies:

If you are the only name above the title on the poster and the movie is about you, then you are a *star*. If you are one of several names like that, then you are a *co-star*.

If you are in a main role throughout the whole movie but the movie is not about you, then you are a *lead*.

Everything else is a *supporting* role.

Los Angeles-style billing for television:

If you are one of the stars of the series, i.e. the team of cops, then you are a series *lead*.

If you are in just about every episode but not a lead, i.e. the coroner, then you are a *series regular*.

If you are the main character in a multi-episode story arc, i.e. the chief of police who turns out to be the killer two episodes later, then you are a *guest lead*.

If you are a main character in one episode, i.e. the killer, then you are a *guest star*.

If you show up in more than one episode throughout the series, i.e. that cranky judge, then you are a *recurring* character.

If you have a large role in one episode but are not a guest star, i.e. the mechanic who seems to be the murderer but isn't, then you have a *supporting* role.

If you have a small role in one episode usually with fewer than five lines, i.e. you are the owner of the pet store who answers a few questions, then you are a *co-star*.

For theater, you simply list the character name, i.e. Romeo. For training, the middle column is for the coach you studied with, or the school you attended if it was a degree program.

Pay special attention to the skills section at the bottom of the page. These can get you hired, accents especially. A Standard American Accent most especially. See the next chapter. It's best to break all these skills out into sections so they are easier to scan, as shown.

Attach the resume to the headshot back-to-back with one staple at the top. Do not use four staples. One will do. Confine yourself to a maximum of two at the top corners. You want the two sheets to stay together through whatever storm awaits them, but you don't want to cause the casting director undue hardship when she has to separate them and put them into a presentation binder.

Never print your resume on the back of your headshot. You might think you're saving paper (and you'd be right), but you are also showing yourself to be a true ignorant amateur. We never do this. Ever. The headshot and resume must be on separate sheets so *they* can separate *them* if they want. And *they* want. Plus, if you are any kind of actor, then your resume should be growing so fast that it would be simply impractical to print it on the back of the photo. You would have to toss out the photos every time you book a new job. So just do not do it.

Agents often have resume templates for you to follow, and sometimes they want to make your resume themselves to avoid problems. Let them.

One of the more important items on your resume is at the bottom: that you are proficient in the Standard American Accent.

The Accent of the Movies

Let's say, you live in Podunk, Canada.

Most of the shows you want to work on either originate in the USA or are destined for the US market where the Canadian accent doesn't play. *They* just don't get it. It sets *their* ears on edge. It doesn't match the other actors. It is usually waaaaay too fast and just not as dramatic as the good ol' US way. Plus, like it or not, the US way is the global standard for movies. The whole world expects the movies to sound that certain way.

So job number one is to master the good ol' US way. Nothing else you do in that audition room will fly if the accent isn't right. In most every case, *they* will simply go on to the next actor.

Bugged by this?

Don't be.

If you were an actor coming out of Texas or the Bronx—not to mention the UK—then you'd have to do it, too. Your problem living in Canada is that you hear the American accent on TV all day long, but you speak with your Canadian one. Many of you are convinced you have no accent at all. No difference. Sorry, I mean *sari*, but you do. The

American producers, networks and studios can hear it like a siren in their ears.

What to do?

Take a good class.

Watch TV like a hawk, listen like a safecracker, and then copy until done.

Watch the news anchors like Anderson Cooper—pure Standard American.

Move to Ohio.

Hang out with Yanks in your own country.

Check out a CD from the library.

Check out the many websites available, such as The Speech Accent Archive: http://accent.gmu.edu/

Then practice.

Do it all day. The beauty of living in Canada is that nobody will notice your new accent. Your own mother might not notice the difference since she is so tuned in to hearing the accent on TV all the time. You want it to become second nature so you don't have to use up half your brain thinking about it in the room or on set.

My own story: I once had to do a *callback* (second audition) just to demonstrate that I could say the word naughty the *right* way. The producer was from New York, and she wanted to know for sure that I could do that one word the way she wanted it before she would give me the job. I had done the rest of the scene bang on, but that one word stuck out for her. I went in, said *naughty* seven different ways, including hers, got them laughing, and got the gig.

Demo Reels

Your demo reel is a fabulous, descriptive advertisement showing them what you look and sound like, that you can act, that you are what you say you are, that shows *them* how you might look on their show, and that you have a certain *something*. It makes *them* want to buy you knowing you will contribute to *their* movie or TV show artistically and financially.

Don't think of it as a demonstration of your acting ability; think of it as a commercial. A teaser. A trailer. Make it succinct, focused and energetic. Make it move. We live in the YouTube generation where people have an eight-second attention span. So give *them* eight seconds of brilliance, and then a totally different eight seconds of brilliance. Make the whole thing end before *they* realize it, i.e. not more than two minutes long. Shorter is better. One minute will be excellent. Do not complain.

My reel has ten different characters in ten different movies in one minute and 22 seconds. Average scene length: 8.2 seconds.

Do not argue.

Do it.

Adapt as necessary, of course. If you only have two movies to your credit, then go ahead and use two scenes from each movie if you want to make a 40-second reel. Fine.

Yes, *they* will know what you've done.

Your reel will focus entirely on you, not your scene partners or the cool stunts or the stars who were in the movie with you. So don't get carried away. Most actors have a hard time editing themselves, so you might be wise to hire somebody to cut your reel. If you want to do it yourself, then cut it down until it is as short as you can tolerate. Wait a day. Cut it in half. That will be about right.

Open with your best scene—right in your power zone, well produced, and well acted. Again, do not get carried away. The first shot should be of you listening, reacting, and delivering a line or two. Cut to the other guy for a line or two, then back to you for your big speech, or your funny bit, or your clincher line. Done. You do not need the whole scene. You do not need the whole movie. Did I mention that? You do not need your big stunt. You do not need to show that George Clooney was in the movie. This is your reel, not George's. Just give *them* what *they* want. What do you look like and sound like in that role? Can you act? Do you have a certain something?

Then add a scene from the next movie, not the next scene in the same movie (unless it is radically different, i.e. your character is playing a different character). *They* have seen that movie already. *They* want the next one, the next look, the next character, the next iteration of you as a cool, slacker comedy leading man. Do the same thing: a short scene, a few lines. Then on to the next movie.

Next, put your name and contact info on screen for a few seconds at the head and tail of your reel. Do not use your address and phone number. You do not need a stalker on your patio. Use your e-mail address or your agent's contact info.

What if you have nothing? No movies at all to use for your reel? Do not panic.

If you can afford it, get a fake one made. There are services, such as CreateYourReel in LA, that will do this for you for a fee. They write and film three short contrasting scenes starring you, i.e. a funny one, a dramatic one, and a romantic one. The goal is to sell you and your brand. The quality of these demos is very high. They make it look like you booked the roles on major TV shows. Don't think you can do the same thing with your HandiCam. Pay to have it done right. You can see samples on their website and on YouTube.

These high-quality fake demos are entirely legitimate and accepted in the biz.

Why?

Jeez.

They just want to see what you would look like and sound like on their show, that you can act, and if you have something. *They're* trying to get a feel for you and to decide if you might be right for a role in *their* show or some future show. If you are right, then *they* will audition you for that specific role. If you are right, but wrong for *their* show, then *they* will remember you for some future show.

Reminder: these professional fake demos are totally acceptable. Real demos are better, meaning clips of you in a speaking role in real movies, TV shows, and quality short and independent films. Never use background (extra) work, or scenes from a class, or some theater show you did, or some modeling or newscasting you did. Never. You will be temped. Don't do it. Either real stuff you were in as an actor or professional fake stuff.

Agents and Managers and Publicists, Oh My

Agents and managers are crossing over into each other's territory more and more these days. I'll tell you why in a minute. First, the traditional definitions.

A publicist promotes you to people in the biz and to the world at large. If you're not famous, then she will try to make you famous by getting you on the cover of *Maxim* magazine, by getting some paparazzi to photograph you next to George Clooney, and by getting Orlando Bloom to take you to the Golden Globe Awards as his date. She will try to raise your public profile and your profile within the biz, so that more people know who you are, take you seriously, and want to hire you. Remember in the section on breaking into the Hollywood vault when I said "If you want to get work, get famous as soon as possible?" This is what she's doing. She is getting you exposure and building your brand as much as she can so you get work.

Very often you will see the BFSs out in public with their entourages. One of those people will be the publicist who probably set up the outing, who then will coach the BFS on what to do, who to talk to, and what to say. Then she'll guide the BFS to the photo opportunity. Then she'll try to prevent the BFS from getting arrested on the way home. If the BFS does get arrested, then she will try to get even more publicity off of that and somehow spin it in favor of the BFS, so the BFS gets even more work.

For this service, the publicist normally takes a percentage—often ten percent—of the BFS's total income, not just acting gigs, but everything. Some publicists will work for you on a trial basis for a monthly fee like 1000 bucks.

Agents represent you to employers (producers, directors, networks, studios). They are the connection between you and the people who hire and pay you. They stay on top of where the work is, do their best to get you considered for that work, and manage your contracts and money if you get hired. Think of them as your other half; you do the show, they do the business. Together you are a showbiz team.

Smaller agencies keep tabs on what's shooting, and then submit you for appropriate roles online as we have already seen. If the casting director wants to see you, then your agent will send you the info: breakdown, sides, and script. You prepare for and do the audition. If you book, then your agent negotiates your contract (money, work conditions, credits, etc.) and makes sure you get paid.

Bigger agencies might have the clout to bypass the submission process and promote you straight to the employers: "Hi Al? It's Harvey over at Superstar Fifteen Hollywood Agency. I hear you're doing a new

KitchenMan movie. Well, I got this new girl from France. You gotta see her. She's perfect for The Spatula." Al might agree simply because of the power wielded by the agency. Superstar Fifteen Hollywood Agency might also represent several Big Fat Stars, so if Al ever wants to hire one of them, he had better listen when they promote the new girl. Plus, she might be the next Big Fat Star, which would only be good for him.

Once *you* become a BFS, your agent will start fielding offers instead of submitting you. He will also look for other sources of work and income for you, such as commercials in Japan and celebrity golf tournaments in Dubai.

Once you are represented by one of the four A-List agencies—CAA, ICM, WME, and UTA—they will also try to *package* you. They represent BFSs of all kinds: actors, writers, directors, producers, golfers, singers, politicians, speakers, comedians, etc. When they get involved in a movie, they try to get several of their clients on the same project and make it a package deal. All or nothing at all. "You want this director? Well he comes with this writer and these actors. Take it or leave it."

For their services, LA agencies take ten percent of your pay. They also need to be licensed and bonded by the state to protect you against any monkey business.

A manager is your career coach. He works with you personally to build your success. Your job will be to hone your acting chops and network. His job will be to take all those contacts you made and try to turn them into work. He will get you invited to parties, help you strategize, make decisions, and get training. He might coach you before auditions, hang out on set with you and make sure you do the scene right, sit in on your headshot session, console you when you're down, and generally hold your hand as you go along.

For this, he will normally expect another 10 or 15 percent of your acting fees, or sometimes of your total income from all sources. Suppose somebody pays you one million to show up at a golf tournament —your manager probably wants his hundred grand.

Managers do not have to be licensed and bonded by the state, which means *anybody* can call himself a manager. Beware the shyster. But good ones can be invaluable to your success.

If you have all three—agent, manager and publicist—then you will pay them up to 30 percent of your earnings each time you work. That's a lot. Some enterprising agents are expanding into manager territory, some managers are expanding into publicist territory, and so on, so they make more money and have more influence.

How to Get an Agent or Manager

Okay, here's the top ten list of how you do it. At the top are the best but hardest ways; the bottom are the worst but easiest. Any one of them can work.

Come to them with a deal: "I've just booked the role of Han Solo in the new *Star Wars*, and I need an agent to negotiate the deal for me."

Have *heat*, which is to be a much-talked-about, but terribly mysterious, emerging star (and money-maker) who just won the top award at Cannes and whose LA agent just died in a freak plane crash, and be sure everyone knows how to get in touch with you.

Be personally referred by your coach, another manager, or any of *them*: star/agent/director/writer/editor/composer/producer/executive. Hollywood functions by referrals.

Shine in a magnificent indie film at a festival, hope *they* are in the audience (possibly because you invited *them*), and then shine in the lobby afterwards.

Shine in a class/workshop/showcase/comedy club/play, hope *they* are sitting in the back (possibly because you invited *them*), and then shine when *they* talk to you afterwards.

Shine in a web series, hope *they* see it (possibly because you invited *them*), and shine when *they* phone.

Consistently shine in class, and then be referred by a classmate.

Send a *query letter* or e-mail (see below) that displays credibility and a professional package.

Shine at a film party, industry event or round of golf, and hope to bump into the right person.

Be 17 years old, stunning, talented, and new in town, and sit at the counter in the right soda shop and cross your fingers.

How to Write a Query that Works

A *query* used to be an introductory letter sent to an agent asking to be represented. Now, it's typically an e-mail.

It used to be a fairly involved and descriptive one-page letter. Now, it's usually just a teaser that directs *them* to your website if *they* are interested in knowing more.

It used to be pretty standard. Today, tastes vary a lot.

Nevertheless, there are some common rules:

Only query agents who want to be queried. You can find lists online.

Address the agent by name. No general queries.

No text-message spelling. How you write the letter foreshadows the kind of client you will be.

Don't be overly formal either. Be a colleague, not a wannabe.

Lead with your credibility, not your name.

Keep it brief. Very brief. Three or four lines are usually enough. All the details should be on your website.

No attachments.

Provide all your links.

Done.

Example Query E-mails

Example One

Bonjour Brian,

For the past five years, I've been a top-rated, award-winning television actress in France. My show, Maude Poubelle, was number one in five countries. You may have heard of it. My agent in Paris, Marc Chagall, suggested you and I might make a powerhouse combo in LA. Would you look at my site, and let me know if you'd like to meet? I'm here until the end of June.

Best,

Isabelle Etoile
www.website.com
www.imdb.com
e-mail address
Phone number in LA

Example Two

Hello Brian,

I recently did a key role in Michael Bay's new film, Transistors,
which shot here in my hometown of Sydney. On set, Michael took
me aside to tell me I was very marketable in a Zooey Deschanel
sort of way, and I should get myself to LA. I am a dual citizen, a
union member, able to make the move, and very interested in
doing television. I really like your roster and your fantastic rep, and
I'd love to be able to work with you there. Here in Australia, I'm
with Ralph Wallaby at the Hazel Nut Agency. Feel free to call him.

I look forward to meeting you.

Sally Stunning
Website
Imdb
E-mail
Phone

Once you Get an Agent or Manager

Most actors think once they have an agent, they can sit back and watch the
money roll in. That's just dumb. Getting an agent is just the beginning.
Once you've signed up and started working together, do the following:

Be marketable, with potential to be a star. Everybody in LA is looking for the next Brad Pitt. All actors think they're the next Brad Pitt. Be objective.

Be ready—not in development. Be in the game, proven and packaged.

Have raw, natural talent. This gives everybody confidence. *They* want to know that you can do it every time. So do you.

Work your butt off—you keep 90 percent of your money so do 90 percent of the work. Never be home; be taking classes, networking, promoting yourself, having lunch meetings, or losing those pounds in the gym. Your agent will not only love you for this, but also he will expect it from you.

Be a good client—be honest, available, reliable, collaborative, hardworking, professional, rational, likeable and always exceed their expectations.

Mind their reputation. Reputation is gold in the biz. Everything counts, remember? Best policy: protect your reputation and everybody else's. That starlette you hated is 'fascinating' and that caustic director is 'eccentric.'

Make them money. Money is the alpha and omega. It means you get to stay and play some more. When it starts disappearing, so you do.

Do not confuse an agent with a manager or a manager with your Mom. They are happy to do their jobs, but they really hate doing other people's jobs.

Understand the biz, and be all about the biz.

Succeed on set. Do a great job, always. Everything counts.

Get a clear working relationship. Find out early on how they like to work, communicate, and do business, and then find a way to work together happily.

Okay. Congratulations. You've come a long way. Now: the important stuff.

STORY AND SCREENWRITING, DON'T SKIP THIS

A good script is a miracle.

—Hollywood Proverb

The Foundation of Everything: Story

Somebody, somewhere along the line, almost got eaten by a lion.

We're talking several hundred thousand years ago when we were still living on the savannah.

He got home all winded and terrified and he shouted: "Lion. Almost got me!" And his family all went back to flint knapping and sleep napping, because clearly it was in the past, and he was okay.

Frustrated, our ancient brother started to act it out. "He leapt out from behind a bush! He hit me with a left, and I went tumbling into Dead Man's Ravine!"

What happened then?

People started to listen.

So our boy backed up a bit and started again: "It was a dark and stormy night. I was hunting gazelle with the guys, but the guys did not have the courage to venture into the Plains of Peril. An ill wind blew black dust in our faces, but I brushed it away and went on alone, my feet burning in the powdery sand, my eyes scanning the horizon, my will set on one objective. For hours I walked on alone, when suddenly…"

When suddenly everyone in the camp is sitting around the fire with popcorn. Why? Because the fact has become a drama, and the drama conveys more than the fact. It conveys the experience of life. People feel the tension and the sand in their toes. Their bodies are taken over by it—which is fun because there is no real danger—and their brains suck it up as a lesson in case they're ever stuck out there in the Plains of Peril themselves. Hence you have: 1) group bonding; 2) physical enjoyment; 3) an explanation of what the hell is going on in the world; 4) relief from the tension of actual life; 5) relief from future tensions; and 6) real Darwinian survival value.

And thus was born the story.

My guess is it arose together with language, one spurring on the other.

Following that came other stories building on the first, soon creating an over-story explaining not only the lions, but the origin of the world, and pretty much everything else, and guiding the people in their quest for food, love, safety, community, the experience of life, and the desire for it all to make some kind of sense.

That's what movies do today. Remember that. Seriously. Highlight that last paragraph.

Basics of Structure

Skip this part at your peril.

What I am about to give you is a seriously abridged lesson in screenwriting. Even though I have an MA in screenwriting, have written many scripts, and right now have one in active development with a producer of 3D movies in Los Angeles, I find it hard to define screenwriting. To me it's kind of like composing music. Either you get it or you don't. Even though it uses words, it is in a profound way beyond words. My writing hero, William Goldman *(Butch Cassidy and the Sundance Kid, Misery, Maverick, All the President's Men, Marathon Man, The Stepford Wives, The Ghost and the Darkness,* and a little thing called

The Princess Bride) has written extensively on the topic. So, take my advice: at some point soon go buy his books, or the many others on the subject, and/or take a good class. In the meantime, soak up this brief summary. Your future in the biz depends on it.

Repeat: your future in the biz depends on it.

Repeated again: your future in the biz depends on it.

Just like the foundation of the oil business is energy to make things run, the foundation of the movie business is story, which, as we have seen, entertains and explains the experience of life. The love of story is the reason why we all work so hard and why the audience pays its money. It is all things. Since you, the actor, are the very face of the story, you must become an expert. So let's begin.

As a general rule, one page of script is equal to one minute of movie. Talking scenes move faster; action scenes move slower. The average movie nowadays is just about 100 minutes long, meaning a script of about 100 pages. Not long ago, scripts were in the 120-page range, but they're shrinking, possibly due to the shrinking attention spans of studio executives. Epics, like *Lord of the Rings*, will be longer; comedies, like *Blades of Glory*, will be shorter.

The story will have a beginning, a middle, and an end—Act I, II and III. According to the standard American film paradigm popularly illuminated by Syd Field in his books, Act I is about 25 pages long, Act II is 50 or 60 pages long, and the end, or climax, or Act III, is the rest.

Take a joke as an example of why this is. We want the set up to be short and sweet:

My uncle Morty in Pennsylvania was trapped in a flood.

Very quickly we know who's involved, what's happening, and what the problem is. If we're not interested, then we haven't lost too much. If we are interested, then we are prepared, even eager, to listen to a big middle part knowing it will be even more interesting, and there will be a fun surprise at the end.

The neighbor floated by in a dinghy and invited Morty to join him. Morty said, "No thanks. I have faith in God. He brought me here, He'll get me out." The neighbor shrugged and kept going. The flood waters rose. Morty was stuck on the second floor. The cops came by in a speedboat to take him to safety. Morty said, "No thanks. I have faith in God. He brought me here, He'll get me out." The cops shrugged and went off to save other people. The waters rose even more. Morty had to climb onto the roof. The Coast Guard sent a helicopter to get him, but the same thing happened. "No thanks. I have faith in God. He brought me here, He'll get me out." There was nothing they could do, so they left. The waters rose some more and Morty drowned.

This is the point of highest tension in the story. Morty is dead. How could there be any more story? What now? We got to caring about Morty, but now we're baffled. And now we sense the funny bit is about to be revealed: the surprise ending that we didn't see coming, but which makes sense and makes us laugh.

In Heaven Morty had a few words with God, "Hey, I had faith in you. You were supposed to get me outta there." God shrugged and said, "I sent you two boats and a helicopter."

Funny, but also kind of inevitable. And also instructive. Whoever made up the joke wanted to say something like faith triumphs, but only if you act on it.

But people don't really listen when you say things like faith triumphs but only if you act on it. They tune out. It's too intellectual. It doesn't seem to apply to them. They have better things to do than listen to old sermons.

So just like our caveman ancestor, the writer cleverly put the message inside a parable about people's misfortunes (always a hit with a crowd) and capped it off with a funny punch line. He added entertainment value. He got an audience. They laughed. With a little luck, they also got the message.

This is exactly how movies are written. A screenwriter starts with a moral message of some kind that he or she is passionate to communicate:

Self-respect is the ultimate victory (*Rocky*).

The forces of good will always prevail (*Star Wars*).

Justice wins because the good guys are badder than the bad guys (*The Punisher*).

True love overcomes all obstacles (*The Princess Bride*).

Then he or she wraps it up in an interesting premise that builds logically to a point of crisis, which precipitates a thrilling, surprising but inevitable climax. And while the audience's brains are off and their hearts are open, he or she slips in the message. Most of the time, the audience isn't even aware of it. But the movies they love are the ones that inform them about their lives. And inspire them. Who knows how many people took up boxing because of Rocky, or how many have tattoos of Rocky on their skin, or how many play the Rocky theme when they have to accomplish something nearly impossible, or how many got the courage to talk to the pretty girl and find love like Rocky did. The city of Philadelphia thought enough of Rocky to erect a statue of him, just like the ancient Greeks and Romans built statues of their gods.

Movies and stories and myths are messages from these gods telling us how to better live our lives. Just disregard the fact that they are created by people.

Incidentally, this is the best way of knowing when you've written something really good. People disregard you completely. You no longer exist. In fact, they are actually kind of angry that you are there, because they have in their hands a message from the gods in manuscript form. The fact that it was written by a human contradicts this belief, and therefore you, who only invented it, must go. The destiny of the screenwriter is to vanish. Tell me, how many screenwriters can you name? Don't flip back to see the name of my screenwriting idol, who is only one of the greatest who ever lived. How many can you name without help? I suspect the answer is close to none. This is why.

The Hero's Journey

The beginnings of this need for story go back to Mr. Caveman, as we have seen. Many things are common to all human cultures throughout history, like the use of fire, cooking, some form of marriage, and the division of labor. Another one is joke telling. And then there is story or some sort of mythology explaining the world and how to live in it. It is common and probably essential to all human cultures and human beings. Moreover, we all tend to tell the same types of stories, and the same basic story over and over again. That story is the mono-myth, or the hero's journey.

Star Wars is the classic example. George Lucas famously designed it to be exactly that—the hero's journey in space—basing much of it on the work of the renowned scholar of world mythology, Joseph

Campbell. Pick up his book, *The Hero with a Thousand Faces*, and you will see how the same tale is invented and told again and again by virtually all people throughout history.

It starts out with a person living a normal life (Luke on the farm) who is then given a call to adventure (fight the Empire) which he usually resists ("It's not up to me, it's too far, I have responsibilities.") but eventually, either by choice or by force, he accepts (his aunt and uncle are killed by the Empire) whereupon he meets a mystical counselor (Obiwan Kenobi) who informs him of his noble birth (Jedi) and presents him with a special weapon (light saber) and helps him cross the threshold of the unknown (Alderon) and into battle against vast forces of evil (Darth Vader and the Empire) in order to be reborn ('as a Jedi, like my father'). The hero must undergo a road of trials (escaping the Stormtroopers, getting captured by the Death Star, confronting Darth Vader), meet a goddess of perfect love or temptation or both (Leia), face an ultimate test (the destruction of the rebel alliance) and come to death and resurrection ("Luke, let go, and use the Force.") and reach some sort of atonement with the father (defeating Darth Vader) to accomplish the goal (destroy the Death Star) and make a dangerous escape (outrunning the explosion) with the help of a powerful rescuer (Han Solo) to bring a boon or benefit to his people (freedom and the Force).

You can see this same structure underlying ancient Greek myths as described in Aristotle's *Poetics*, in movies of all kinds, plays, novels, and comic books. Heroes all tend to be born of kings or gods or saints, have special weapons or knowledge or powers like Excalibur or a cloak of invisibility, and then they meet mystical helpers like Merlin or Gandalf or Alfred the butler, do battle against great villains like Lex Luthor or Hades or Sauron, and they have to undergo a spiritual or physical death and rebirth like Hercules, Superman, and Westley who dies on The Machine in *The Princess Bride*. Then they return to their people with boons like love and fire and safety for another day in Gotham City. The hero doesn't have to be a warrior—he or she can also be in a love story, a western, a comedy, or virtually any other kind of tale.

For those critics of formulaic American movies, I point out that the formula is not American, and that it has almost certainly been around for the 100,000 years since modern humans left Africa and probably a good million years before that. It happens to be what we humans want to see and hear. It's somehow basic to our DNA.

Genre

Remember, we want to see the misfortune of others. That's the only way we can learn anything. Get it? A guy with a nice happy life doesn't teach us anything; we want to know how he got there.

In the simplest terms, a screenplay is about a person with a problem. It's best if the person is someone we like or identify with or care about. Same with the problem. For this reason, smart writers don't write about things that happened to them, like when they lost a job or got a traffic ticket; instead, they write about universal problems that all people can identify with, like finding love, or dealing with heartbreak, or finding your path in life.

Movies tend to fall into three very broad categories: 1) Warning movies, which are often scary, and which warn us all about the way the world is going and invite us to maybe do something about it (*Enemy of the State, I Am Legend, Die Hard, Independence Day, World War Z*); 2) Better World movies, which are often quite a bit happier, show us visions of a better world, and invite us to be part of it (*It's a Wonderful Life, Legally Blonde, Love Actually, Pay it Forward*); and 3) Mythic movies, which are about gods or archetypal heroes who teach us the great life lessons, like how to be heroes ourselves (*Spiderman, Star Wars, 300, Lord of the Rings*). Genre is not an obstacle here. We can have Warning zombie films (*28 Days Later*) and Better World zombie films (*Shaun of the Dead*).

Certain kinds of problems are best dealt with in certain kinds of movies. This is the basis of genre—as in western, romantic comedy, murder mystery, thriller, and horror. If you are interested in lifting spirits with love and laughter, then you're probably writing a romantic comedy. If you are interested in extolling the classic American virtues, like independence and rugged nobility, then you might be looking at a western. Each genre has developed over the years a set of rules that define it.

In the romantic comedy for example, we need to see boy meet girl, boy lose girl, boy get girl back again. These rules correspond to the structure we have been talking about: Act I, Act II and Act III.

Since they're my favorite movies along with action comedies, let's use the romantic comedy as an example. What is at stake: life or death of the heart. If the lovers unite, then they will be truly alive, otherwise they will be the walking dead.

The leading man is usually a millionaire (*Pretty Woman*) or the Prime Minister (*Love Actually*) or an heir to a fortune (*The Proposal*) or the greatest writer in history (*Shakespeare in Love*) or just a prince of a guy (*Sleepless in Seattle*). Usually, we meet him in his happy life and then almost instantly throw it out of balance by having his wife die (*Sleepless*) or getting him dumped by his girlfriend (*Love Actually*) or having his stable job threatened (*What Women Want*). As he is grappling with this little problem, he sees the eyes of his true love at a party *(Bridget Jones' Diary)* at work (*Groundhog Day*) or in a restaurant (*As Good As It Gets*). This is his call to adventure. Usually there is a lot of resisting because she's engaged to someone else (*The Wedding Singer*) or she's impossible to win (*There's Something About Mary*) or she is unlikely or wrong for him somehow (*The American President*). At some point he accepts the call (in *Sleepless*, he actually accepts the phone call) and then soon bumps into his quirky neighbor (*As Good As It Gets*) or the whacky roommate (*Notting Hill*) or odd-ball pal (*Along Came Polly*) for advice and information and often some kind of special weapon that is usually nothing more than some courage or some insight into himself, or both. Then the special helper sends him, or them, over the threshold to adventure. In *The Proposal* for example, the helper is the Immigration Agent who sends them to Alaska to get fake-married. Sixty minutes of fun, games and trials for both of them ensue, during which they each grapple with the problems of love and their own inability to deal with it. The escalating pressure makes them grow and change for the better, but not fast enough, because pretty soon boy loses girl. This usually means she leaves town: she goes back to New York (*The Proposal*) or home to Portugal (*Love Actually*). The boy is in crisis. He has lost his love and hence his life, and there's no way to get it back. Except to die to himself. Most often his dumb ego needs to go (*The Proposal*) and he realizes that a man's got to do what a man's got to do (*Love Actually*), which is closely followed by a race through an airport or onto an actual plane (*The Wedding Singer*) where the lovers face off again, always in front of a crowd (every romantic comedy ever) where they replay their struggle in miniature, put their egos aside for something bigger—love—and eventually, after a lot of milking the moment, kiss to wild applause (*Elf, Never Been Kissed, Music and Lyrics, The Wedding Singer*). The lovers then return to their people embodying the boon of love, which usually causes everyone around them to start kissing too, old enemies to make up, and so on.

The End.

The girl in these stories has her own hero's journey too of course, and sometimes we see the story mostly from her point of view, as in *While You Were Sleeping.*

Act One

Most good scripts open with what is called a primordial image that sums up the mood and world of the story and is often connected to the forces of antagonism or the bad guy. Recall that in *Star Wars* the first image is stars against the blackness of space, and then, whoosh, an Imperial Cruiser that seems to be five miles long. In the next image, we see that it is chasing and trying to obliterate a tiny, helpless, nice-looking space ship. In these first few seconds then, we are shown the world of the story (stars and wars), and we're already inclined to be rooting for the guys in the nice-looking ship.

In the very next images we meet our hero or heroes, and see their lives go out of balance. In this case, Darth Vader blasts a hole in the nice-looking ship and marches inside looking for the Princess. She quickly hides the Death Star plans in R2D2's memory banks. Less than 60 seconds into the movie, we already know the basic story, and we're already on a rocketing rollercoaster ride.

Movies can't take ten minutes to get started; they need to start on the first page. After a minute or so, we decide if we're interested. After reading a page or two, studio executives decide whether they want to keep reading or drop it on the reject pile. If they're nice, then they might give you ten pages. Usually they're not so nice.

As the story is ripping along, we meet all the other key characters, and we watch as our hero is pulled toward a fateful meeting with his or her antagonist and the crossing over into the unknown. That moment when he or she, or sometimes they, take that step into the unknown, which usually has life or death consequences, is called the First Act Turning Point, or the Inciting Incident. There are other terms, too. In any case, this is the moment at which we know the hero's life is never going to be the same, that there is going to be a life or death struggle between the forces of good and evil, and we want to see it play out. Often, actual life or death is on the line, but not always. As we have seen, in the love story it's the life or death of the heart. In the coming-of-age story, it's the life or death of one's future. The inciting incident also states the central question of the movie: Will Luke save the Princess and the Rebel Alliance?

In *Legally Blonde* we meet Elle and see her life. She's ditsy but we like her. Then her life goes out of balance when Warner dumps her and goes off to Harvard. She decides she has to go too, to prove herself to him. So she gets accepted herself, and then she's faced with having to actually go into the unknown, a blonde at Harvard, risking the life or death of her heart.

In a western, it's when the bad guy says, "This town ain't big enough for both of us, Sheriff. Main Street. High noon." Actual life or death by six-shooter is at stake.

In *Alien*, it's when the alien creature jumps onto Kane's face. Life or death for him and soon for everyone on board the ship.

Act Two

Our hero undergoes a series of trials on the road to his or her goal. Each time she tries a tactic—i.e. when Ripley tries to fry the alien with a flamethrower—it doesn't work, and the door closes on it so she can never try it again. The risks get riskier, and the stakes get stakier. Tension builds as it appears that victory is impossible.

Ripley and the crew try everything they can think of to get the alien critter off Kane's face in one piece. They want to save it for study. But nothing works. Finally, after discussion and argument, they agree to cut it off. Snip, snip. There's blood, which turns out to be acid, which eats a hole through four levels of the ship's hull. Not trying that again.

That door being closed, the crew has to think up something else, something riskier, and more dangerous. Typically, all of Act Two action follows the hero, and it is based on the rule of cause and effect: one action leads logically to the next in an ascending staircase of riskier moves that don't pay off. Each move also has moral implications, which illuminate the heart of the protagonist and thus the central theme of the story.

Round about the middle of the movie there is usually another major event or revelation called simply enough the Mid-Point. In the first half of Act Two, the problem spreads out. Everyone gets involved and is under threat. Back to our *Alien* example, Mother, the ship computer, gets in on the action saying they must preserve the specimen—orders from the Company they all work for back on Earth. Once this story is spread out as far as it can go, the writer typically needs something to start bringing it all back in again towards a conclusion: that something is a Mid-Point event. In the case of *Alien*, the writers let everyone relax for a few minutes by having the critter release Kane all by itself and die. The crew members then have lunch, relax, and talk about money. Then the next stage of the creature busts out of Kane's chest and runs off into the depths of the ship. That's what you call a Mid-Point. One of them is now dead and the peril is increased. Now they have to hunt it down and kill it, whatever it is. Soon enough they find it, and it's just about the most horrible creature you can imagine and it likes to munch on people. One by one, they all die, except Ripley.

The end of Act Two is called the crisis, or the darkest moment. It is the point of highest tension, the moment of death and transcendence. Sometimes, as in the case of Westley in *The Princess Bride*, the hero actually dies and is resurrected. In most cases, the hero almost dies for real but certainly dies to his or her old self, and it is reborn in spirit or character or heroism. And in almost all cases, it involves the hero making a conscious decision to let go of his old self and embrace death and whatever may come as a result. It is this decision that we, the audience, really came to see, and that the writer worked so hard to deliver. It is this one decision that carries the meaning of the story and conveys it to our open hearts. We have a hero at the darkest moment of her soul, confronting death, and we get to see what decision she makes, and what happens as a result. It's thrilling and inspiring, and it helps us to know what to do the next time we are (figuratively or literally) stuck on a spaceship with an alien.

In our example, Ripley re-animates the head of the robot, Ash, and asks, "How do I kill it?" Ash replies, "You can't."

Stuck on a spaceship in the middle of nowhere beyond all help, alone, with an alien that eats people and can't be killed. That's what you call a dark moment. Then we get to see her decision: I will sacrifice everything to survive and protect humanity. She sets a nuclear bomb to destroy the ship and blasts off in the escape pod.

Climax or Act Three

In the final movement, the whole story tends to play out again in miniature. This is beautifully exemplified in *Alien*. Ripley thinks she's safe in the pod and that the creature is a cloud of radioactive dust, but instead she discovers that it's onboard the pod with her. The exact same story plays out again: there's a deadly alien on your ship that you can't kill, but now it's bigger and you're on a smaller ship. Yikes.

Now what?

Time to confront the bad guy directly, usually in spectacular fashion: in a battle, a boxing match, a chariot race, a shoot out, or a trial. This spectacle demonstrates the truth of the story. In the case of *Alien*, Ripley forces the thing out into the open (after climbing into a space suit) and then opens the back door. The critter is nearly sucked out into space but not quite. She shoots it with a space spear gun (wherever that came from) knocking it outside, but it grabs on and starts to pull itself back in. More tension and a chance for a secondary, and even more thrilling, end. Ripley ignites the main thrusters, frying the alien in the jet stream and sending it whirling into space.

Many screenwriters use this technique, called the false ending, to ratchet your nerves to the breaking point. You think it's all over, but wait a minute… In *Terminator*, for example, we think the Terminator is dead and burning up in the flames of the exploded gas truck. The tension comes off for a moment. We relax. The heroes are okay. They're fine. Whew, what a movie. Then… Oh crap… the Terminator rises up out of the flames, now just a metal endoskeleton, and he's really mad and coming in their direction.

We want to pee our pants.

James Cameron, who wrote and directed it, then has the gall to do it again a few minutes later! Our male hero, Reese, in his final act of self-sacrifice while trying to save Sarah Connor manages to stick a pipe bomb into the skeleton and blow its legs off. Whew! She's safe. He died saving her. What a movie.

Then the damn thing wakes up and starts crawling on its hands and broken torso after Sarah again!

I imagine many people did in fact pee their pants at this point.

Alone now, Sarah has to use her new skills, awareness, and self to defeat the villain or perish. Recall that in the beginning of the movie she was just a regular girl who was pretty much afraid of her own shadow. At the end, she's a Terminator terminator, a warrior in the battle against the Machines, and a suitable mother for the savior of humanity.

The Tag or Dénouement

Sometimes all the loose ends of the story are not tied up completely in the climax, so the screenwriter will add another scene to do that. Sometimes, for example, the love story couldn't be finished up until the main conflict was over, so he plays a little moment where the lovers come together and announce their love. In *Terminator*, there's a final scene in which Sarah Connor drives away in her Jeep and sums up her feelings and fears into a voice recording meant for her unborn son. In *Star Wars*, it's the scene in which our heroes all get medals strung around their necks, dramatizing the boon they've won for their people. In *Rocky*, it's the ten-second resolution of the love story after the prize-fight where Rocky sees Adrian: "I love you Adrian!" "I love you Rocky!"

The tag also gives the audience a moment to come down emotion-ally from the movie before the lights come up and reality hits them in the face. In a love story, it's the time to dry your tears before everyone sees you were bawling your head off.

Other Forms of Structure

The three-act structure is the basic form of the story, but writers and theorists come up with options and augmentations all the time.

Have a look at *Pulp Fiction*. Tarantino keeps going back in time to tell the same story from the point of view of different characters. Some writers do everything in five acts, as Mr. Shakespeare did. According to the sequence system popularized by Frank Daniel, some people think the best way to write a movie is in eight, ten-page mini-movies, each of which is structured in three acts, and each of which sets up the next. Still others think it's best to do away with all notions of structure entirely and just let the characters determine the story. Then there are movies that are flatly anti-structure.

But you can't go wrong with the good old three-act happy ending.

The Building Blocks of Structure

And now a little tidbit from the world of fractal geometry: if you look at a leaf under a microscope, you will see that it is composed of thousands of smaller structures that have exactly the same shape as the whole leaf. The tree found a structure that worked for it, and then simply and very intelligently multiplied it to create the finished leaf, which then has all the characteristics of both the small and the large. You can see this same pattern in all kinds of natural objects like snowflakes, and coastlines, and vegetables.

And since the stuff of story is another natural thing—human life—you can also see it in screenwriting.

If you analyze a good script, then you will find that every part of it, every act, every sequence, every scene, every beat within a scene, every character, every subplot, as well as the story as a whole, all have the same structure intelligently multiplied to create one brilliant glowing living thing. Story. It starts with an active and compelling beginning, an inciting incident, a mid-point, a crisis, a surprising turn, which is either an action (a punch in the mouth) or a revelation of some kind ("I love your sister.") and an inevitable ending. This is one of the secrets of good screenwriting: it's the same simple structure intelligently repeated in such a way that it grows logically into a whole of the same shape. Each little piece carries a bit of meaning; the finished story carries all the meaning plus a combined transcendent meaning in one simple and yet also very complex whole.

Most screenwriters start by structuring their overall meaning, the concept they want to communicate to the audience. This concept is carried by the hero so that his or her structure comes along with it. Then they give each character the same treatment, and then each Act, and so on down the line.

Let's do a short example. We have a war movie. You've seen this character many times in war movies. He's the great guy who dies early. We meet him very early in the movie, usually at the same time we meet the hero. He's a great guy; everyone loves him. Usually, he just got married and she's pregnant and his dad is the Senator from Colorado, or something like that. Then we throw his life out of balance by sending him into battle with the hero. When he gets on the threshold of the unknown (war) he decides he must do his duty and be the best soldier he can be. He meets his advisor, a Captain perhaps, who reminds him of his noble American birth and who gives him a new rifle. The battle begins. He kisses a photo of his wife and then jumps off the landing craft. He faces untold trials trying to take the beach. His buddies are dying all around him. They are clearly outnumbered and losing. He tries an escalating series of things that don't pay off. It becomes clear they will all die unless someone takes out the enemy bunker. Crisis. Alone behind a little pile of sand, we watch him make his decision. It needs to be done or everyone dies. He calls for backup from the other guys. No one comes. They're too afraid. He's alone. He faces the decision again. He could decide to be afraid too, and maybe he'd survive. But that would make him a coward and he'd have to live with that which he just can't do because he's a great guy. He couldn't do it to his wife, to his father, to his country. He checks his weapon. He decides. He'll go it alone. He dies to his old self, and he is reborn a hero. He scrambles up the slope, bullets flying, dives into the bunker, and takes out all the bad guys. Seeing this from the beach our hero is taught a lesson about courage and the call of duty in the face of insurmountable obstacles. But then the tanks arrive, and one of them is turning its big gun on the bunker. The great guy can't get out without help. Our hero charges up there to save him, blasting his machine gun, dodging bullets. But it's too late. Kaboom. The great guy dies in a blaze of glory and shrapnel not five minutes after crossing the threshold. A hero.

You feel terrible, don't you?

Well, that's the idea. Our great guy lived his whole story, the entire structure we've been talking about, in the first fifteen minutes of the movie. His story is done. But, of course the writer did that to further teach the hero, to raise the stakes of life and death, to show what could happen to the hero, and to make the audience side with him in his quest to defeat the enemy and get justice for America as personified by the great guy. If you were cast as the great guy, then that would be your dramatic function.

The writer continues to build up his tale like this; one story made up of many other little stories, blending together, circling around the main theme, defining it, resonating it, magnifying it, and showing its opposite.

A Story Told in Pictures

Put on a great movie. Turn the sound off. You should be able to watch and understand and enjoy the whole thing that way. Why? Because a movie is a story told with pictures. Not with words as in a novel or with dialogue as in a play or with song as in an opera. It is told with pictures. As in a movie. Think of pure action movies such as *Rambo* or *James Bond*. You might see a little bit of set up, and then it's 90 minutes of spectacular story told with pictures. Every now and then Bond stops for a moment to utter a *star line*, like "He won't have the stomach to do that again," and then he's off on another speedboat.

Yes, there are movies that are full of dialogue, but the nature of cinema, its essence, is a story told with pictures. If you ever get a chance to see a silent film, like *Joan of Arc*, or *Battleship Potemkin*, or *Birth of a Nation*, then you will witness pure cinema. These films are visually masterful and amazingly moving.

What this means to you, the actor: the story is told with the *pictures*. Not the *dialogue*. Untold numbers of actors come into my classes freaking out about the words. Must get the words right. It's all about the words. Some of these folks are just beginners who don't know better, and some are theater actors for whom the text is all things and absolutely sacrosanct. Understood. That is the good and true tradition of theater. But we are making a movie and movies are different. They are stories told with pictures. Most of those pictures are *close ups* of your eyes and face. That means that what you *do*, and what you *feel*, and what you *think*, and how you *react* (because the camera sees all those things, and they are part of the pictures) are more important than what you say. The pictures carry the story.

Scene: man and wife in the kitchen.

> MAN: Coffee?
> WOMAN: You're kidding.
> MAN: I can't offer you coffee?
> WOMAN: I can't question something I've never seen?
> MAN: I happen to love you.
> WOMAN: You're starting to grow on me, too.
> MAN: This afternoon. We cut class. Skinny dipping in the pool.
> WOMAN: Mmmm. I suppose we should get some use out of it.
> MAN: Two-thirty then?
> WOMAN: Agreed.

The bad actor, thinking it's all about the dialogue, plays it all cheery and chirpy like a couple flirting in the morning. *Oh, honey, let's go for a swim.*

The good actor knows that in their next scene together, the man is going to drown his wife in the pool because he read the script and because he gets it. This scene is not "let's go for a skinny dip." The scene is "I'm luring you out to the pool where I'm going to kill you 'accidentally' for the insurance money so I can pay my gambling debts and not get killed myself, and how ironic that you think it will be fun." That's what's going on. And since you know that, what you think and feel and how you speak and react in the scene will be different than in the chirpy version. You will be playing the sub-text, in other words, the real meaning of the scene that is underneath the lines. Sub the text.

What the scene *means* in story terms is something like this: husband is beyond redemption because he will murder the one person he loves, the one person who believes in him, to cover up his miserable cowardice.

This may very well have been the sentence the writer started with before she wrote the scene. I need to show that the husband is beyond redemption so the audience will accept it later when I have him run over by a steamroller. How am I going to do that? Well, I could use the pool where he made his first bad bet earlier in the story. That would be ironic. He could make it look like an accident. I could set it up that she loves the pool, maybe he bought it for her, or maybe they met at the beach. What a schmuck.

Get it? The story is in the sub-text, which is what we see. The pictures. The look in the eye. The subtle reactions. The movements. The hiding. The writer then very cleverly uses the dialogue as *counterpoint* to the truth of the moment. It's like a sprinkle of spice on top of the scene that is in contrast with the main flavor: murder. You've probably heard it said that acting is reacting, that Oscars are won on reaction shots, and not for delivering dialogue. This is why.

Of course, good plays are written this way as well, but in cinema it is beyond paramount; it is the very nature of the thing itself.

No sane writer would do the scene like this:

> WOMAN: You never pour me coffee.
> MAN: That's right. I never pour you coffee. But I'm being nice to you this morning so I can lure you behind the pool and kill you.
> WOMAN: To pay your outrageous gambling debts to Lefty, and Luke, and Petey the Knife?
> MAN: And your sister, Meghan.
> WOMAN: Goodness. I suppose you'll try to seduce me too?
> MAN: You always fall for it.
> WOMAN: Yes, I do. And you think I won't suspect anything?
> MAN: Why would you? I've always been good to you.
> WOMAN: True. Yes, I suppose I would fall for it.
> MAN: Two then?
> WOMAN: Can we make it two-thirty? I want a few minutes to say goodbye to Fluffy.

The characters are speaking the sub-text—what we call *on the nose* writing—and the thrill is gone. Instead, it becomes a ridiculous comedy.

So, get busy learning to act for the camera by understanding story and screenwriting and by telling the story with the pictures. The casting director will want to have your babies.

But does it Play?

After the writer has bled onto his keyboard for months doing the many impossible tasks that you will read about in the books you're going to get, he has to make it *play*. For those people who are used to reading novels, this can be a tough concept because a good script is nothing like a good novel. A novel is a work of literature. A screenplay is more closely akin to a work of music, as I have said before. A symphony for the camera. When people read it, they should see the movie in their heads and hear the music in their ears. In their very eyes, they should see the movie itself rolling by *exactly* as it would on the big screen and exactly in time. A 100-page script should take exactly 100 minutes to read. If the reader sees *words*, then the script has failed. It's only a movie script if they see *pictures*—what appears to be the actual movie playing in front of them. If you doubt me, then go online and look up the script of *The Princess Bride*. You'll see what I mean.

The screenplay is not a description of the movie as so many people seem to think; nor is it a blueprint of the movie, nor is it a set of instructions on how to make the movie (although it is partially all of those things). The screenplay is more like the score that plays out in time. It carries you like a wave, sometimes up, sometimes down, but always forward, and never stalled or choppy or out of line. The notes of the symphony can't be all jumbled up in one place. That is not music. The notes have to unfold at exactly the right time and in exactly the right relationship to the other notes in volume and texture and feeling and in the right relationship to the piece as a whole. It has rhythm, and a certain key, and a defining theme that unfolds. It doesn't play on your brain; it plays on your emotions. It bypasses your brain and immediately causes you to feel and imagine.

So, if as an actor you pick up a script that instantly turns into a movie against your will, then you have found a good one. When you get to the end, go back to the beginning and start examining it in detail, like a pianist, to understand and be able to play it on your instrument: you.

Format

Over the past 100 years of Hollywood, a standard presentation format has emerged. Scripts are written on letter-sized, three-hole punched, white paper, in 12-point Courier font, with set margins for the various elements such as action, character names, and dialogue, feature very taut succinct writing styles meant to express the story as efficiently as possible in the present tense, and are held together with two heavy brass brads at the corners. No brad is to be put in the middle hole. Adherence to this format distinguishes the amateur from the profes-sional. Amateurs always seem to think that if they mess with the for-mat they'll get noticed. Well, they will, just before their script hits the trash.

There is a reason for the format. A producer can flip through a properly formatted script and learn a lot about the film just by looking at the pages as they go by. First of all he can see that it's 104 pages long meaning a 104-minute movie on average. That is important informa-tion when an extra minute of movie can cost an extra 500 grand. He can see if it's full of action or dialogue, or a good mix of both. He can get an idea if the story is properly structured, too, since most movies are heavy on the dialogue at the beginning and then move more and more towards action at the end. If he wants to read it, then he can eas-ily remove the brads and lay the script out on his desk. Since it is in standard format, he can easily compare it to others he has read. If he likes it, then he can quickly replace the brads and send it off to actors or the photocopy room.

Once the script goes into production, the actors will start prepping, the rest of the crew will start numbering the scenes and analyzing it for props and sets and number of space ships, and all their methods are based on the standard script format. During production, the script supervisor will take copious notes on the script itself on behalf of the editor, and these notes too are based on the standard format.

Go online and look up a few scripts from produced movies and you'll see this standard format. For those of you who are thinking about writing a script yourself, you can easily buy software that will do the formatting for you.

Okay, those are the basics of screenwriting. Go buy some books, remembering that none of this stuff means a thing if you can't audition properly.

YOUR FIRST AUDITION

What are we looking for? We are looking for real; simple as that. No acting, no shtick. We are looking for the person that we believe, both physically and verbally, in that role.

What goes into that is a longer answer. For me, a very natural delivery is key. Body language, eye contact and volume should all be what they would be in real life. Actors tend to either be too "on," getting perfect posture, perfect resonance, and Hannibal Lecter eyes in an effort to perform well, OR they will over compensate and do nothing, mumble, slouch and look at their shoes, in an effort to be "simple." Both ring false. Real life is often loud, often messy, often active. It is almost never perfect, nor does it fall flat. Perhaps the single biggest indication to me, in the room, of a great reading is that I truly believe the actor is listening to me as I read with them. The old, tired cliché of "Acting is Reacting" is very true. Even when the reader is giving a dull, lifeless performance, that actor needs to listen, react to what is there (or hear something better in his head and react to that if need be). Again, perfect line delivery is not what we are after, it is a real, living, interaction. Wardrobe is important, but not crucial. Dress the economic class and circumstances of the character, and we will fill in the rest. Anything that feels like a costume will take us out of the reading much more than it will impress us and draw us in. Lastly, we can tell if the actor has "set the stage" in his/her mind. "SEE" the environment you are in, place people, object, places in your environment (do it quickly please.) Once the scene starts, it makes us feel that you really are there. If you believe it, then so do we.

— Andy Henry, casting director (CSI, Percy Jackson - The Lightening Thief)

Okay, now that you have survived your first day as a screen actor, discovered what *they* are looking for, and understood story, it's time to get working. I mean, time to audition. Rarely does it happen that you book a job without auditioning. Well, actually, it does happen in two ways:

Your husband is a director.

You are a mega-star.

Absent these two conditions, you will almost certainly have to audition for every part you ever get. *They* have to see you in the role to know if you're the best choice. This is the reason why the audition is so difficult.

In the audition, you sell yourself to *them*. In the movie, you sell the story to the audience. Different. Similar, but different.

Film acting attracts a lot of weirdoes, so there is a list of unwritten audition rules—I call them *land mines*—which pros know about but which amateurs don't. If acting on a film set involves advanced pretend, then the audition is pretend squared. You have to invent the whole scene standing in one spot in a room the size of a closet for people who often don't care or are sick to death of actors and scenes and closets. And yet you still have to make them lean forward and love you and believe in the story and in you. You have to wait in a small room full of people who look just like you or better, and they probably have vastly better resumes and are reading for the same role. Usually, an enormous amount of pettiness, jadedness and repressed rage wafts in the air. You have to transfer confidence to the casting people in the room so that they will pass your tape to the producers. As Andy says: "Your performance in the room gets you on the tape; your performance on tape gets you in the movie." You have to prepare for auditions and do them without pay. And a lot more.

It is its own little art form, which is similar to working on set but also very different. Kind of like the Portuguese and Spanish—they can mostly understand each other but they are different languages.

Which one should you learn? The one that gets you booked. The audition. Master it first so you have a chance of working.

Getting the Call

You will get a phone call from your agent. Seeing it's her on your call display, you will think, "Damn. She hates my headshots. There's another 300 bucks down the drain." And you'll answer with "Hi Sandy."

And Sandy, your agent, will say something like this: "Hi. I have an audition for you on Monday the 12th at noon with casting director Rhona Bambalona. It's for a movie of the week called *Lord of the Wings* about a dwarf named Fred O. Baggings who overcomes his fear of heights by becoming the world's first four-foot tall fighter pilot. Rhona wants to see you for the part of Calvin, the aircraft mechanic who secretly gives Fred a leg up toward completing his training. I've sent you the breakdown, the sides, and the script, okay?"

You will be a bit stunned. You will let it all sink in. You will realize that you didn't really hear most of what Sandy said. You will say okay anyway.

If she's a nice agent, then she might at this time say, "Congrats."

Then she will hang up. You will process the info, trying to remember what she said. You will recall that she said something about Monday the 12th. You will swear, probably aloud, because that's the day you're supposed to be in a daylong meeting at work. Never fails. Also, any time you leave town, and I mean any time, you can count on your agent to call as you're boarding the plane. You may not have heard from her in months. You want to take two days and go see your aging mother in Dubuque, Iowa, but suddenly you have an audition the very next day.

You can learn two important lessons from this: if you want to hear from your agent, then book a flight, and along the road of your acting career, you are going to have some hard choices to make.

If you are smart (and you are) then you will not panic. You will download the script, the sides, and the breakdown, and see what you'd be missing if you flew to Dubuque.

The Breakdown

This little baby is a summary of the project including information on what kind of project it is, where it is destined to be shown, who's making it, who's casting it, when *they're* shooting it, when the auditions take place, its union status, what the story is all about, which characters they are looking to cast, and so on. Study it. You might find that it's a feature film, which could be very good for your career.

Features are the mac-daddies of projects. You want to do as many of these as possible. You want to do *only* these if you can because only people who do movies get to be movie stars. It's what we all aspire to. You will not see Brad Pitt on television except for the odd episode of *Friends*, and only then because it was a lark, and he liked Jennifer Aniston. You see Brad in movies. If his star ever fades to the point where he can no longer get hired for the movies (unlikely), then you might see him starring in a TV show of some kind like countless other former movie stars are doing, but not before. In the meantime, he's holding on to cinema as long as he can.

If you get cast in one movie, then you could get cast in another one, and that all means there may be a place for you in the cinema landscape. That is a very good thing. Plus, many people around the world will see your work, which is good for the building of your brand. Plus, many moviemakers and Hollywood types will see you, which is good for your industry profile. (Please note that many name casting directors don't do auditions for key roles; they make phone calls to your agent having seen you in something.) Plus, movies are usually full of movie stars, meaning you might—in fact, you probably will—get to work with one of them. Your average two-line part in a feature is usually played opposite one of the stars. This is good for your demo reel, good for your acting chops, good for your confidence, and good for your career in a whole lot of other ways. Who knows, you and Megan Fox might become fast friends. That couldn't hurt. *Plus,* you will get to work with a top director. *Plus,* you can pretty much count on it being a great script. *Plus* a lot of other good things. *Plus,* you can go see yourself at the local cineplex with your girlfriend and shrug coolly when she sees you on the big screen.

So, if it turns out to be a feature film, then starting thinking about changing your flight.

In some ways television is even better; especially nowadays. As I write this, a huge number of movie actors are doing television: Sigourney Weaver, Dennis Quaid, Richard Dreyfus, Cathy Bates, Josh Lucas, Laura Linney, Christina Ricci, Ashley Judd, William H. Macy, Glenn Close, and Kevin Bacon. And many others. This never happened before. The reasons have to do with:

- Studios making a much smaller number of movies, most of which are bigger budget sequels, remakes, animation, and comic book movies;
- Shrinking movie-star salaries;
- Growing television salaries;
- The economic situation in the US;
- The expansion of the TV universe, specialty channels like HBO, AMC, etc.;
- Great writing for television;
- The trend toward home consumption of entertainment (downloading, streaming, Netflix, YouTube, etc.);
- The rise of new powers in the movie world, namely China and India;
- The rise of the independent filmmaker. Anyone with an IPhone and a Mac can make a feature film now.

Basically, the new media is expanding. The cineplex is moving into the living room, and the stars are moving with it.

If your audition is for a TV series, then you might be looking at steady work, possibly for years, and a great deal of money. Features pay you once while television pays you over and over again, potentially forever. People like that sort of thing.

Hmmm.

Better investigate this audition.

Start by looking up the people involved in the project. Go to www. imdb.com and search. If you're not aware of this site, then go there immediately and have a look around. It is a comprehensive database of every single human being who ever worked on any movie or TV project at any time in the modern history of humanity. If the people of Atlantis had movies, then they will not be listed. Everyone else is. I'm there. Go look me up. Go look up Brad Pitt and you'll see his entire resume. At the top of his listing, you will see titles with little red status notes in parentheses, i.e. (in production). These are the projects he is working on now but they have not yet been released. Your goal as an actor is to get a listing on IMDB, to build it up to roughly the same size and scope as Brad's and to always have several items in red. That means you're working. And the fact that you're working means you can work more.

IMDB is resume central for everyone in the biz. Any time I call anyone new in LA, I can hear them typing my name into IMDB and examining my photo and credits. It's just what we do. If you sign up for IMDBPro, then you can access all kinds of other useful information, including the STARmeterTM, which uses some kind of big-brained algorithm to track every actor in the world and rank them on a scale of one to one million. Actually, four million. Or so. It changes every day according to who's hot, who's in the news, who has a movie opening, who's being searched online, who just got married, and so on. It is very useful for casting directors and producers. *They* use it all the time to find rising stars who *they* can get for cheap dollars or falling stars who *they* can get for cheap dollars, or BFSs who *they* can consider for huge dollars. It is searchable as well, so you can ask it to list all the blonde actresses who are 18 to 25, play ping pong, and have a certain STARmeterTM ranking. I once reached number 6,695 on the STARmeterTM. I am currently ranked 74,612. Considering that when you get your first credit you will be ranked somewhere north of 4 million, I'm doing pretty well. I am in the top two percent of actors worldwide having once been in the top fraction of one percent.

Sounds pretty good doesn't it?

Well, it ain't.

It basically means I have a pretty good resume, I'm employable, but I have absolutely no traction. No buzz. Nobody's going to ask me to be on *Dancing with the Stars*. I live in the outlands somewhere, and occasionally I book a job or two. Once in a while, I get lucky and land a good-sized role working with somebody like John Voight for a few days. I feel validated. I do not make a living doing it. No big agency is looking for me. Because I have a sizable resume with work in production, I can properly call myself a film actor whereas most everyone below me can properly call themselves wannabes.

And I'm in the top two percent.

To be a real *working actor*, I'd need to consistently be in the top one percent, or approximately one of the top 35,000 actors on planet Earth. Those are people who are really in the game, probably live in LA or London or New York, and work regularly enough to kind-of make a living. They work several times a year, maybe more, have a profile in the industry but probably not in the public eye, and keep their STARmeterTM up by appearing in higher profile movies and TV shows than I do. (I no longer live in LA.) Sometimes they struggle. Any day now, they could drop out of the biz and sadly no one would really miss them. But at least at this time, they are working.

To be a real *contender*, you need to be in the top 1/10th of one percent or the top 3,500 or so. Go ahead and look up number 3,500. My guess is she'll have a sizable career but you probably won't recognize her name. She will have been the lead in a TV series maybe. She will have appeared in a number of high-profile movies. That sort of thing. You will also see dead people on this roster. Yes, people like John Wayne and Elizabeth Taylor are still in this group and making money—kicking your ass— even though they are no longer with us. Holding place number 3,504 today is Scoot McNairy. Most of us don't know Scoot. We have nothing against Scoot. In fact, we admire him. He's kicking our butts and making a living. Proper respect. He has done some television and many movies we may never have heard of, we have never seen him on a talk show or magazine cover, but he's a serious contender. He's on the way up and could break out any minute now and become a household name. Maybe by the time this book is published, he already will have, but right now he's hovering on the verge. And he's in the top 1/10th of one percent.

Along with actors in the top 3,500, there is a special category: *name actors*. There are two kinds: names known in the biz and names known to you, the audience.

The first kind are people like William Fichtner, a fantastic actor with a huge and enviable resume and tons of respect. If you saw *Date Night*, then you saw him as the crooked DA who made Tina Fey and Steve Carell dance in the nightclub. He has eight movies in production and 41 past credits including little things like *The Dark Knight* and *Mr. and Mrs. Smith*.

The second kind are names known to you. Example: Number 3,500 today is Dwight Yoakam, who is a country music star but not a movie star. Nevertheless, he is a name you recognize. Names like this get hired because they know what they're doing and because they might help the movie make money.

To be a Big Fat Star, you probably need to rank in the top 1/10th of 1/10th of one percent—the top 350 or so. What defines a BFS? Money. They can make money at the box office. You put Tom Hanks in your movie and it's going to make money. At the very least, it's going to *open*, meaning a lot of people are going to come on opening weekend to see the latest Tom Hanks movie. After that, it might bomb. But probably not with Tom in it.

Again, several categories of BFS: rising stars, falling stars, passing stars, movie stars, mega-stars and legendary stars.

Example of a rising star: occupying the number 350 spot today is Danielle Panabaker who was in *Piranha 3D*. Not a household name, but she's a name in the biz at this time and is likely to star in something else soon.

Example of a once-falling star: Mickey Rourke. He found his way back in so I don't feel so bad pointing him out. Having once been the toast of the town, Mickey spent 15 years in exile and was looking for work in construction. But even as a fallen star, he still had some value. Given exactly the right movie, he could make money again. That movie was *The Wrestler*.

Passing stars are usually young things who get lucky with a franchise movie of some sort, who make money there, but seem to have zero value beyond it. They are stars of the moment who come and go.

An example of a real movie star would be Greg Kinnear, a terrific actor who is incredibly likeable, rich, famous, proven, and sought-after. His presence will help a movie make money, but it will probably not open a movie. People won't line up around the block just because he's in it. For that you need a mega-star.

There are a handful of these guys and, yes, they are virtually all guys: Cruise, Hanks, Will Smith, Will Farrell, Bruce, Harrison, Denzel, Brad, George. A small number. Now and then, a woman like Angelina can open a movie. But it's mostly the boys. The handful. Two or three dozen, maybe. It's probably one of these mega-stars that inspired you to want to become one too. I don't want to be a downer, but your odds of breaking into this group are pretty slim: possible, but lottery-slim. It's mainly because these guys last. 30, 40, 50 years sometimes. So there are not many openings.

Still expensive, but always worth it are the legendary stars like

Clint, and Jack, and Sean, and Gene, and Morgan. And, of course, Meryl. They give a movie not only money but a certain legendary status that draws people around the world. Again, there are only a few dozen of these, and one of them is always Clint. They are probably the top 10,000th of one percent of all actors on Earth.

So, that's the line up. That's what you're dealing with.

Your odds may be long, but you definitely won't make it if you don't get started. To get a credit on IMDB and a ranking of four million in the world, you need to appear in a project that gets some kind of approved screening, i.e. it makes it to theaters, or on TV, or is accepted to a film festival. (You can't wave a little camera around at Thanksgiving dinner and expect an IMDB listing.) Your credit will appear automatically provided the producers have listed the title. If it doesn't appear, then you can take steps on the site to let them know you were in the movie and would like to be credited.

Okay, back to what you were doing: looking up the people on the breakdown. I advise you to find them all on IMDB and check them out. With a little clever hacking, you might be able to find out who the stars are (they most likely won't be listed on the breakdown). In any case, you will find the producers and the director, and you will see how much clout they have and how likely it is that this project will be great. You will learn enough about them to have a conversation (if you get that lucky). This will help give you confidence and calm you down. Plus, you might learn a thing or two about the kinds of films they do, and therefore the kind of performance they want from you.

Remember that there are different styles of acting like there are different styles of playing the guitar. There are also different tones within each style. You can play the guitar classically or you can rock out. Different styles on the same instrument. Then you can play different tones like Chicago blues, dance blues, or bluegrass blues. These are the same basic style with different tones or sub-styles if you like.

The same is true of acting. Maybe you see yourself as suited for romantic style, but are we talking about straight romance, or romantic comedy, or screwball romantic comedy, or black comedy? They're different. They ask for different styles, different choices, and different ways of doing things. Once you advance a bit in your career, you'll start to get good at these different styles and tones, and you'll find the ones that work best for you. If you happen to live in LA, then you can take classes in all these different styles—you can go from your soap class to your sit-com class to your primetime drama class. For now, see if you can identify the style and tone that's right for this audition by reading the script and the breakdown and then doing a survey of the people involved. Many directors lodge themselves in a certain genre—romantic comedy for example—that you can see if you study up on them. Rent their movies. See what they're looking for in terms of style and tone.

Example: Romantic comedy acting is all about the idea of awkwardness. Everybody in a romcom is awkward, out of place, slightly embarrassed, pretending to be okay, clumsy, kind of pitiful, but very charming at the same time. It's this awkward charm that makes it funny. Think of Hugh Grant. See what I mean?

Example: a television series will strive to have a unique look, feel and style to distinguish it from every other series out there on the tube. You have to look and feel like you belong on that show, not to mention act like it, or you won't get the job.

Okay, back to the breakdown. Examine the rest of it for clues, information and encouragement.

You might want to check out the pay scale, for example. A little two-day part might net you five grand depending on where you live and which union presides. If you are in the US, and your two days are three days apart, then you will most likely be paid for the *intervening* days as well according to SAG rules, so you could make fifteen grand. If it's an episode of a popular TV show that also pays residuals and syndication, then you might net $30,000. That could take the sting out of your cancelled flight to Iowa. On the other hand, if it's an ultra-low budget feature, then you might be in for 100 bucks a day plus a piece of the action in the (unlikely) event that the movie makes money. Pay scales vary according to the size and scope of the role, the movie's budget, and your agent's ability to negotiate on your behalf. They also vary from country to country, and union to union, and sometimes from union branch to union branch. Talk to your agent.

The breakdown should also tell you when and where your audition will be held. Put the time and date in your iPhone and set the alarm so there is no way to miss it. Then do an Internet search on the address and print out a map. Or better yet, do a drive-by so there is no way to get lost on the day.

The Script

The script is the script. It will come in .pdf format so you cannot make a few changes and say you wrote it. You will read it all, carefully. If it's a high-profile thriller, *they* may only give you the first 90 pages so you won't know who-dun-it in the end and can't blab to all your friends on the Internet. In other cases, such as when it's a *very* high-profile movie, *they* won't give you the script at all, and your audition scene may not be from the script at all, so there is no possibility of a leak. But normally you will get the whole thing. Needless to say, don't post it and don't go blabbing about it. You will be tempted, I know, but posting and blabbing about it is unclassy and a clear sign of an amateur who is not destined to move forward in his or her career. If anyone finds out that you are up to these sorts of shenanigans, then your career in this town is over. Plus, I will kill you. So, keep it to yourself. If you must talk, then talk to other friends in the biz or your coach.

Next, find your scene or scenes. Review them closely according to the section of story and screenwriting to find out why are you are in the movie. What is your dramatic function? The writer put you in there for a reason, a story reason, not just to give you a part. What is that story reason? Why are you there?

Let's do an example exercise. Read the following page of script. You are being asked to read for the agent—not a Hollywood agent but an agent of doom. The script calls for a big Asian dude, but we are looking at everyone of every age, and gender, and ethnicity for this part. Okay? That includes you.

You should be able to read this one page and tell me: what the movie is about, what kind of movie it is, who the hero is, which stars are likely to be in this movie, where the scene happens in the movie, what the central question of the story is, what happens next, and why you, the agent, are there. If you are very clever—and you are—then you should even be able to guess the title of the movie. Read it and don't stop pondering until you have answered all the questions.

AGENT

Mortally ashamed, Charlie can't face his father.

            BIG DRAGON
        Shoot me if you want, but let him
        go.

            RED EYE
        Oh, we're not going to shoot you,
        Doctor. That would be very
        unpopular. No, no, for you, and
        your little Dragon, we're going do
        something much, much worse.

                            DISSOLVE TO:

INT. GREYHOUND BUS - DAY

The desert of Nevada, in June. Hot June.

Guarded by two SECRET SERVICE AGENTS in clumsy 'American'
clothes, the Dragon and Charlie stare out the bus window
as the endless, empty desert rolls by.

            CHARLIE
            (to the window)
        Man, was he ever not kidding.

            BIG DRAGON
        What?

            CHARLIE
        It's not so bad. There's lots of
        sun. And room. And dead things.

EXT. THE STEEL FARM - MOMENTS LATER

The bus stops in front of a decrepit farm house, owned by
a decrepit American couple, the STEELS, who are standing
out front waving as the bus arrives.

Charlie and the Dragon are nearly pushed out by the
agents.

            AGENT
        Have a nice 'life'. If you are
        ever seen in Hong Kong again... we
        cook your family!

The agent throws their luggage at their feet, and boards
the bus. As it pulls away the Steels approach, and help
with the bags.

            MR. STEEL
        Long trip? Okay, this would be
        the house. Those are cows. And
        that's the rest of the place. Come
        on in.

Cheater.

I said read it over and don't stop until *you* have answered all the questions. Don't look at me. I won't be around when you have to do this for real. And you will have to do this for real every time you audition or prepare for a part, and no one will be there to help you. In fact, this is probably the largest and most important part of your job as an actor. Your job is to read the script and perfectly interpret it in your performance using whatever tools God gave you. Don't show up looking pretty and ask, "What are we doing?" That is not your job. You must interpret the script. Therefore you must get the script. Therefore you must go back and actually do the exercise and see how good you are at this point. Okay?

Try again.

Hmmm. I suspect you cheated again. But if you didn't, congratulations. Here are the official answers.

What's the story about?

Clearly it's about a young boy who has sorely disappointed his legendary father, the Big Dragon, who is also a doctor, and who must regain his respect by getting them both back to Hong Kong. Look at the scene again. It's all in there.

What kind of movie is it?

Clearly, since it's about a young boy and his dad, it's a family movie. But more than that, we can tell that it's a comedy ('Lots of sun. And space. And dead things.'). And it's also quite apparent that there is potential for action: the comic book names like Big Dragon, and Red Eye, the Secret Service Agents, our heroes getting pushed around, the dialogue like: "Shoot me if you want, but leave my son alone." Since our heroes are Chinese we can assume we have some kung fu on our hands. So there you go. Family, action, kung fu comedy. *Spy Kids* with karate chops.

Who's the hero?

Clearly, it's who? Altogether now... Charlie. The son. The kid. As in kids' movie. He is clearly responsible for getting them in the mess (Mortally ashamed, Charlie can't face his father) and clearly has to find a way to get them out if he is to regain his father's respect. He'll do it with comedy and roundhouse kicks.

Who is likely to be in it?

If this is a feature film, then it needs a star. The kid playing Charlie won't qualify. Probably he'll be a newcomer with great kung fu skills. Therefore we are looking for a Big Dragon. Someone with star power and *gravitas*, someone who can do comedy, someone who can sell doctor by day and crime fighter by night: the Big Dragon. An Asian Batman or Robin Hood. Clearly we are looking at a Jackie Chan vehicle. If he's booked, then we can imagine it with Jet Li or Chow Yun Fat.

Where does this scene happen in the movie? Clearly, it happens on page 23. And having read the section on screenwriting, you know that that is pretty darn close to the end of act one in the traditional paradigm. Knowing that a change in acts is usually accompanied by a change in location and a major restatement of the central question of the movie, we can rightly conclude that we are at the very end of act one and the very beginning of act two.

What is the central question of the movie?

Clearly, it is this: Will Charlie win his legendary father's respect and get them on a slow boat back to Hong Kong?

What happens next?

Clearly, since they don't bat an eye when a thug drops off a couple of Chinese 'guests' at their place, the Steels are working for the bad guys. Clearly, they are not farmers ("Okay, this would be the house. Those are cows. And... that's the rest of the place.") And clearly, they are going to try to further come between Charlie and his dad, since that's the story, and take them even farther away from their destination, which will clearly involve comedy and action. We can expect a comic brawl in the barn.

Why are you in the movie?

Clearly, you are there to physically and verbally restate the problem: "If you are ever seen in Hong Kong again, we cook your family." The screenwriter thought it was imperative to have someone actually say those lines at this point to remind the audience of the central question and raise the stakes on our poor hero, Charlie. As if things weren't bad enough, now he's got to win his father's respect, get them back home to the other side of the world, and then keep his mother out of a wok (reminding us yet again that it's a comedy).

You can guess the title.

It's about Charlie. His dad is the Big Dragon. He wants nothing more than to be like his dad. Red Eye actually calls him the Little

Dragon at the top of the page. Hmm. Has a nice ring to it. It suggests action, comedy, and family. Hmmm. The one thing you can't guess from this page is that Charlie is going to team up with a cute little American girl named Cammy, who has father troubles of her own, and together they are going to do some kung fu and some comedy and resolve the story. Therefore… *Little Dragons.*

Acting style?

Action comedy, like every Jackie Chan movie ever made.

Tone?

A bit campy, and just a bit tongue-in-cheek.

There, you did it. You figured it out. You now know exactly what you're doing. And you can now see exactly why it can be so hard for you to book these 'little parts.' Because this part, even though it is brief, is not little. You are there to spin the entire story into the second act. You have to represent the forces of antagonism, scare both Charlie and the legendary Big Dragon as well as the audience, close the door on any hope of escape using the bus, show us that the Steels are working with or for the bad guys, restate the central question, raise the stakes on Charlie, and do it all in a campy, funny, action comedy way. That is your job. That's why it's tough to break in. Most actors have no clue about any of this and therefore have no hope of breaking in.

But not you.

Well done.

You must now do this same work on every script that crosses your desk or table at the café for the rest of your career. By reading one page of a well-crafted script, you should be able to deduce all this information and more. That is your job from now on. At least, it's the first part of your job. If you remember the opening pages of this book, then you have a few more.

The next thing you must do is apply your brand. But before we do that, let's finish up this section by taking a look at the sides.

The Sides

I don't know the etymology of this term, but I do know it means the pages from the script that have your scene on them, the scene you do for your audition. If you have a one-line part, then you will have only one page of sides. If you are lucky, then you might have ten pages and three long scenes. Your sides will be marked up with info about the audition as in the previous example. The casting director will have shown you where to start and where to finish. She may have given you some extra pages from the script, which have information marked FYI (for your information) that you should know. She may have crossed out a section of the scene in the middle that she wants you to ignore for the audition. And so on.

It's these sides you learn and take with you into the audition. I'll tell you what to do with them in a minute.

Sending Regrets

Seeing that you have a shot at doing an important though small role in a big Jackie Chan movie, you should have rebooked your flight to Dubuque and committed yourself to this audition. It could be a big break. Hopefully your mom is well, and she's happy to see you at a later date. You have made the hard decision to put your acting first whenever possible.

Good on you.

If you *did not* rebook your flight, then your agent will have to send your regrets to the casting director. Although this does happen, it's not very good for you. Since you read the first part of this book, you know that your agent did some work to get you submitted for this part, and as a result you became one of 25 people chosen out of 2000 for an audition. And then you went and said, "Sorry. Maybe next time." This will annoy your agent and potentially irritate the casting director. She too went through a lot of trouble in selecting you. Neither one might want to do it again. And they both have long memories. Next time, they might just leave you off the list altogether. There are plenty more actors where you came from.

The sending of regrets is a well-known bee in the bonnet of many people. You want to keep bees out of their bonnets when it comes to you. So, do not send regrets. Go to the audition. Change your flight if at all possible. The mistake you made on this occasion was not telling your agent you were going to Dubuque in the first place. Then she would not have submitted you, and you would not now be in this predicament. The only legitimate excuse for sending regrets is this: after your agent submitted you, you booked a job on something else. You can't come in because you are working as an actor on something else. You're booked. That's a good regret to have, and a very respectable one, and the only one you should ever use, unless you got run over by a truck the previous day. Getting an audition in the first place is a minor miracle in most cities, so respect it, and your career, and the people who made it happen, and go.

Of course, in this case you didn't go. You went to Dubuque.

If you have a very good agent, and if the casting director forgives your regrets on this occasion because you are somehow perfect for the part, then you might be able to put yourself on *tape*. In other words, when you get to Dubuque you are going to get a video camera and a friend, do the audition yourself in your mom's living room, and e-mail it to the casting director. The term comes from the olden days (ten years ago) when we only had videotape cameras and FedEx. No matter. We still call it *putting yourself on tape.*

Note that it is not as easy as it sounds. And even though it's good that you have permission to do it, and even though more and more casting is happening by tape these days, you are at a disadvantage in the competitive process. The actors who go in and do it live and in person have the upper hand. The casting director can see and feel them, talk to them, coach them, see the truth of them, get confidence from them, and size them up in all sorts of little ways. Moreover, the director and producer might also be in the room—which happens more and more often in first auditions nowadays—so you'll miss out on that as well. You're starting a notch down by sending your regrets in the first place. And, if you are like the vast majority of actors, then you are going to do a truly crappy job of putting yourself on tape. Most likely, they are going to cast from the room not from the tape.

But stranger things have happened.

That being said, casting from tape is happening more and more often these days as the technology improves and the actors figure out how to do it properly. My guess is we are going to move more in that direction over the next few years until most casting happens by tape. So, now is the time to learn.

The two advantages tape gives you are: the calmer nerves and the retake. You can do it 30 times if you like to get it exactly right. And you should. Knowing that you are starting from behind, do anything you can to make it perfect. The casting director knows that you have the advantage of retakes and will expect more from you anyway. Typically, the only time *they* look at the tapes is if *they* haven't really found what *they're* looking for in the room. Then *they* kind of stretch and groan and look at each other and say, "Do we have any tape?" Then *they* watch. To give *them* enough confidence to hire you from tape, your audition has to be two levels of amazing higher than what *they* saw in the room. Then you have a chance.

How to Put Yourself on Tape

The easiest way is just to call up a service and have them do it for you. Most bigger cities have services (often local actors) who are set up for this work and who will do it for you for a few bucks. They will act the scene with you, shoot it, and send it off. Some will also coach you if you want. Call the local branch of SAG, or an acting school, or a friend, or get on the Internet to find people who know what they're doing.

If you can't do it this way, or if you just want to set yourself up with the gear for the future, then here's how to do it the best way possible.

You will need the following: a grey-blue bed sheet, some duct tape, a bright light or two or three depending on how finicky you are and how good you want to look (the best ones are LED lights from a camera store), a couple of white sheets of foam-core from an office supply store (the stuff you would mount a poster on with some spray glue), your smart phone, or a consumer camera as long as it communicates with your computer, your computer, some kind of video editing software that comes standard with most computers now, a tripod, your *sides*, two chairs, a quiet room, and an actor friend.

Tape the sheet to the wall as a backdrop. No one wants to see your mom making lunch in the background or all the traffic in New York City out your window, especially if it washes you out. Do not under any circumstances try to make a little movie out of your audition. *They* are not interested in your filmmaking skills, and they probably don't want the competition. Blue-gray is the best neutral color, and it matches the wall color in most audition spaces so your audition will look roughly the same as everyone else's. This is good for you. You will stand four or five feet in front of this backdrop. Three or four feet in front of that, put the two chairs, one a bit to your left and the other a bit to your right. Take the white sheets of foam-core and lean them up against the chairs facing you at about eye level. Shine one light onto each sheet of foam-core so the light bounces off the sheet and lights up your face. Bounced light is diffuse light, which makes you look lovely. Hard direct light, like sunlight, is the least attractive kind. It shows every blemish and crook in your nose. If you are bit richer, then you can do away with the foam-core by buying more expensive LED lights or photo lights with little *umbrellas* or *soft boxes* on them like you see at a photo studio, which do the same trick as the bounce boards. These are more portable as well, in case you want to go on the road with them. If you are very ambitious, then place a third light behind and above you so it illuminates the top and back of your head, but doesn't shine in the camera lens. This *back light*, also called a *rim light*, is almost always used on a set to give you a little glow from behind, which lights up your hair a little bit, and separates you from the background so you look like a star. Set the camera on the tripod in between the two sheets of foam-core so your face is lit from both sides.

Now, have your friend put you in a loose *close up*, meaning we should see your head and shoulders down to about your bust line. Make sure there is no extra space above your head; we are only interested in you, not your halo. Have your friend stand next to the camera so his eyes are next to the lens and at the same level, and I mean not more than a foot away to one side or the other. Doesn't matter which side. Make sure the camera is not in wide-screen mode. You will be tempted to make your audition look like a real movie, but don't do it. It's not the standard, and many of the websites where it is destined to go don't like the format.

Have him push the record button. Do the scene together.

Use all the audition techniques you will read about in this book.

Check out what you shot. Tweak the lights and the performance. Check that you got good sound. Repeat until satisfied. The biggest technical mistakes people make are poor sound quality, poor lighting, and poor framing. Make sure you can be seen and heard as well as possible. Make yourself look good. Your eyes are what sell you, so make sure we can see them clearly.

The biggest performance mistake actors make in putting themselves on tape is this: they don't understand the scene. They don't get it. They read it over once, throw it on tape, and expect love and admiration. It just doesn't work that way. You have to deeply get what's going on.

Simple example: I recently put a young actress on tape for a sci/fi show on television. It was a lead role. The character was eighteen but very sharp and capable. The scene had her begging the captain to take her down to the planet on the latest dangerous mission. He eventually relents. Fine. The actress did the scene like an 18-year-old begging her dad for the car keys. Not fine. Can you see what might be wrong here? How she didn't get it?

Here's how to do it: it's a lead role in a series. Leading characters do not beg and whine and stomp their feet unless they are five years old. The dialogue has to sound like she's a teen, but the performance has to be grown-up, courageous, able beyond her years, quite probably sexy beyond her years, and possibly dangerous beyond her years. Why else would the captain take her into a battle against the aliens? Why else would the audience root for her and want to be her? Why else would she get fans and a salary worthy of a lead in a series?

Deeply getting what's going on is 90 percent of the battle when putting yourself to tape. More on this as we go along.

If you're totally lost and not sure what to do, then record your two strongest choices and send both. Most casting directors won't mind. It is a cop-out, but it can be done. (I mean, I wouldn't do it. I don't want to suggest I don't know exactly what I'm doing. Anyway…) You will only send *them* the best version of each. In other words, send two takes of the same scene that are different enough to justify sending two takes. Do not send five takes; *they* will not watch them, and you will look like an impossible bozo.

Do not do your audition scene without a partner. To see you doing a long scene with nobody reading the other lines just freaks people out. Have a *reader*—the off-camera actor—doing the scene with you. If you can't find an actor friend, then use Mom and cross your fingers.

If you can't set this all up perfectly, then do the best you can. Try to get a plain, neutral background. Try to get some diffuse light on your face so that you can be seen. Make sure it's quiet and that you sound good. Keep it in a *close up*. Keep your *eye line* close to the lens so *they* can look deeply into your magnificent eyes. Eliminate all distractions.

When you are satisfied with your one or two versions, you typically need to do a *slate*. This means you are going to look directly into the lens and introduce yourself to the casting director and anyone else who might be watching. Be warm and open and friendly—have the *it factor*—and say: "Hi, I'm Rachel StarMaterial, I'm with Superstar Fifteen Hollywood Agency, and I'm reading for the part of the Prom Queen." Then smile warmly. Do not act. Do not be the character. Be yourself. *They* want to get a feel for the real you.

That's the basic slate. Kids will usually be asked to state their age. Occasionally, *they* will want to know your height and have a look at your profile as well, because 1) your height is an important casting consideration (don't lie), and 2) some people look lovely from the front and circus-freaky from the side, which could also be an important casting consideration. So then say, "I'm five-foot six, and here's my profile." Turn to one side to show your profile. Turn back to the front and smile, or glow, or just be yourself—whatever is right for your brand and the role.

The major mistakes you make when doing a slate are these:

You look somewhere between uncomfortable and terrified, which is not good when you are trying to give *them* confidence. So, get your alpha dog going and exude confidence and personal power.

You act it up and try to push yourself on *them*. Everybody hates that.

You look apologetic. Everybody really hates that.

You do it in character so they have no idea about you personally.

You talk way too fast. You may know your name, but *they* don't. If you rip through it at light speed, then the rest of your slate will go by before *they* decipher your name. Slow down. You're a movie star, right? Make *them* remember your name.

If at all possible, have your friend start to shoot your slate in a *long shot* that shows your whole body, and then zoom in rather quickly, but smoothly, back to the close up. This gives *them* a look at the whole you, and it gives *them* confidence that you're not hiding anything like a huge butt or a conjoined twin.

Don't laugh; it has happened.

Import your slate and your two best takes into your computer video editing software. Put the slate first, and then the one or two takes. Some skilled individuals will type their agent's name and phone number on screen at the end.

Convert the file to .mov or .wmv format at the highest quality you can send over the Internet; most people prefer H.264. Depending on your e-mail server, you might be able to e-mail it directly. You can also try one of the file sending sites, such as Hightail or Mongofiles or Dropbox. These sites allow you to upload large files and send them to any person with an e-mail address. That person will simply get a notice in the person's inbox saying you have sent a file and a button to download it. In other cases, you might be able to put your audition up as a private video on YouTube and send off the link. No matter which way you choose, you should also send a copy to your agent to prove that you actually did it, to show her how good you are, and to find ways to improve for next time.

The Room

If you decide to stay in town to do the audition live and in person, then you are heading for the *audition room*. It will be part of the casting director's office or a rented space somewhere. Sometimes it's a high-tech room dedicated to casting sessions; sometimes it's somebody's closet. I've auditioned in a curling club, a TV studio, a guest bedroom, a boardroom, a hallway, a trailer, a theater rehearsal hall, a rented office in an industrial manufacturing park, a car, and in a third-floor office in a skyscraper. Oddly, this last one was the hardest. The casting director had leased an office in a tower on the busiest street of an insanely busy city with no parking available anywhere within a country mile. I think I wound up paying 20 bucks just to park for 30 minutes. I could hardly believe it. Each and every day, 50 or 60 actors had to make this harrowing journey, and then find their way up the elevator in a tower full of lawyers and oil companies to get to his door. The moral of the story: be ready for anything.

The waiting area is called the *green room*. Nobody knows why. It's just the waiting place with chairs and a few forms to complete lying on a table. More on this in a few minutes.

In the small and stuffy audition room, a camera will stand on one side, possibly accompanied by small lights and flanked by a table with a TV monitor and a laptop. A few feet in front of the camera, some tape on the floor will look like a small 'T.' That's your *mark*. You will stand there, or roughly there, as you do your work. Normally, a camera operator and a casting director will sit in there waiting for you. Sometimes, an assistant also helps with collecting actors and fetching lunch. Occasionally, a reader will join you—a reader is another actor who plays the scene with you from off-camera as the casting director watches. In my experience, the most typical version includes the casting director and the camera operator, with the casting director reading the other side of the scene. And that's it. If it's a first audition, then that's typically the whole affair.

You wait in the green room until called, you go on in, audition, and leave.

If you are called back to audition a second time—known as a *callback*—several other people will sit behind the table: the director, a few producers, and sometimes the Big Fat Star.

In the coming pages, I'll explain the process for you step by step, and give you a roadmap to success.

Let's start by taking a look at audition room protocol, and then we'll look at how to learn the scene and prepare your read.

The Audition Land Mines

There are a lot of standard ways of doing things in the audition, so mastering the technique is paramount. Get used to it and get with the program. They are simple and don't require any talent. They are designed to level the playing field so *they* can get a better look at you and your potential.

Can you imagine if *they* didn't do something to level the playing field? Actors would be riding up to their auditions on ponies trying to get 'noticed' and writing their resumes in the sky. It would be an impossible freak show. So, over the years, standards evolved to level things out and allow *them* to get things done.

The lovely by-product of these levelers, these little *land mines*, is that ignorance of them is an easy way to spot the *wannabes*. Your complete knowledge of them tells *them* you have been around and know what you're doing, and gives *them*... guess what? Confidence.

The main thing you are trying to do in this, your first audition, and all subsequent auditions, is to give *them* confidence in you. The main way to erode that confidence is by making simple technical mistakes (stepping on the land mines) and by 'acting.'

We have already established that you are not going to do any acting, so all you need to focus on now are the bits of technique or protocol. The land mines are your main enemy. Every time you step on one, a little explosion goes off in *their* heads, and you get a big X next to your name. When you're just starting out, one X might be all it takes to put you out of the running.

This may be news to you, but movie acting attracts weird people: oddballs, psychos, wannabes, fame-seekers, stalkers, the emotionally unbalanced, and the not-ready-for-prime-time players. These people are not welcome. They creep everybody out, and they have the potential to destroy a movie and waste millions. While *they* do want to find good, professional actors, and great, new, young talent, *they* want to keep out the weirdoes. Therefore, much of what *they* do is about blocking you, preventing you, and discouraging you. You might be a weirdo. Worse, you might be a weirdo who can act. That would be really bad. You could fake your way onto a set and then sucker-punch *them* right out of Hollywood. *They* don't want this to happen. So, *they* plant these little protocol land mines to trip you up. Professionals know where the land mines are, and they step around them. This is how they declare themselves. Weirdoes who can act step right on them and give themselves away.

Thank God.

The good news: all this technical stuff has little or nothing to do with your acting, as I mentioned. It doesn't take any talent. You just have to learn it and do it, step around the land mines, don't be a weirdo, and you're home free. It's simple stuff, like don't wear the cop suit and don't bring the beer.

Protocol

If you really want to see protocol in action, then spend a day in court. Everyone follows tightly prescribed rules of procedure and conduct to ensure a fair trial and get the job done. You are strongly encouraged not to break these rules. Call the judge "Buddy!" for example, and you're likely to spend the night in jail, even though you did everything else exactly right for the previous eight weeks.

Audition protocol works the same way.

Film auditions have been happening for about a century now. With literally millions of them having been done, a protocol has arisen. You could say that by design audition protocol makes life easy on the auditors, not on you. If they wanted to make it easy on you, then *they'd* come to your house for a spot of tea first. But it's a two-way street. For example: when you enter the room, you will normally see a little 'T' of tape on the floor. That's where you stand, with one foot on each side of the trunk of the T. Forget that the T makes life easy for the cameraman and instead realize: 1) that is where the lighting is best; 2) that is where the mic catches your voice best; 3) that is where everybody else stands so no one has an unfair advantage; and 4) it's one less thing for you to worry about. You are also free to ignore it if you like, but at least then it will be an active choice. Complete ignorance is not an excuse.

Thus, the protocol levels the playing field and gives you a fair shot at showing what you have to sell. Similarly, it allows the auditors a pleasant and meaningful shopping experience. *They* can shop and compare without distraction, and *they* can hope to hire the right actor for the right role. Think of it all as your way of getting a fair trial.

I say *modern protocol*, because it is not static. It keeps evolving as we go along, not to mention it varies from place to place and casting director to casting director. Some don't use the T, for example. One of your jobs when you're just starting out is to learn the basic protocol and the variations used by each local casting director where you are setting up shop. This knowledge will make you look like a pro in front of each of *them*, and it will relax you completely so you can do the real work of the audition without any worry.

For example, consider: slates. I already explained the slate to you in the section on How to Put Yourself on Tape (page 126). You have to look into the lens of the camera and introduce yourself. The slate used to be common practice in all auditions, and thus it was integral to the protocol. *They* needed a slate and you knew *they* needed a slate. You did it as a matter of course. If you didn't do it, or worse, you asked, "What's a slate?" then a rather large explosion went off in *their* heads. But slates are tough to do, especially when you're all keyed up, and very especially when you're trying to focus on the impossible scene you have to do next. And you always had to do the slate first. Tough.

One of the local casting directors in my neck of the woods thought it was overly tough so he started doing the slates for us. When we entered and hit the mark, he'd stand beside us, put an arm over our shoulder, and do the slate for us. "Hi, this is Paul FamousDude, he's with Double Giant Happiness Talent Partnership, and he's reading for the captain." As a bonus, the director could easily see how tall everybody was just by comparison to the casting director. Then he'd jump out of the shot and start the scene. Wow. Nice of him. But that could really throw you if you weren't ready for it.

So what you do is learn the basics—coming up—and then confer with your agent and all your actor buddies. If there are more than a couple local casting directors, then start a little scouting report on each of them so you don't forget and so you aren't thrown off. You can take classes offered by casting directors and ask them. You can ask the casting director's assistant on the day of your audition, if you catch him or her with a moment to spare. "Does she do slates? How does she work in the room?" Where necessary, you can even be brave and ask the casting director herself once you get into the room as long as you do it in a way that gives her confidence.

By the way, slates have gone out of common use in the room. *They* simply type your name at the bottom of the screen or attach it to the video file in their computer. Much easier on you. However, you will still have to do one when you put yourself on tape, and you will still have to do one—showing both your profiles—in every commercial audition.

If you are not sure, then ask. After you hit your mark, say: "Do you need a slate?" It gives everybody confidence.

Basic protocol originates in LA since it is rightly the center of the movie universe, and because more auditions happen there than anywhere. For example, not long ago it became forbidden to shake anyone's hand in the audition. Did you know that? Absolutely forbidden. Came from LA. I don't know if it was fear of the Bird Flu that started it or if maybe someone just used Bird Flu as an excuse to stop having to shake 100 sweaty-actor hands a day. Who knows? However it happened, it happened, and now it's part of standard audition protocol. Shake no hands with LA-types, dear actor, especially with casting directors. Even though shaking hands feels proper, polite, and natural upon meeting a colleague in the business, shake no hands. If you try, *they* will likely recoil in horror and shoot you a mean look. Chalk up a bunch of amateur actor points for you.

Sound bizarre? Maybe it is, but it is also the prevailing audition protocol and they're not going to change it for little old you. You need to adopt it like your very own child, love it, and get to know it intimately. Thus, you will appear professional and current, and you'll get a fair trial.

Note: if someone *does* offer you a hand in the room, then shake it warmly, look them in the eye, and smile. Try not to have sweaty-actor hands. Maybe we'll win them back.

In the meantime, walk in with a glint in your eye, say hello, and keep your hands to yourself. Add in a little bow if you are so inclined.

The casting director was hired by the producer to bring in professional actors not amateurs. Take my advice here. Make the protocol second nature so you can focus on staying calm and confident and on doing a great audition, and so that you don't wrack up too many Xs that cause your headshot and resume to land in the garbage. It doesn't matter that your actual audition was good; she lost confidence in you and doesn't want to risk moving you forward in the casting process. It could have been a couple of simple things: you incorrectly stapled your resume to your headshot and then cheekily tried to shake hands. Horrifying.

If you didn't know that these were mistakes—and the casting director is certainly not going to tell you at the time—then you'd just go on making them and not getting hired. Then you'd get discouraged. And then you'd give up acting over some silly little things having nothing to do with your talent and ability.

This, we don't want.

So, master the protocol, keep up with it as it changes, and do your best to find out the little variations preferred by each casting director.

The following are more of the basic rules. Let's start with distractions.

Don't Distract Them

Now, pay very special attention: The whole journey of screen acting is toward freedom and self-acceptance. That's why kids are so good at it; they haven't yet learned self-loathing like the rest of us. Your job is to embrace yourself and share your true, deep, honest self with others.

What that means is that you must *resist and defeat any temptation to distract them with things other than yourself.* Things like extra lipstick, perfume, freaky facial hair, and crappy accents. That kind of thing might work in a bar, but in the acting game it is truly the oldest trick in the book. Plus, what you think looks good in 'real life' probably looks ridiculous on camera. The camera is a magnifying glass. You cannot rely on your old tricks to divert people's attention from the real you. Remember the chapter on How to Determine Your Brand (page 59)? It's about the deep you, which you can focus by refining your look. It's definitely not about covering up your true self with all kinds of paraphernalia and hoping *they* don't notice. *They* can see from a mile away your little attempts to distract *them*, and *they* will start giving you X's before you even cross the threshold. Take heed.

You must have easy confidence and present yourself simply and clearly, and you must be appropriate to the character. *You must not do anything that will distract them from the real you.* If you are not strong enough to present the real you, then do everybody a favor and get stronger first.

The Basics

Do not overdo the *makeup. They* are not interested in your talent in this area, and they are certainly smart enough to spot the two pounds of concealer. Not knowing what you really look like, *they* will shake *their* heads, sigh and put a big black X through your name. Wear just enough to be appropriate to the character.

Keep your doggone *hair* out of your face, boys and girls. *They* are not interested in your hair! Lots of people have hair. It does not distinguish you. More likely, it hides you. Women, if you are reading for the sexy chick, then leave your hair down but keep it back off your face, and preferably behind your ears. Thus, you are sexy but we can see your face. If you are reading for the sexy professional, such as the lead cop in a series, then consider putting your hair half up and half down, making sure it's not in your face. Thus you look sexy and professional. If you are reading for a professional woman, then put your hair up. Thus, you don't look like the judge in a porn movie. Those are the general strategies; adapt as necessary. Just keep it out of your face, and for the love of God, out of your eyes.

Guys, how many stars can you think of who regularly have *facial hair?* Think about it. If you are young and hope to be a leading man, and you are sporting the latest facial fad, then time's a-wasting. Shave it off. Otherwise, you look like somebody who's trying to be cool and who's face we can't see. Want to be a star? Don't cover your face with a sweater. If you are an older character actor, then leave it, but realize it is likely going to restrict your roles. Suppose you want to specialize in cowboys. The giant mustache is probably a good idea in that case. It makes you look like the guy *they* want, and it saves time in the makeup trailer. I just want you to be aware of what you're doing. Don't think "I'll just shave it off if *they* want." Most likely, *they* won't ask. *They* will cast the next guy who doesn't have the 'stache in the first place.

Do not wear *distracting clothes.* Do not wear the colors black, white, or pinky-red; the camera hates these colors. You will tend to look like a blob. And stay away from medium gray as well since that is the color of most audition room backdrops. Do not wear any patterns or stripes or logos unless you want *them* reading your shirt instead of watching your performance. Ditch the Metallica t-shirts, the hoodies, the giant leather jackets, and the cowl-neck sweaters that make you look like a sea turtle. If you are putting something on because you think it'll be cool, then it isn't. Take it off. Go with simple. Go with clean. Stick with blues, and greens, and sometimes purples. Put yourself on camera and try out different colors to find your best.

Do not wear anything that makes *noise* like corduroys that crunch when you move. This includes shoes; wear quiet, soft soles wherever possible. If you must wear the stilettos for the character, then go ahead, but you better hope you are not auditioning on a hard floor. You tend to shift around when you are nervous so all *they* hear is clackity-clack. I know things like this shouldn't matter, but they do. Remove all dangly, jangly things, such as the 60 bracelets you've been wearing because, again, you think they are cool. In an audition situation, they are painfully, irritatingly distracting.

Take out your nose ring, earring, eyebrow ring, cheek ring, and tongue ring. All f*acial jewelry* must go unless it is native to the character. Do not think *they* can't see your tongue ring. *They* can and *they* will. Lose all excess jewelry and *puka shell* necklaces from Hawaii.

Do not under any circumstances douse yourself with *colognes* and *perfumes*! The room is small and stuffy, and *they* are stuck in there all day. By leaving your scent, you remind *them* just how much *they* hate their job and you.

If you are a *smoker*, then have your five cigarettes at home. Then take a shower. Then go. Sorry to tell you this, but one of the people who is universally despised by casting directors is the one who nervously smokes five in a row outside then walks in smelling like an ashtray. And, yes, *they* can smell it. A lot. And yes, *they* can smell it a lot for a long time after you leave.

The other universally dreaded distraction is the *boobs*. Ladies, please leave the *girls* in their holster, especially when auditioning for lawyers and pastors. Cleavage distracts everyone and does not add to your performance or depth as an artist. The boobs say, "Look at me, not her." By leading with the boobs, you give yourself two more mountains to climb before catching up with the rest of the pack. Plus, every audition room cameraman is trained to frame out your glorious *boobage* anyway. The casting director doesn't want the girls influencing *them* while watching it later. That is, if *they* move you forward that far, which *they* won't. Unless specifically called for in the breakdown, excess boobage means excess X's. For example, Charlene is a busty, blue-collar bimbo, a size 12 in a size 2 shirt, who loves to flaunt her cleavage. Then go ahead, being mindful of how distracting they are. Nobody's going to hire you just because you have boobs. If the character requires nudity, then you will be asked to get the girls out in the callback. For now, leave them out of it and show *them* you can act.

Props

If you need to appear to smoke, then bring a cigarette and wave it around all you want. Just don't light it up and don't take a drag on it, lit or unlit. It's distracting. The script might explicitly say: She sits, sullenly puffing on her cigarette. But this is the audition, remember? It is not the movie. *They* do not expect you to light up. *They* do not want you to light up (distracting, stinky, dangerous, and possibly illegal).

Want to make a call? Bring your cell phone. Just make sure you don't get a call from your mother during your scene. Turn it off.

Coffee? Pencil? Map of Bulgaria? Bring it.

Realize that this advice only applies when the scene *requires* the prop, as in the case mentioned: you must answer the phone to talk to the detective.

Forgot your cell phone? Now you are in a bit of a pickle. Now you need it but don't have it. Do not panic. Instead of using it, you are going to *mark* it. Marking a prop is when you show *them* where the prop goes, that you know you need it, but that you don't have it right now. The best way to mark a phone is to tap your ear with one finger making it appear as though you are engaging your *BlueTooth* headset. Bingo. You are talking on the phone while not being distracting by holding up an invisible cell phone. Get it? You marked the phone. You can also mark movements, actions, and kisses, as we will see shortly.

If the prop is *optional*, or just something you invented to help your sense of reality, then I recommend against it. It depends what you're going to do with it, how well you do it, whether it's distracting or adding to the scene. The basic rule is: don't distract them. A cigarette does not a performance make.

Oh, and for the love of God don't *pretend* to have the cigarette.

Don't *mime* it. Almost nothing on Earth is more laughably distracting than somebody smoking an invisible cigarette and drinking an imaginary cocktail. You might think you are making it play on the mark in a close up but you would be wrong. You don't have a cigarette! You don't have a martini! This means the scene doesn't play. *They* will probably be mesmerized by how badly you are miming, and *they'll* again forget about watching your scene. Tape yourself doing it and you'll see what I mean.

Special note: some casting directors love miming and encourage it in all cases.

Sorry. That's just how it is.

Two quick stories.

A casting director friend of mine, who must remain nameless here to protect the innocent, tells the story of a young actor who was reading for a waiter in a bar. When his turn came up, he entered the room carrying a full tray of beer—we're talking about eight one-pint glasses, full, on a tray. Apparently he thought it would help with everyone's sense of reality and help him book the role. It didn't. No one in the room could take their eyes off the beer because it was distracting, rattling because of his nerves, likely to fall, and perhaps *they* were thirsty. Definitely there was also all of *them* thinking: "Where the hell did he get all that beer and how did he get it in here and what kind of lame-ass actor does that?"

No one saw his audition at all; *they* were all waiting for the whole thing to come crashing down. And even now, years later, his story is being told as an example of what never to do. Don't let this be you.

Just show *them* you can play the scene, please.

In another instance, I was working as a reader on a movie of the week. The script called for an elderly lady with a sick dog to show up at a clinic. The director decided he wanted to see not just elderly ladies but all ages and types, male and female. He wasn't sure who he wanted and who would help the story the most, so he went shopping for everything. Maybe the scene would be more touching if it wasn't a lady but a huge truck driver nearly brought to tears over his sick little dog. Maybe it should be a kid. Or a soccer mom. So he literally asked for the works.

The little dog was key to the scene. He was not just in the scene, the scene was about him and how sick he was. Therefore, he was an essential prop. Knowing this, the casting director brought in a prop to stand in for the dog—a big furry frog I think. All was well for a while until all of a sudden, no frog. Someone had walked out with it. We were auditioning all the different roles, not just the dog lady, so we had no idea who had purloined the amphibian stuffy. For the rest of the day, the actors reading the dog scene had to mime the dog, or use their rolled-up coat, or some other such distracting option.

Unfortunate.

Except for those smart ones who knew the prop was essential and who left nothing to chance by bringing it themselves. These people all had a distinct advantage at the end of the day. Their scenes looked better, and they themselves looked like pros. They gave confidence.

On the other hand, somebody made the obvious mistake of bringing in an actual, living dog. You know how actors say you should never work with children or animals? There's a reason. Actually, at least four reasons: they are difficult to wrangle; they are unpredictable; they are adorable; and no matter what, everyone will be watching them and not you. This person did not book the role. Again, she was memorable for all the wrong reasons.

Another lesson to be learned from the dog scene: If you are 35 and male, and they call you in for the elderly lady, then do not be an idiot and stay home. Go. Do not play it like an old lady. *They're shopping. They* don't know exactly what *they* want, so they are shopping around looking for someone to catch *their* eye. Play it like you, in your power zone, and cross your fingers. You might book it. If you don't book it, then you will have made an important investment in your future. You will read more about Shopping on page 170.

So know all the necessary props and either bring them or mark them. *Never bring* animals, children, guns, machetes, chainsaws, food, or things that are on fire. Do not bring beer. Do not mime unless you have no other choice.

It's just common sense. Do not distract *them. They* want to see you, not your tinkling glasses. *They* will not confuse chainsaws for talent. And *they* do not want to think you are so desperate that you'll rent a dog for an audition. It's just creepy.

Important aside designed to inform you not intimidate you: some casting directors get understandably miffed at actors who make these kinds of mistakes, and *they* will put your name on a *hate list*. Meaning, *they* won't see you again for a year or so. Or forever. Remember, *their* job is to supply professional actors to professional productions. *They're* just cutting down *their* risk by keeping track of who is ready to move up and who is not. You don't want to be on this list. For a complete run-down of what might get you on this list, see the Appendix, 50 Stupid Stunts in the Audition Room, and don't do any of them.

Wardrobe

As best you can, dress in the economic status and situation of the character. When you walk in the room, *they* immediately read your look and feel, assess the way you present yourself, and then ask *themselves*, "Do I believe it?" In other words, do *they* believe that you are the cop, the soccer mom, the senator, or the waitress? Your wardrobe should point *them* in the direction of that belief. And you need to look comfortable in it, not like you just put on a costume.

Do not overdo it. Do not rent the cop suit. Whenever *they* see the cop suit walk in, *they* know *they* are going to be subjected to terrible acting. A special kind of person goes to all that trouble: the bad actor. He seems to be the same guy who brings in the gun, the dog, and the beer. His *desperate factor* is through the roof. Don't do it.

If you have the cop suit in your closet—possibly because you are a cop—then fine. Some people in casting like to see the full wardrobe, so if you have it handy, and it looks like it belongs on you, go for it. Just make sure your acting measures up. Otherwise, don't do it.

Instead, go to your closet and pull out your own suit for the lawyer role. Pull out your blue-collar shirt for the blue-collar role. Grab your jeans for the western. Simple. Help them imagine you in the role without going overboard and looking like a wannabe. Believe it or not, filmmakers have imagination. *They* also have costume designers.

Since we're telling stories, I can't resist the pirate tale. Many years ago, I was called in to audition for a pirate in a TV series, a comedy about people who got transported through time and space. This week: a pirate ship. There were three salty pirates in a scene together so they brought three of us actors into the room to play off each other.

Oddly, one of them brings in a backpack. Before the casting director can say a word, this guy pipes up: "I brought the wardrobe."

She says, "That's okay, we don't need it."

"It's really great. I made it myself."

"That's okay."

"It'll only take a second."

And then he proceeds to strip down to his underwear and put on a crappy pirate outfit. It took him several minutes. I saw steam rising from the casting director's head. She sat boiling until he was done. Then we did the scene. Then, guess what? He took another several minutes to change back.

Truly amazing.

None of us got the part of course. Not only did he ruin our chances, but I believe he went on the hate list for all time.

Why didn't she just kick him out?

Professional Courtesy

Don't get me wrong here: some people in the biz don't care too much about professional courtesy, and *they* will kick you out hard for this kind of behavior. But these folks usually live and work in the big centers of the world, like LA, where there is an endless supply of new talent, where *they* don't seem to care that much about burning bridges sometimes, and where occasionally *they* just get fed up. Still, in my experience it is relatively rare. Most people believe in professional courtesy and maintenance of good relationships even when you're a jerk.

This is one of the reasons it's so hard to improve your audition skills: you don't know what you are doing wrong. Casting directors usually won't tell you. *They* will be polite, watch your stupid stunts, and thank you. And then *they'll* drop you from *their* list.

The reasons for *their* professional courtesy:

Actors are known drama queens, for one thing, prone to having fits and tantrums especially when they feel rejected. Nobody wants this happening in the room.

On the contrary, *they* generally want to do everything possible to make you feel flattered and confident so *they* get the best performance out of you.

It would take way too much time. *They* are casting a $60-million movie, not giving acting classes.

It would take way too much focus, and it would potentially derail their efforts to cast *their $60-million movie.*

It's politically unpalatable, meaning *they* don't want to offend you, your agent, your manager, or your pal Knuckles, or risk having you blab all over town about how *they* insulted you when all you wanted to do was put on your pirate outfit, which you made yourself.

It's simple professional courtesy. Who knows, maybe you meant to do that ridiculous accent. Maybe you consciously chose to wear a Speedo to the audition—for the Senator. *They* want to respect you as a professional actor who knows what he or she is doing, so *they* will most likely just watch and say thank you and later say something like, "Wow, that was weird."

It's just easier, that's all.

The only option you have when it comes to feedback is to ask your agent to ask *them.* This will usually happen by e-mail in the days after the auditions. This will usually result in very little. Mostly nothing. Maybe *they* will send back a little note saying: "She did fine." And that's it. The reasons for this are basically the same as the above plus they don't want to get it wrong. *They* see sometimes 80 people a day, and it's easy to get confused and forget who was who. Plus, *they're* kind of busy casting a $60-million movie. It is not *their* job to give you feedback. So, get educated, confer with your team, and use your head. Watch the trade papers and your e-mail to see if *they* are giving any classes in the future, and think about taking one. That is the time to ask questions.

"Hi. I was the guy with the pirate suit. Bad idea?"

How to Learn Lines (and Story)

Okay, those are the basics. Soon, I will take you through the audition step by step. But first you need to prepare your read.

I was doing a Kirstie Alley movie once, playing the manager of a trailer park. The first scene was pretty long and complicated. The camera was to crane down from the sign on the roof of my dingy office to find me coming out to meet the young leading lady, have a conversation, and then walk away together. *Action* had already been called. I could see the camera craning down. I timed my exit perfectly. And then I heard, "Cut, cut, cut."

The director rushed up to me saying, "Sorry, I rewrote it last night. I forgot." And he handed me the old scene with all the new lines handwritten in the margin. He bustled away to reset the camera and call the roll. I had about two minutes.

Having to learn lines scares many new actors, and having to learn them quickly can be horrifying. Actually, it scares off many potential actors before they even start. But if you do it right, then it's one of the easiest parts of the job. It needs to be. If you're doing a movie, then the script is likely to change just about every day or every minute like it did for me. Each day of the months-long shoot, you need to show up knowing the new day's pages. If you're doing a TV series, then the shoot lasts most of the year. If you're doing a sitcom, then you need to learn a new episode every week and shoot it in front of a live audience. It's like staging a whole new play every seven days. But by far the line-learning champions of the actor world are the soap actors; some of them make an hour-long movie every single day. Can you imagine? Shoot a long difficult scene, rush off to your dressing room to learn the next one, go shoot it, then do it again, then do it again, and then do it again, every day of your career, which for some of these folks lasts 30 years.

Obviously, it can be done. So, let's put your minds at ease, and show you how.

When you get your script, read through it once to experience the story. Get the overview. Then read it again applying everything you learned in the Story and Screenwriting – Don't Skip This section (unless you did, indeed, skip it against my advice; if so, then go back and read it right now).

Think about these questions: What kind of movie is this? What genre? What's the central question? What is the crisis? Where are all the points of structure? Why are you in the movie? Sean Connery (*the* James Bond) spreads the script out page by page all over his office so he can see how all the parts fit into the whole, and then begins breaking down the story line by line. Remember, because it's a movie, the story is in the pictures and the sub-text. By definition, the sub-text is not written down. You need to read between the lines to fully understand the story, which then illuminates the text.

To learn a particular scene, you first apply everything I told you about story, and then you must work through the scene line by line, going back and forth between the text and the sub-text to find out how they are related and why they are in the movie. Thus illuminated, you find that you don't have to memorize the lines; you already know them.

I hear you scratching your head, so let's do the example. I'm not even going to tell you the story. You should be able to figure it out as we go along, like you did in the *Little Dragons* scene. This time, you're learning story and lines.

INT. BIG BOBBY'S BOWL-A-DROME — DAY
Thirty busy lanes of bowlers. Every second, another ten pins CRASH to the ground. There's a large banner hanging over the center of the lanes: Welcome to the BETTY BROOKLYN INVITATIONAL. The foyer is packed with CUSTOMERS. The WAITRESSES in the restaurant are run off their feet. It's NOISY, and CHAOTIC. Donny stands by the check-in counter taking it all in, and wondering how anyone could possibly manage all this.

Now, stop reading and start figuring. What's going on and why? What's the meaning of this? What's going to happen next? Do not neglect the obvious.

The slug line tells us we are inside (INT. as opposed to EXT.). We are in Big Bobby's and it's daytime. Bobby seems to be hosting a big tournament having something to do with Betty Brooklyn. It's a seriously money-making enterprise. Why? Why is this scene happening in the first place? And why in a bowling alley? What does it have to do with the story? The writer goes out of his way to tell us how chaotic and noisy it is. Why? And who is Donny? We have met him before, otherwise his name would be in ALL CAPS LIKE THIS. Who is he and why is he standing there being bombarded by everything? Why does he care about who manages it all? What's going to happen next?

Sit with these questions for a minute or two until you come up with some answers. They don't have to be right at this point; they just have to be. We are training you to analyze a scene line by line.

JENNIFER O.S.
Donny?

Stop reading again. Who is Jennifer? What's going on and why? What's the meaning of this? What's going to happen next? By the way, the O.S. by her name means *off screen*. In other words, we don't see her yet.

Well, clearly, Jennifer knows Donny. Right? Do not neglect the obvious. She knows his name. Who is she and why is she interested in him, especially now? Come up with some answers. Just guess if you have to.

Donny spins around to see JENNIFER LANE, a lovely brunette with a bowling ball bag, lurking in the doorway to the woman's lockers.

Stop reading again. Were you right? Yes or no? Maybe you thought Jennifer was one of the waitresses or perhaps his mom. Were you right? What's going on and why? What's the meaning of this? What's going to happen next? Why did Donny spin around? Why didn't he just turn? Why didn't he just ignore her? How did he hear her over the din? Why did the writer want to let us know that she's lovely? What's she doing with a bowling ball? Why is she lurking?

Answering all these questions *is your job*. This is what an actor does. Perhaps you've only seen actors on screen doing the *results* of their work. This part is the *actual job*. The bad actor skims over all this and then desperately starts trying to jam the lines into his memory banks. He's in for trouble. It is very difficult to remember a string of words that are not connected to anything, that don't mean anything to you or the story. But this is what most actors do. Terrible.

But now you know better. You will carefully and painstakingly analyze the story as you go along, word by word. If you do this right, then the script and your educated actor mind will tell you everything. You will only have to do it once, and you will know your lines and the story, and therefore, and most important, your performance of the scene will be perfectly informed. You will not be able to do a bad performance.

Literally just keep asking why until you run out of whys.

Okay, clearly we can already see that Jennifer is a hot number, and this is the first time we've met her, because her name is CAPITALIZED. She knows Donny, and she's meeting him again at an important time. She's a bowler herself. Maybe she's in the tournament. Why is she lurking? She's lurking because she's shy, or because she's been watching him and has a plan of some kind. Why did he spin around? Probably because he knows her too and recognizes her voice. But so what? Why spin just because you know somebody? Unless… it's somebody you have an emotional connection too, like a sister maybe? But the script says she's lovely, and doesn't mention anything about her being his sister. So, maybe a love interest? What's going to happen next? Hmmm. Probably he'll say something like, "Hey, Jennifer, wow you look … great.'

JENNIFER
I could tell it was you.

Whoa, wait a minute. She speaks again. Why didn't he say anything? How could she tell it was him? Why did she bother to tell him that?

Apparently, Jennifer knows him well enough to recognize him from behind, and she wants him to know that. That's why she said it. Why? And why didn't he say anything? Maybe he's shocked to see her. Maybe he doesn't want to see her. Maybe she doesn't want him to say anything. She butts in on him. But wait, the lines don't indicate that. Looks like he's shocked, and she wants to remind him of how well they know each other. Hmm.

DONNY
Jen. Uh… hey.

Okay, this is getting interesting. Obviously, he knows her, so we were right about that. He calls her Jen—a nickname—so he might just know her quite well. Then he's stuck for something to say. Then, awkwardly, he just says, 'hey,' which is a very neutral and uncertain greeting. He's definitely not taking the lead here; he's waiting. Why? What's the meaning of this? What happens next?

Come up with some answers of your own.

JENNIFER
(closing the distance)
Sorry to hear about your uncle. We were all shocked.

His uncle? Hmmm. Looks like the uncle died, doesn't it? Then she makes it a point to say *We* were all shocked not *I* was shocked. Why?

She wants to remind him again about how well they know each other and how she's part of his gang? But why? And then she closes the distance. Why? Obviously, she wants to continue talking. What's the meaning of all this? What's going to happen next?

DONNY
Yeah... thanks... uh... I didn't see you at the service —

Goodness gracious, we have a scene going on here don't we? Clearly, she should have been at the service, or at least he expected her there, *he looked for her,* meaning she's part of the family or very close to them at least. If he's so uncomfortable around this lovely girl, then it seems likely they were once a couple. But then how come they're not anymore? Why? What does this all mean? What's going to happen next?

JENNIFER
Yeah, sorry, Darren sent me to Phoenix to look at new design ideas. Since this place has got this new profile going on he thought we'd better spruce up the restaurant a bit. And since I'm hoping to take over one day...

Wow. Okay. She made an excuse, but it was a good one. The bowling alley is just recently taking off financially. She works at a restaurant close by. They both know a guy named Darren. She's ambitious, and she let the sentence trail off about how she wants to take over, meaning either that she's maybe embarrassed by it, or that he already knows that. But how would he know it? What's the meaning of all this? What's going to happen next?

See?

On and on you go to the end of the scene. Don't peek at the next line until you have done all the work on this one, figured out as much as you can, and made a guess about what's coming. Then look at the next line and start again. See how the new line changes your understanding and your forecasts. Keep going. It will take you maybe 30 minutes or so to break down the average scene. About halfway through, if you are doing it right, then you will start correctly anticipating the lines and have most everything worked out. You will only be waiting for the turn at the end of the scene—the action or revelation, which concludes all well-written scenes. In this case, it's a startling kiss on the cheek.

Your goal is to understand everything profoundly. The director should be able to stop you at any point in the scene and ask you, "what are you doing and why?" You should not only have the answers, but also you should know more about the answers than he does. That's your job and why you were hired. You are the specialist. If he's the brain surgeon, then you are the neurovascular surgeon called in to attach the arteries. You need to know more about that character and that scene than any person on Earth, even the writer. You make the word flesh.

Bonus: By the time you are finished this process, you will know the lines.

I do this exercise in my classes with a three-page scene. Working it like this, with all the class discussion, can take an hour. Then I spring it on them: I ask the two actors in question to drop their sides and do the scene from the top. Guess what? Ninety percent of the time they are ninety percent perfect. At least half the time, they do it perfectly and with great ease, and not only that, the scene is perfectly performed because they know what they're doing. They know the story. They know all the sub-text. *They don't have to think about either the lines or the sub-text, so they are free to be present with each other, to connect, to live the scene on a very intimate level, and to hit their marks.*

This is possible after only one reading. If I give them a minute to run it quickly a few more times, then they are virtually perfect 100 percent of the time.

Next, I ask them to do it again but this time to put a *cherry on top*.

By this, I mean to remember to apply their brands, their personality, and their power zone to the scene. The second time through, the scene is everything it was before *plus* it is full of their own colors and shades and interesting choices. If I then ask them to add some *special sauce*, by which I mean some extra appeal such as sexiness or charm, then the scene veritably pops and sparkles.

And it's easy.

It may have taken an hour to prepare, but from then on, the scene is virtually as good as it can be. They could not improve the scene; it even snaps and crackles. If I happened to be the director shooting this, then I would be the happiest man in the world.

The other benefit of learning the scene like this is flexibility. It becomes so easy to jump around the scene, start in the middle, pick up the ending, whatever. Plus, you know the other person's lines so well that you can help them save the scene if there is a stumble. And because you're not desperately trying to remember lines, there's room in your brain for direction, like "Can you start by the tree over there and get to the railing when you say the line about your uncle?"

Plus, you will not forget the scene. For proof of this, the next day, or sometimes the next week, I'll ask *two other people* in the class to stand up and do the scene from the top with no script. All they did was participate in the discussion the week before, and even they can do the three-page scene with ease.

Reminder: this is your job. Maybe you come out of theater where you spend eight weeks slowly wading into the script, having discussions, and asking questions. But you are in dire straits if you bring that attitude to the movies. I explain all of this in detail in the next section, but for now realize that there will be no rehearsal. No rehearsal. None. The director will not explain anything to you. He's too busy or he's a writer with no clue about how to talk to actors. You will not meet your scene partner until about 30 seconds before you go on. Your number one job is to be ready, having already done the work yourself. You prepare on your own and figure it all out. You know the story, the scene, the sub-text, the lines, the performance, the actions—everything— long before you get on set and meet anybody. You are a professional and this is what professionals do. If you want to be a movie actor, then this is what you're in for. If you don't do it, then you'll find yourself back in theater or working at the car wash in no time.

I am harping on it because of something I see happen over and over again. I show this technique to my actors. They go, "Wow, that's amazing, and so easy!" I give them a different scene to prepare for the afternoon session and what happens?

Correct.

They go right back to their old habit, trying to jam lines into their skulls with no idea what's going on in the scene. Amazing.

Learn this technique, commit to it, and never do it any other way. Okay?

Punctuating the Text

While breaking down the scene like this, remember also to play the punctuation. The writer put it in there for a reason. If you see a comma, then pause. If you see a full stop, then fully stop. It is in there for a reason. It is not optional. Play it.

Example: I once wrote a short film in which a regular guy becomes the target of an assassin. But the assassin misses his shot. Our guy digs the bullet out of a wall and takes it to a gun shop for analysis. The gunsmith asks, "Somebody took a shot at you, huh? You in some kind of unsavory business?" My guy replies, "Yeah. Advertising."

See? The full stop after 'Yeah' firmly acknowledges that our hero thinks he is in an unsavory business. It tells us a lot about his character and perhaps the sudden awareness of what he's been doing with his life. And it provides a nice pause, the right timing, for the punch line: "Advertising." It lands hard with a full stop too, making it funny. There is a lot of character information and a joke in two words of dialogue, but it works only if you play the punctuation.

Comedy is all about punctuation. Comedy writers hear the joke in their heads, and then write it down with the same emphasis and punctuation. If you do it that way, then it'll most likely be funny. If you don't, then it won't.

Normally, if you see a dash like this—after a sentence, then it means the character is inviting someone to finish his sentence, i.e. "Was that you I saw dancing with, um—?" If you see an ellipsis, like this…, then it normally indicates a sentence that trails off or is interrupted, i.e. "Honey, how's the new girl, um... She seems nice."

The bad actor would just run right through this without thinking. The smart actor asks, "Why is that in there? What does that mean? I need to play it. So, what is it?"

After some thought she might realize that this scene is about a woman who suspects her husband of cheating with his new secretary. Perhaps it is the first time she has ever doubted him, which would be painful and difficult, and perhaps because of that, she'd be a bad liar. All of this is in those three dots, and it needs to be played. It slows you down, it makes you find the pauses, the sub-text, and it makes you play the subtle thoughts and reactions.

This is film acting, remember? Academy Awards are won by reaction shots, by what you do when you are *not* speaking. It's in the tiniest details. Begin your education in this department by learning to play the punctuation, and do it faithfully from here on. "Who are you calling sweetheart?" is a lot different than: "Who are you calling, Sweetheart?" There may be mountains of information in the tiny dots of ink or the blank spaces.

In screenwriting, a comma is a comma and a period is a period, but beyond that each writer tends to have his or her own style when it comes to punctuation, so you'll have to be a bit of a sleuth with each new script you are handed. But no matter what, play it. Stomping all over the punctuation is the hallmark of the amateur.

Punctuating the Sub-Text

Since we are on the subject of punctuation, we shall now discuss punctuating the sub-text. Because of all the work you just did, you are probably already doing this naturally. I just want to point it out so you are aware.

Watch a great actor. You'll see that the person tends to do one thing at a time, and everything has meaning. Everything without meaning is removed. You must learn this technique as well.

For example, say you have one line: "Oh, I like her." The inexperienced actor plays the one line, not knowing it is much more than just a line. There may be five, six or seven mini-beats needed to effectively deliver that one line. Maybe you enter the shot. That's one. You do not talk while you are entering; we'd miss the line, and/or you'd look weak and insignificant. You enter. That's one. You see the woman in question and react to her (how else do you know what to say about her?). That's two. You say the line. That's three. You react to having said the line. Four. You turn to the person next to you, and react to seeing her. Five. She reacts to what you said. You react to her reaction. Six. You turn on your heel and leave. Seven. So, there are seven mini-beats to this one line. If you had three lines, then there might be fifteen mini-beats.

Watch any good actor and you will clearly see all of these mini-beats. They play the punctuation in the text, and they add their own punctuation to the sub-text. This will have the effect of slowing you down and making your performance sharp and professional—not to mention easy to edit.

Example: you suddenly see someone off screen, *cut* to that someone, cut back to you for your reaction. Thus we have a complete mini-story. If you do everything at once, then your performance will be sloppy, meaningless and impossible to cut, meaning you will be cut out of the movie in favor of the actor who did it right.

In my classes, I call this punctuating the scene, but I also call it rolling in the Jell-O for some reason. It seems to give people the right mental image. Have a good time and go at a natural pace. Slow down because it's all squishy and yummy. Point out all the important stuff. Enjoy the doing instead of trying to get to the end. Have fun rolling around in it. If you don't love your work, then how can you expect others to love it?

You will do this with every scene you have to learn for the rest of your career.

Okay?

Don't argue.

Say okay.

I'll wait.

Okay.

Want to practice? Here's the rest of the scene.

DONNY
`Design ideas?`

JENNIFER
Phoenix IS the restaurant AND bowling capital of
the world.
DONNY
Right. Forgot.
JENNIFER
So, are you still working at that casino in…
where was it?—
DONNY
Mesquite.
JENNIFER
Right, Mesquite. Still there?
DONNY
Well, actually I've been on the road playing
tournaments, and… that all kind of depends… I hope
so… but… what's with you? You're looking good.
JENNIFER
Yeah, well I guess your absence does me good.
DONNY
Right. So, are you… um…
JENNIFER
What?
DONNY
You know…
JENNFIER
With somebody?
DONNY
Yeah.
JENNIFER
Yeah.
DONNY
Ah.
JENNIFER
Ah.
DONNY
Not Pierre is it?
JENNIFER
It's not Pierre.

DONNY
Good. Cause that guy…. I have to go see him about the legal… actually, and… man… if I knew…
JENNIFER
You broke up with me.
DONNY
Right. Exactly. Yes. Well… Good.
JENNIFER
Good.
DONNY
And… I'd better go…
JENNIFER
See Pierre.
DONNY
Right.
JENNIFER
Who I'm not dating.
DONNY
Yes.
JENNIFER
(kisses him on the cheek)
You look good too, Donny.
And she goes, leaving Donny shaken and perplexed.

Did you get it all? Hint: Donny's uncle died leaving him the bowling alley, which he has no interest in or ability to run. He'd clearly rather play poker. But now he's forced to deal with it, and his past, his ex-girlfriend, and his nemesis Pierre who seems to be a lawyer who also has an interest in the bowling alley and possibly Jennifer. Jennifer clearly is mad about being dumped, which is why she stabs him a few times with little insults, but clearly she wants him back—which she seals with a kiss—even though she's dating someone else.

This is the overview of the scene. If you want to be great, then your analysis should be detailed down to the microscopic level.

How to Make it Audition Friendly

The next thing you have to do is make the scene *audition friendly*. Suppose in your scene you have to kiss somebody. Do you do that in the audition? Do you walk up to the casting director and kiss her on the lips?

It's in the script.

Do it?

Answer: yes, if you want a slap in the face and a knee in your naughty bits.

So, no.

Don't even think about it.

Instead, you need to find a way to make the scene play while staying on your mark in a close up. Because it is the audition, not the movie. Get it? Commit this to memory for all time: the audition is the audition. It is not the movie. You will not be kissing people, shooting people, or jumping off cliffs. This is the audition. This is where you play the scene on a mark in a little room so the casting director can get a look at you in the part. Feel free to treat it as if it was the actual performance, but do it as if it was an audition. Make it play on the mark.

You are expected to do this.

Every professional actor knows this and does this.

This is part of the reason why the audition is its own little art form and why it is so difficult to master.

In a callback situation, you may be asked to do some kissing or fighting or butt-baring for the director and possibly the star, but that will be covered later. For now, for the typical first audition, you must make it friendly.

Example: the kiss. You have several options: 1) Kiss the casting director, which we have already determined would be dangerous to your life; 2) Kiss the air, which would look silly, probably make us laugh, and distract us from your performance; 3) French kiss the air, which would be hysterical and make you the talk of the town; 4) Ignore the kiss altogether, which could work but might be distracting by its absence; 5) Find a way to play the kiss in a non-distracting way. For example, tilt your head to one side and close your eyes romantically. Do not purse your lips. Do not stick out your tongue.

Voila. One kiss. Not distracting. The scene plays. You look like a pro. *They* watched your performance not your wagging tongue. Everybody is happy.

What you just did was make it *audition friendly*. You showed *them* everything they want to see—your confidence, that you get it, that you are technically proficient, that you have made choices based on your brand, that you can sell the scene—without distracting *them* by running around the room and French kissing the air. Simple.

Earlier, I explained how to mark a prop. Now we are talking about marking actions, reactions and bits of *business*, like handing someone a 50-dollar bill or taking a gun out of the trunk of your car.

The term *marking* comes from the world of dance. You go through the routine in miniature showing that you know all the choreography. Therefore, everybody knows that everybody knows, making everybody happy and confident.

So, go through the scene determining what actions, reactions, and bits of business are necessary, and be sure to play them or mark them all. Simple. Does the scene indicate that you enter and sit? Do that. Just walk in from the side of the shot and sit in the chair provided in every audition room. Do you need to survey people coolly, look at a fire, address certain lines to certain people, pet a dog, shout, shoot down an alien space craft, lose an arm, tiptoe through the tulips, show somebody your business card, and exit? Prepare all that stuff. Some of it you can do, but some of it you need to mark. Most of it will be fairly obvious because somebody wrote it down for you in the script. Imagine that. But some of it *they* leave to you. Say you have a long speech delivered to your two angry lovers. Which lines go to which lover? Which go to neither? Maybe you're talking to yourself? Prepare all that.

Next, if the scene requires some physical object or bit of business, then do the same thing: either bring it or mark it. If one of your lines is, "You see, detective, I put my ring on my middle finger, like this," then be sure play it or mark it. You know *they're* going to look. Once *they* see it, and it's there—even if it is only in *their* imagination—*their* attention will come back to you for the rest of the scene. If it's not there, then annoying thoughts tend to run through *their* minds, like: "Didn't she read the scene? Is this one of those people who is never prepared?"

If one of your lines is, "You see detective, I can turn into a slimy green blob at will," then you will definitely need to mark that. Get it?

Finally, do not under any circumstances add anything to the scene to show yourself off or make them 'remember you.' If the scene says *the bartender pours a shot of whiskey*, then just pour a shot of whiskey. Do not take an extra five minutes to set up your bar, clean your glasses, and demonstrate your kung fu skills. *They* will remember you as an example of what not to do for the rest of *their* careers. Tell the story as written in the script. Do not write yourself a bigger part. Be remembered for doing good, professional work, and get out of the room.

I cannot possibly give you the audition-friendly alternatives to every possible problem, so you are going to have to get used to doing this on your own just like all the rest of us. Just know that, sooner or later, you will have to deal with punching people, getting punched, wrestling, kissing, shooting guns, opening doors and windows, and transporting yourself to distant planets. The rule of thumb is simple: make it play on the mark in a close up without distraction.

If in doubt, then ask the casting director. But it is far better just to understand the concept and do it. Commit to it. If you come into the room baffled and sobbing, then *they* will lose confidence in you. Come in courageous and firm, do the scene, and head for the door. *They* are far more likely to be impressed and want to help you if you did happen to get it all wrong.

The Choreography

Once you have made it friendly, rehearse the *choreography*—the little dance of the scene. You just determined *what* to do in the scene; now you need to *practice* so you can actually do it in the audition. Make a list if you have to.

Example: Enter the shot. Seeing the entire board of directors waiting for me, pause. Acknowledge them, one by one. Sit when the chairman gestures to the chair. Notice the documents on the table in front of me. Confirm with the boss that they are for me to read. Put my glasses on. Open the file. Hide my reaction to the photograph.

Forget about the 'acting' for now. Rehearse just the choreography of the scene until you know it as well as you know your lines. Make it as detailed as possible. Realize that the choreography is not optional; it is the collection of acts that make up the scene. A collection of scenes makes up a story. Your job is to determine those acts and do them. Act the acts. They don't require much talent. They are the spine of the scene. Learn them and do them.

Think of the scene choreography as ballet choreography. The steps are not optional. You must do them all. You must point your toes or it's not ballet. You can't do every other step, or just the big steps, or your personal selection of steps. You have to do all the steps.

The difference between the two is that whereas the steps of *The Nutcracker* are set, only some of the steps in the movie scene are obvious. Only some of them are written down for you, because the writer doesn't have space on the page to tell you every little thing, and he's leaving room for you as a fellow professional. The unwritten ones have to be figured out by you and your keen actor analysis.

Do not try to *wing it*—do your best without preparing—in the room. Few people have enough brain power to do that successfully. Learn the choreography. Make it one less thing to think about. Thus, when the camera rolls, you'll have enough brain to connect, to believe, to be alive, and honest, and to tell the story.

Nobody wants to watch you trip over your feet in the *pas de deux*. Learn the dance.

The Cliché

I usually hate it when authors tell little life stories, so I'll make this one brief. At one point in my career, I was making a few bucks working as a reader for a casting director. A reader, as you know, is the supposedly good actor who stays in the room all day reading with the actors auditioning for all the various roles, just like your friend did in Dubuque. I would stand beside the camera acting opposite the actors as they auditioned. One minute I was the bad guy, the next minute I was somebody's mom, and then I was a kid, all day long. If you get a chance, do this job at some point early on in your own career. Not only is it a terrific acting exercise, not only are you getting paid, not only are you gallivanting around with a casting director, but you will learn what it showed me: that most actors suck. You will also see *why* they suck. You will also get to work with many actors who don't suck and great actors who just aren't right for the part. This will sober and calm and reassure you. You might also get a chance to meet the producers and directors, get a backstage pass to all their secret goings-on, and hear what *they* think of the contenders. This couldn't hurt one bit. *They* might get tired of watching tape and just hire you. Also not bad.

An aside: you may have heard the now-famous story of how Harrison Ford booked the Han Solo gig. Ford had worked for George Lucas before, in *American Graffiti*, but then he went back to his day job as a carpenter. He was hired by Francis Ford Coppola to build an entrance to an office, where George Lucas just happened to be doing the auditions for his new flick: *Star Wars*. At some point, George asked Harrison if he wouldn't mind being the reader for the various Lukes that came in. Pretty soon, George started listening more to Harrison than to the Lukes, and the rest is history. You can actually go on YouTube to see many of the original *Star Wars* auditions, and you will hear Harrison Ford off-screen as the reader.

If you never get the chance to do this job, then just read on. I'm going to fill you in as best as I can. But if you get the chance, then do it. How? Just get on your laptop and start communicating your desire to do the job, "Hi, Ms. Casting director, I'm Shelley GonnaMakeIt. I wanted to let you know I just landed in town, took a few fantastic classes (my teacher thinks I am a young Audrey Hepburn), I'm really excited about my career, and I'm even more committed than ever. Here's my headshot and resume. And, if you ever need a reader, at any time, for any reason, then please call me. I'm very flexible and reliable and eager. Thank you."

Okay? Then just keep bugging her occasionally, politely but assert-ively, until she breaks down and calls you. This might take a while. If she uses readers (many don't), then she already has one, so you'll have to wait until the job comes open. When it does, leap. Do not hesitate— you will get one chance and one chance only. If it's three in the morn-ing and you are at a party at somebody's mansion, then politely excuse yourself, and go do the job. Knowing people in the biz is infinitely bet-ter than knowing people in the pool. Once you get your hooks in, hang on for dear life until you sufficiently expand your skills and contacts, and even then do not burn your bridges. This is just a reminder. We went over all this in the section called Everything Counts on page 11.

Back to my story about being a reader. Remember, I'm playing the boss and reading opposite the prospective executive assistants. The first one comes in and does fine and all, but she's just a bit boring. The second one: same. Third one: more of the same. By the forth one I realize that they are all doing exactly the same thing, the same performance over and over again. Different girl, same performance.

I wonder if it's me.

It's not.

It's them.

By the 26th one, I want to murder them all. I'm so stultified, and bored, and baffled, and mad. Did they have a meeting out in the green room and decide to play a practical joke on me?

Doubtful.

How then is it possible to have what we had, to see what we saw? Twenty-six times exactly the same performance.

Any idea?

No?

Here's what happened:

The cliché.

A cliché is something that is overused, predictable, and lacking in original thought or expression. In other words, when these 26 girls and women looked at the role, they saw a cliché version of the executive assistant they have seen on TV a million times. The boring, old stereotype. And immediately they thought, "Perfect, I'll just do the boring old cliché again. Surely that will excite them and land me the job."

Actually, I doubt they thought that much. They just saw executive assistant on the page, and they immediately went to the cliché and never even questioned it. They learned their lines, performed the cliché assistant and left, most of them probably thinking they did a darn fine job and would be booking that part in no time.

They didn't.

The boring, old stereotype is not exciting. It lends no color, no spark, no drama to our story because of the fact that it is boring and old. And when we see 26 in a row, it also makes us mad thinking that no one wants to take five minutes to read the script and do something unique and true to the story and interesting and dramatic and sparky. Our hearts sink, because even though we know better we start to wonder if our story is any good. The actors don't even get it. Maybe the whole thing is a stupid cliché and I should never have become a director and should probably go out to the parking lot right now and breathe fumes straight from the exhaust pipe. That's what you, and your lazy-actor ass, make us feel: a little bit closer to death. That's not a good way to score points and get hired. Not a good way to build your business. Not a good way to have fun doing what you love to do. Not a good way to help the movie, the story, the filmmakers, or the casting director who went out on a limb for you. It's lazy, lax, dull, and dumb.

What do you do instead? How do you get all sparky and avoid the dreaded cliché? Very, very simple. You apply your own brand to the role. You remember your brand? The thing about you that's unique and fascinating which others want to buy from you? The thing that sells you? The thing that adds cool colors and fascinating choices to the scene?

That.

You apply that.

The Story and You

Look at the role again, and this time, see yourself and your fascinating brand playing it. Add the *you* to the part. No one can do you as well as you can, right? So this is your secret weapon. This is your way to make the performance unique, interesting, colorful, and sparky. This is how you differentiate yourself from everyone else and stand out. This is how you avoid falling onto the smelly heap of clichés. This is also how you help the story and the filmmakers, and Hollywood and the world.

Play the role in a way that suits both the story and you.

Play the role in a way that suits both the story and you.

See, I repeated it so it might have a chance to stick in your head. Wait a minute, I feel something important coming on.

Play the role in a way that suits both the story and you.

Obviously, if you're not helping us tell the story, then we can't use you. Sorry, maybe next time. But if you're not using your unique gifts to help us tell the story, then we can't really use you either. Another guy in the green room will use his unique gifts, and our story will be that much richer. And if we get lucky, then that guy will become a star someday, and our film will have a whole new life because of it. So, we're hiring him.

Who says the executive assistant can't be sassy? Sexy? Impatient? Motherly? Girlish? Threatening? Judgmental? Weird? Creepy? Odd? Brilliant? Comic? Kooky?

Who says?

You and I have both seen executive assistants just like any of these. That's kind of how life is. People are different. Sure there is, somewhere, a perfect cliché TV executive assistant, but let's forget about her until she's not a cliché anymore and then go back to her. In the meantime, let's look at the five million other ones, and say yes, they can be any of those things. That's life. That's real. That's interesting.

And one of them is you.

So, remember your brand. What is it? Kooky sexy co-ed? Fine. Now apply that to the role and what do you get? Kook, sexy, co-ed executive assistant. Who wouldn't want one of those? Quirky, lovable executive assistant? Bring it on. Soccer mom executive assistant? Why not? There must be thousands out there.

Read the scene again, and start seeing it as soccer mom executive assistant—your brand meshed with the story. Imagine how you could play it, how soccer mom influences your acting choices. Soccer moms are tidy, for one thing. They're on time. They clean constantly because they have to. They have a certain sobriety born of dealing with silly little humans. They speak clearly so you understand them the first time. And so on. Then ask what is it about *you* that sells you most as soccer mom? Are you insanely finicky? Where can you use that while playing the role? Sure, let a little bit of the old secretary cliché creep in there too. Why not? That too is real. But mix it with soccer mom. Make sure everything you do contributes to telling the story and is the right style and tone. Then go for it. Work through the whole scene. Apply, apply, apply.

These choices are often known as *choices* in acting circles. "She just makes really interesting choices." You've probably heard it 1000 times. I think most people don't really know what they're talking about when they say choices; they just know them when they see them. But now you know where they come from.

Your choices happen when you do what's best for the story while applying your personal brand and your creative intelligence at the same time.

What's the sense of trying to do it like Jim Carrey or Angelina Jolie? There already is a Jim Carrey and an Angelina Jolie, and they are presently getting all the Jim Carrey and Angelina Jolie parts. What you want are the *you* parts. And you want to start building that brand now, right from the beginning because it's best for the story, it's best for you, and it's best for your business.

And why wouldn't you want the best for everyone?

And now a word of warning.

Remember what I said: your choices have to be best for the story and for you. The story comes first. Suppose your brand is smart sexy professional woman, but it's pretty clear the story can't handle the sexy part. It would be inappropriate. Maybe the story is about a noble man who gets caught up in a criminal investigation, but he is eventually vindicated. That kind of man probably wouldn't have an overtly sexy executive assistant. Most likely that would work against the story, against his noble profile as a good man and good husband and good father. Right? The audience might suspect something was going on between them or that she was somehow significant in another way, which is not the case. You probably would like to have a bigger role, but that is not in the script, the story. Your job is to help sell this story, not the one you have invented in your mind. You must tell this particular story in which the assistant might be warm, or yummy, or sweet, but cannot be sexy.

So, now what?

Do you go ahead and use all your sexiness anyway?

There are two answers to this question.

Answer number one: if you want the part, then the answer is a capital NO. Your performance would be wrong for the story, it wouldn't be helping, and you would know that. The casting people and the director and the producers and the network would know it as well. Almost certainly, you wouldn't book it. As I mentioned before, casting is subjective, so just about anything *can* happen, but most likely, 99 percent of the time, you wouldn't. They would move on to the next girl whose performance didn't work against the story. This only makes sense. If you happened to be stellar in every other way, and if *they* were completely out of options, then *they* might hire you, but be assured *they* would have a little chat with you before shooting where *they'd* ask you to please turn down the sexy bit. But most likely, you wouldn't get it.

So the answer is: if you want the part, then turn the sexy down in the audition. You can do that both internally (by turning down your sexiness) and externally (with clothes and makeup). Just apply your brand minus the overtly sexy part knowing that this is the best thing you can do for the story and for you.

Answer two: if you don't care too much about the part and want to declare your brand as loudly as possible, then go ahead and keep the sexy part in there. Turn it up, in fact. Again, you won't book it, but you will leave *them* with a strong impression of where they might be able to use you in the future. Think of it as an investment. It's possible *they* might even think of you for a different role in the same movie, most likely a bigger one, provided the rest of your performance seemed to merit it. This has happened before and will happen again. Or *they* might be back in town in a year with another movie and will call you up then. Or *they* might talk about you to friends in the biz.

On the minus side of the equation, *they* will likely know exactly what you are doing, might be put off by it, and might never want to see you again. *They* will put you in the reject pile for doing an inappropriate audition and your nefarious plan will have failed completely.

My general advice here is to do what's right for the story, book it, make some money, get a credit on IMDB, impress your agent, and build your career step by step. Introduce your sexier aspect in a later, larger role where it is appropriate. Work. Learn. Grow.

Others will disagree with me. That's the biz. And there is one case in which I disagree with myself.

If, for example, you have clear star potential, then you might be wise to hold out for bigger offers, trying to do only lead roles to build and preserve your star mystique and keep your price up. This is a valid career-building strategy for a star actor. If you only have leading man credits on your resume—even if they are all short films and student films—then it naturally makes you look like a leading man. It gives people confidence. You are therefore likely to book another leading man role next. Your agent can use it as ammo when she is promoting you: "Brian is a young leading man. Check out the resume."

But in this case you would most likely have to be 17 and beautiful or 21 and handsome, and incredibly talented as mentioned in the bit about the inevitables, and represented by a top-notch agent, and be turning heads wherever you go in LA. Most likely.

But again, not necessarily. This is where the breaking-into-the-Hollywood-vault speech I gave you in the first section of the book becomes very important to you. All kinds of people have made it big in all kinds of ways. So evaluate your assets and liabilities and draw up a plan. Let it flow and evolve day by day. Get some good advice. Be smart about it. Don't be a pain in the ass egoist. Good luck.

Just please, on behalf of all of us in the biz, care. Care as much about us and the story and the audience as you do about you and your career. We'll all get along famously.

And now for the Meg Ryan story. I helped promote a workshop given by Jane Jenkins of The Casting Company in LA. Jane and her partner Janet Hirshenson are legends in the *biz*. They've done *Jurassic Park* movies, *Harry Potter* movies, *Transformer* movies, *Da Vinci Code* movies. They've written a book. But the big draw for me was this: way back in the *day*, they did a little thing called *The Princess Bride*. (Thank you, William Goldman, for inventing it.) I got to chat with Jane for 30 minutes before the workshop, and all I wanted to know about was *The Princess Bride*. She shared a lot of insider stories, but here's the one that matters at the moment.

They needed Buttercup, the leading lady. *They* couldn't find her. *They* looked everywhere: actresses, models, singers, beauty queens, here, there, everywhere. Nothing. At one point, Meg Ryan came in to audition. A teenager at the time, Meg was simply the most adorable girl in the world. Jane showed Meg's tape to director Rob Reiner, who reportedly said something like this: "This is the most adorable girl in the world. Unfortunately, the script calls for the most beautiful girl in the world." No matter how fantastic she was, she just wasn't right for the part. It eventually went to Robin Wright (in another interesting story) who truly was the most beautiful girl in the world and absolutely perfect as Buttercup. I couldn't imagine the role with anybody else.

The point is they remembered Meg because she had delivered her adorableness, her brand, in the audition. And they remembered it for years until they happened to be doing another little movie, this one called *When Harry Met Sally*, which needed the most adorable girl in the world. And they called Meg. And Meg became the most adorable female star in the world.

That's how it works. You show *them* you are in the game, you show *them* where *they* should put you, and you wait. Rinse and repeat until hired.

Doing it 'Right'

All those hopeful executive assistants back there who performed the cliché did so for one basic reason: fear of doing it wrong. They see *assistant* on the page, and they want desperately to do it *right* so they can book it. Then, recalling all the assistants they have seen on TV, they conclude that that must be the right way to do it, and so they copy that performance.

"There, I did it right."

Wrong.

Which brings me to the following very important point: There is no right.

Let me repeat: there is no right way to do a role. It is useless and counterproductive to try to do it right. You will only come up with a cliché or *careful acting* (where you are watching yourself and trying hard to do it right) or you will overwhelm yourself with anxiety until you crash and burn completely.

There are plenty of ways to do it wrong, however, such as: work against the story, work against yourself, be technically off, do the cliché, be uneven, be disconnected, etc. But there is only one way to do it right, and that is *your way.* No other way will do.

To do this, you must have confidence.

Nevertheless, virtually all novice actors are consumed with the desire to do it *right,* meaning the way *they* want it.

That is an impossible goal. Please burn that into your brain.

The following are several reasons why it is impossible.

There will be one director and probably two or three producers on any project. *They* are all different people, with different tastes and different goals.

The producers want to find distribution and make *their* money back so *they* can make another movie. *They* have already spent a bundle on the star who *they* hope will help open the movie. (Star casting is a completely different enchilada and is not discussed in this book. We're here to get you hired after your first audition.) What the producers want from you is bang for the buck. *They* want you to help tell the story and get the movie made and/or help them politically somehow, i.e. calm down the local actors' union, and/or to fit the wardrobe *they* just rented, and/or 100 other things. *They* are making this up as they go along, so what *they* might want and need from you on Monday changes by Tuesday. It is hopeless to try to second-guess them.

The director would like the movie to be successful too, but he would prefer to hire someone he can work with on set, someone whose very presence helps him tell the story. Or someone with a sense of humor to lighten the mood. Or someone he just has a good feeling about. Or someone who doesn't look anything like his ex-wife.

If there is a studio, or a network, or in the case of commercials an advertising agency, then *they* also have a say. *They* have goals of their own, which you may have no clue about. There is no way to do it right for *them* beyond telling the story.

The word *right* suggests that the *rightness* is external to you; that is, that you have nothing to do with it. You seem to think that there is some kind of judge up in Heaven who knows how this scene should go, and that he is watching you. And he will punish you if you do it *wrong*. I suggest to you that there is no such Heavenly judge, and even if there is, he has better things to do than watch you read for the hot dog vendor.

Yes, in the world of accounting there is a right way. You add up the numbers, and they go in the box. That is correct. Anybody could do it. You are a functionary of correct answers. And, yes, if you could put the numbers in a box, then it would make success in acting a whole lot easier. Sadly for you, *they* are not looking for functionaries. If *they* were, then *they* could just get anybody off the street to come in and play the role. *They* are looking for artists, sensitive people who plumb their humanity and express it in a uniquely personal way. In acting, the scene has no correctness: in fact it has no life at all; it does not exist outside of your expression of it. It lives through you. And in screen acting the character will only be played *once*. No one else will ever play that role. You are the very definition of it, the only ever expression of it. Therefore, the only right way is your way. Get it?

So, if *they're* not looking for actors who do it right, then what are they doing?

Shopping

They're shopping.

They don't know what *they* want until *they* see it.

It's as if *they* just bought an Armani suit and *they* need a tie. *They* have a general idea of what *they* are looking for. First of all, it must be a tie and look like a tie and work like a tie. That's a given. So now *they* want to browse the racks and see what's on offer, see what might work in this particular case, see what catches *their* eye and suddenly makes *them* say 'yes.' It could be something muted and traditional or something hot and trendy or something completely unexpected. Who knows?

They don't even know.

See what I'm saying here?

They all have different tastes and needs, and *they* themselves don't even know what *they're* looking for. Many times, *they* haven't even thought about the hot dog vendor (for example) up to this point. *They* have been busy trying to get the damn movie funded and set up a production office, and find a location, and get shooting permits, and so on and so on.

So, *they* shop. *They* hold up different ties. *They* argue.

It's hard enough shopping for yourself. Try shopping with three girlfriends at the same time. It's hell. It's a battle. Most of the time, *they* find one great and perfect tie, but only three out of four of *them* believe that. The fourth likes the green one. *They* argue some more. Eventually, *they* get sick of arguing and settle on the blue stripes. You know deep down inside that that's how it works.

You Are a Tie

Now listen carefully. Even if you were a chameleon tie that could read minds and change designs instantly for each and every producer and director looking at you, then you still won't be selected. Here's why:

* You don't know who you are.
* You don't stand for anything.
* You are wimpy.
* You have no confidence, no authority.
* You are not trustworthy.
* You make people uneasy.
* We can't count on you.

Now listen even more carefully. The only way to win here is to be profoundly and honestly what you are, do your best work, and let the chips fall. That's it. Make your own personal tie statement, stand up for it, and wait for the right suit to come along. You know deep down this is how it works.

Look, even if you are the world's perfect tie and you are sprinkled with *magic dust* so that you make it to the final round of judging every time, you can still only win on average 25 percent of the time if there are four people shopping. Right? On average, you will win *them* all over about a quarter of the time. Even with magic dust. That's how it works. You cannot win them all (until you are a huge BFS, and then you still can't win them all), so quit trying.

Forget trying to be *right*, and start trying to be *honest*. Apply yourself, your brand, as strongly as you can, provided it works for the story, and do the scene your way as honestly as you can. This is the one and only way to make it to the final round of judging. You will be up against three or four or five completely different but equally honest other actors. Once every three or four or five auditions, you will book the job—but only if you do it this way. Until you are a BFS, this is the absolute best average you can hope for. The average uneducated actor might book one in forty.

A story told to me by the actress concerned: she was called in for a nice role as a 40-year-old woman. The actress was 32. The casting director was shopping, as I hope I have drilled into your head by now. He wanted to see options for the so-called 40-year-old woman. But the actress took it personally. She asked why she had been called in. Did she look 40? Because she wasn't. She was 32. A young 32. She got all emotional. They had a little fight about it. The actress still didn't understand. The casting director asked her to read anyway, and then never, never invited her in again.

'Acting'

Don't do it.

All casting directors everywhere agree that 'acting' is the last thing they want to see in the room. 'Acting,' as it is commonly understood, has no place in your work as an actor. We should never see 'acting.' If we do, then your career is on the slick, short track back to your dad's hardware store.

We want to see you living. We want to eavesdrop on you living a particularly compelling moment of your life when conflict is rife and stakes are high. That's what is interesting to an audience. I hope you can see that as an actor, your job is to not perform. It is to *be*, as if no one were watching. Behaving spontaneously. Totally alive and totally unaffected. Unwatched. If *they* see you acting, it means you are aware that you are doing a scene, aware of the camera and the movie. You are definitely not having a private moment in a public place. You are not letting *them* secretly watch you in your personal world. Therefore, *they* cannot hire you. To be an actor is to be unaware of these things and very definitely not 'acting.'

You already learned everything you need to know about the story and the scene when you analyzed the script, so you don't need to act it; you simply need to be relaxed and confident and just do it.

Easy.

Aren't you glad you bought this book?

Now, let's go through your audition day step by step.

Getting Ready

Scrub yourself clean of all things that might be distracting to the eye, the ear, the nose, and the blood pressure. Just make sure you are fresh and clean, dressed accordingly as discussed in the Wardrobe chapter on page 142, and packing the right props where necessary.

Do not get drunk, either the night before or the day of. Do not self-medicate in any way, because: *they* can tell, and you will suck.

Turn off your cell phone so it doesn't ring when you walk in the room.

You will be required to bring one resume and headshot to each audition and sometimes two. Your agent will let you know, but you should be prepared for anything. If you happen to be going out for a commercial, then they sometimes want four: one for the casting director, one for the director, one for the advertising agency and one for the client, who will all be in attendance. The smart actor will carry a small satchel of headshots and resumes in the car at all times. Many LA actors will also carry several changes of clothing in the car at all times in case they spill mustard at lunch or their agent calls with another audition. I knew L.A. actors who sometimes went on four or five auditions a day. They'd get up, clean up, hit the road, and show up eight hours later for supper. Auditioning was a full time job. Every now and then they got to take some time off to do a movie.

Next, you will bring the breakdown and the sides. I usually staple them together because I tend to get absent-minded when going to auditions.

Double-check everything, especially your audition time. It seems easy to get the wrong time stuck in your head. Double-check everything. You are welcome to bring the script with you for last minute reference, but leave it in the car or in your bag. Do not bring it into the room. You are supposed to have read it and done your homework long ago. Don't give *them* the impression that you're just getting to the script now. These little things mean a lot. They add up.

Like it or not, you are being judged on simple and often silly little things, such as the fact that you brought the script. What is it about the script? A) You are supposed to have done your work already, and B) the filmmakers love and cherish the script since it is the basis of everything *they* are doing and the engine of *their* success, and *they* don't like seeing it bandied about or abandoned on a coffee table. It freaks *them* out. It makes *them* think it has already been posted on your blog. You may laugh. Go ahead. But if you want to book a job, then leave it in the car.

Bring only your headshot and your sides.

Arriving

Show up!

The first rule of show business is show up. Something like 30 percent of actors don't show up for their auditions. Nearly one third of all possible auditions are lost. Ridiculous. Not to mention it's hurtful to you and all your creed, because that is 30 percent of the available slots other actors—who'd really like to be there and who would show up—can't have because of you. So, if you're struggling to get an audition, then don't blame your agent, don't blame the casting directors, blame your fellow actors for not showing up. You think sending your regrets is bad? Try not showing up a couple of times. You can buy your ticket back to Dubuque with complete confidence.

Do not be late. This might be difficult. You will have to make arrangements, take time off work, find a babysitter, or battle the traffic. But you will do it, and you will arrive early. Nothing rattles your already frazzled nerves like trying to find the place and park with ten minutes to go.

I suggest you arrive 20 or 30 minutes early. Use some of this time to sit in your car to relax and focus. Rehearse your scene one last time, and I mean it. Once you leave the car, you will do no rehearsing or running lines or anything having to do with the performance. Nothing. From here on, you are to focus on the land mines and the confidence. A great performance marred by two land mines means you lose; a decent performance coupled with zero explosions and lots of confidence means you move forward. Get it? It's about the land mines. *It's about the land mines.*

By the way, it's about the land mines.

Even if it isn't entirely about the land mines, it's best at this point to believe it is.

Focus.

I don't care if you think you don't know the lines. We will deal with that shortly. It doesn't matter. For now, it's about the land mines.

Next, prepare a very brief monologue about how professional you are and how you can make them money. Four or five lines are plenty. It should sound something like this: "Well, I just did the lead in a brilliant short film for German director Dieter Fingerpoken—it just got accepted to the Sundance Film Festival, actually—I'm playing Benvolio at the Santa Monica Superior Courthouse Theater, studying with my coach Oscar OnTheWay, and I just finished reading Peter Skagen's insightful book, *Screen Acting Trade Secrets*, I'm working hard; enjoying it. Oh, and by the way, I just finished a course in horseback riding, which I know is important for this character."

Rehearse this a couple of times so you don't stumble. You will be using it in the room. If you did not recently work for Dieter Fingerpoken and are not playing Benvolio, then list whatever you can that is pertinent to your acting career. Go into a bit more detail about your training and then finish the same way. What you say must be true (the casting director might know Mr. Fingerpoken), although you can embellish a teensy bit, and it must amount to a sales pitch for your career and why they would be wise to hire you.

Leave your stuff in the car. Wherever possible arrive with as little carry-on luggage as you can. It's a big mistake to lug all your stuff into the room and unload in a corner. You waste time, you look difficult and foolish, and you risk a nice big juicy X. If you can't leave your stuff in the car, then leave as much possible in the green room. If you can't leave it in the green room, then bring it into the room, but be ready to drop it as you're walking to the mark. The entire audition is meant to take about two minutes. That's the only way *they* can see enough people in a day. Don't be the *unloader* jerk who takes ten minutes of everyone's time. You might think you are making yourself stand out, but *they* are wise to your games and will hate you for it.

Do not bring children or animals, you doorknob. I was working for a casting director when this actor walked into the room with his ten-year-old daughter. He told her to go stand in the corner, be quiet, and wait for him. Can you imagine? Do you think anyone paid any attention to his audition? We were all thinking about the poor kid and wondering what kind of Dad would do such a thing. Maybe he was really a nice Dad, but just got muddled up? Or maybe he was some kind of weirdo with a dungeon, who… Oh, sorry, did you just audition?

Your audition starts the second you leave your car and approach the building. Remember the 'everything counts' speech? Buildings have windows, for one thing. At one particular audition, I walked into the room and the casting director asked me if I was alright. She'd seen me trudging up to the building and her confidence was already shaken.

The guy having a smoke by the front door might be the director, for all you know. This happened to me in reverse on one occasion. I did my audition, and then bumped into this poorly dressed guy on the way out. I thought he was a crew member of some kind—a grip maybe. Or maybe another actor. He started to chat. I stopped and chatted back. He asked me how I liked the casting director and the audition. Did I like the acting game? I said I did and I did. Then he said, "Well, I really liked what you did in there."

Uh?

"I'm watching the auditions from my office down the hall. I liked what you did, in there. See you on set."

He was the director. He was patched into the video feed. He wanted to see if he liked me or not. Luckily, I didn't stick my foot in my mouth, and I didn't mope away cursing my bad luck and lack of talent. I booked it and had a terrific time.

Just accept that you are auditioning from the time you approach the building to the time you get back in your car at the very least, and you should act accordingly with ease and confidence. Smile a lot. Treat everyone respectfully. Expect everyone to be the casting director or a future good friend. If you are serious about the game, then you will accept the fact that you are auditioning all the time.

The Green Room

Find your way to the green room and enter with easy confidence. You're an actor, right? Land your entrance. You don't know who's in there. Set yourself up for success. Easy confidence. Share your easy confidence with everyone there, including any other actors who may be waiting. Some will be there to read for the same part as you. You will not be concerned because you remember the cliché speech and know that you are not in direct competition with them because you are selling something different than they are. This will add to your easy confidence.

Sadly, some of these waiting actors will be jerks hoping to win by cutting you down or psyching you out. They are small people of low character and little courage or ignorant people who have not read this book. They will give you the stink-eye. Counter with a little nod and more easy confidence. It will knock the wind out of them and is by far the best way to fend off any such attacks in the future.

If you see anyone you know or if anyone wants to gab, then just say, "So nice to see you. I just need to sign in/prepare/focus/compose my thank-you speech." Some actors love to gab before an audition. You may be one of them. If so, then you can gab in a minute. I find that gabbers gab mostly out of a kind of childish nervousness, which you don't need to be associated with. You need to focus. Some gabbers are sneaky jerks who will try to psych you out by pretending to be your pal. Smiling, they ask you, "How is it that you are so good?" You will make some self-effacing remark. Then you'll walk into your audition thinking, "Yeah, how is it that I'm so good? Am I good? I did screw up that last audition for the plumber. Wait a minute…" Your audition is over and he has won. My general advice is to avoid gabbing until after you're done. Even the secret director will respect you for wanting to focus, provided you are civil and full of easy confidence.

Say hello to the assistant. Usually, there is an assistant manning a registration table. Be nice and warm, and exude your easy confidence. These assistants often determine your fate. If the casting director is not sure about moving you forward in the process, then she'll turn to her assistant and say, "What did you think?" Happens all the time.

Same goes in spades for the cameraman in the room. They work as a team. He has seen 1000s of auditions too. They compare notes constantly. You don't want your fate in the hands of a cameraman or an assistant whom you recently snubbed.

Better yet, introduce yourself to the assistant, say, "Nice you meet you, Julie," and ask her how it's going. You will probably be the first all day to do such a thing and she'll remember you for it. If you come in all brooding and boiling with fear and loathing, then she'll remember that too.

Sign in. There will always be some kind of sign-in sheet you need to complete. If it's a union production, then there will be a union sign-in sheet so they can keep track of where you have been and whether you have been abused or made to wait too long. They are the clearing-house for all performers on a union production so they keep very detailed records. Example: if you are a union member, then you are usually required to audition for free only twice. If *they* call you in a third time, then *they* have to pay you.

Often there will be also be a form you need to complete with your contact info, your agency, your sizes, and your availability for the shoot dates. Complete this form truthfully. Every actress in the world seems to weigh 108 pounds on these forms because they're all lying. Don't you think *they're* going to see that you're really 155 when you walk in? Or maybe find out in the costume fitting? Do you think *they* will be happy? Do you think *they* won't fire you?

The other major crime is to claim you are available for the shoot dates when you are not. Don't ever do this. If *they* are shooting from August 24th to 30th, and you are in Hawaii until the 27th, then you are not available. You will write down: in Hawaii until the 27th. If you claim you are available, then you must actually be available. It's a sworn oath. Filmmaking is like going to war on Mars, remember? The rocket leaves on the 24th, not when you get back from surfing. And no, *they* will not plan around you. Are you crazy? *They* are planning around the weather, the money, the release date, the locations, the studio, the script, the special effects, the star, and so on. And the only reason *they* are planning around the star is because she's busy making five other films. She's not tanning in Hawaii. And she's the *star. They* will not plan around you. Instead, *they* will hire someone else who *they* can trust to show up for battle.

The only reason for breaking this sworn oath is the same as before: because you book a job in the interim. Or you get hit by a bus and have a note from your coroner. No other excuse will do. If you lie, and book the job based on that lie, and then tell them all about Hawaii and how you'll try to change your flights, and oh, please forgive me, *they* will 1) be very pissed off; 2) call to scream at your agent; 3) never want to see you again; 4) lose just a little bit more respect for actors everywhere;

and 5) probably take it out on some innocent person three weeks from now. Your agent will then call you to drop your sorry butt from her roster. Thanks for playing. Good luck in the food service industry.

As a director who has been sucker-punched by actors in the past, I'm asking you nicely to be honest. It will take you a long way and restore a lot of faith. And it will save you from my murdering hands when I snap one day.

Next, deal with your headshot and resume. In most cases, the assistant will take them from you along with the paperwork you just filled out. In cases where the assistant only comes out of the room in spurts to collect actors, fill out the paperwork and leave it on the table in a neat stack with your headshot on top, sunny-side up. When your turn comes up the assistant will see your smiling face on the table, grab your stack, and usher you in. In cases without an assistant, fill out the paperwork and bring it into the room with you when you are called, along with your headshot, resume, and sides.

Waiting to be Called

Now, relax. Find a cool corner or comfy chair, focus, and reassure yourself of the following:

You are in the game, otherwise you would not have booked this audition.

You are right for the part, otherwise *they* would not have called you in.

You are already giving *them* confidence with your easy confidence.

You *get* the story, because you are schooled in that department thanks to this book and the other books you bought, and you did your homework.

You know where all the land mines are with respect to technique and protocol, and you will not step on any of them.

Because of your superior technique, your performance will be at least 90 percent perfect. You can relax. And you will have your sides in your hands in case your forget anything.

You will look for a chance to do the monologue you composed in the car on how you can make them money and be professional.

There is nothing more attractive than easy confidence, so you can be assured that everybody likes you.

You are firing on all cylinders. You are doing the best you can, so you can relax. You know that you are going to both win and lose every time you perform, so there is no need to worry. You know that you love acting and would do it for free, so there is no reason to feel anxious. You know that the absolute best you can do is book about one in every four auditions, so there is no need to put any pressure on yourself over this one audition. The only thing you can do to be better at this point is to focus, and relax, and be present. Be here now. Instead of being anxious and lost in the past or the future—being in your head—you are sitting here now, in your body. You have presence. You are an alpha dog, so no one can reject you. You can do anything you want, like explore your imagination in front of a camera, without worry. You dominate, you are generous, and you are enough. You feel free and powerful. You love the work. You let an infinitesimal Buddha-smile unfold upon your lips. You wait.

And then, the Movies call your name.

The Audition

It may be the assistant or it may be the casting director herself. If she uses a reader, then it may be the reader. On rare occasions it's the actor who went in before you saying, "Dude. You're up." Once in a while, it's the janitor. But usually it's the assistant calling your name. Rise up and smile warmly, oozing your easy confidence. Look her in the eye and say, "Thanks."

She will lead you into the room, hand off your paperwork to the casting director, and introduce you. Then she leaves.

You hang onto your sides. Always carry your sides into the room and hold them during the reading (but leave the script in your car). Feel free to refer to them during the reading. This is why they call it a reading. Even though you analyzed the scene and know all the lines perfectly, you are not expected to be *off-book* (completely memorized) at this time. It's fine if you are, but it is not typically expected. So, hold your sides.

My friend Andy Henry, an LA casting director, tells it like this (paraphrasing): "It's like watching a high-wire act. If there's a net below the guy, then you watch his amazing acrobatics with joy and abandon. It's a thrill. But once they take away the net, guess what? All you're watching is the danger, and you're really scared that something terrible might happen, and you're not really watching the stunts anymore."

Your sides are your safety net. They let everybody relax and focus on the reading rather than on your ability as a daredevil. Get it? So, bring them in and use them whenever necessary.

Here's how: hold them in front of you at a height slightly below your manly chest or womanly bosom. Your thumbs should be on either side of the page. Do not hold them out to one side at eye level; it's not done, and you look stupid doing it. The proper protocol is two thumbs on the pages held slightly below your boobs. There is a good reason for this. If there are several pages in your scene, then learn where the page turns are, remember them and practice them in advance: learn that the last line on page one is: "But I never drink milk with my nose." Turn the page. Put your thumbs back where they belong, ready for the next page turn. Practice so you can do this without looking for the whole scene no matter how many pages there are. Get really good at it. In the audition, you will similarly turn the page without looking as you go along so you can keep your eyes up where they can be seen and remain connected with the other actor. This position means if you do have to look for a line, then you'll be on the right page. You don't want to be flipping around trying to find your place.

To look for a line, go like this: stay connected with your reader. Do not stop; do not get all flustered; do not say "oh shit." Wait for him to finish whatever he's saying or doing. Take it in. React. Stay in the scene. Stay connected. Then find your line on the page. Take it in and know it. Bring your eyes back up—still connected and maintaining the reality of the scene—and deliver your line.

There is *never* a time when you are looking at your pages while your partner is talking.

If your lines are short enough, then you should be eyes-up when speaking, too. If you have longer speeches that you can't remember, then just read them—still connected and maintaining the reality of the scene—then bring your eyes back up as you say your final lines.

Do the whole scene like this if necessary. It's done all the time. You can take classes in it in LA. Casting directors will love and admire you, and they will talk about your overarching skill with their colleagues.

Look, sometimes actors go on six auditions a day in LA or New York. You can't memorize everything. Not possible. Everybody knows that, and everybody expects you to use the pages in this way. Okay?

The other benefit of working like this is that you are free. You can live truthfully in the scene without worry because you have the papers if you need them. You can go down and get as many or as few lines as you need. Thus the scene is about two people having a conversation rather than about some actor trying to remember his lines. Get it?

Don't forget it.

Next, walk in smiling and oozing and alpha-dogging. Say, "Hi. Thanks for calling me in." Then head for the mark or the large open area in front of the camera. On the way, nod in an alpha-doggy way to the camera operator and anyone else who may be in the room. Make eye contact with each and every person. Do not shake hands. Say "Good morning." Call them by name wherever possible.

In first auditions, you will generally be alone with the casting director and the cameraman or camerawoman. If a third person is in the room and that person is standing next to the camera holding some sides, then that's your reader. That's who you're doing the scene with. The casting director will watch. Sometimes she will watch you live and in person since you're only eight feet away; sometimes she'll get you started and then watch you on a monitor she has on her desk. This can throw you if you're not ready for it. You might feel ignored. Do not be offended. Remember, she's interested in how you act for the camera, not how you act for the empty part of the room.

In some first auditions you will find the director and producer(s) present as well. This happens a lot in television because they don't have a lot of time, and TV is a producer's medium. Directors come and go every week on episodic TV shows, so it's the producers who mostly manage casting.

You will smile, nod, ooze, make eye contact. If you had a chance to do your homework and look them up, then call them by name. *They* will most certainly wave a little hello and then turn to the monitor. Do not act the smiling and oozing. Be the smiling and oozing. This is not as easy as it sounds.

I once walked into a little room to confront at least a dozen people sitting around on couches surveying me. It felt like a weird, artistic Inquisition. I had no idea who was who, and I didn't see a camera anywhere. It was wacky and nerve-racking. From one side, a young guy appeared, and he stared at me oddly. I concluded that he must be the reader. Not being sure, I asked in an easy, confident way, "You reading?" He nodded. I went into the scene. I finished. This bearded guy then addressed me from the couch. I thought he would be well cast as the director. He was. "Nice. Nice. I liked that." So I said, "Great. Thank you." I scanned the room looking for anyone resembling a casting director. She was off in a corner, but she was nice enough to send me a little signal. I said another thank you, and as I turned to go, I saw the camera hidden behind a plant. This particular group must have thought that cameras make actors nervous. I was more nervous by its absence.

An aside: I hereby recommend we start a lobby group to make every room post its peculiar practices on the wall outside. It would help enormously to know the camera will be hiding behind a plant.

Anyway, I booked it.

These kinds of curveballs will come your way occasionally so be ready with all that easy confidence of yours, but also know that most auditions will be little affairs between you, the casting director, and the cameraman.

As you are hitting your mark, the casting director will be hitting hers next to the camera where she will be reading with you. But first, she wants a little time to remind herself who you are, to make sure you look like your headshot, and to see what's on your resume. Sometimes she will stand there quietly reading. Usually she will fill the void by asking the stock question, which is: "So, what have you been up to lately?" This accomplishes two goals: it buys her a little time, and it gives her a chance to get a feel for you and your potential.

Here is the wrong answer: "Well, not much. My girlfriend just left me, so that sucks. Got nothing left and I mean nothing. I haven't booked a gig in like a year, plus I quit my day job at Audio/Video/Hamburger Shack a week ago, so I like really need this gig or whatever. And I'm hung over."

Clearly, you are not transferring a lot of confidence to the casting director. Two or three, or perhaps four big Xs for you, and your chances now are microscopically close to nil no matter what you do from here.

Who knows the right answer? Anybody? You made it up in the car about 20 minutes ago, and you rehearsed it so you wouldn't stumble.

"Well, I just did the lead in a very brilliant short film for German director Dieter Fingerpoken—it just got accepted to the Sundance Film Festival, actually—I'm playing Benvolio at the Santa Monica Superior Courthouse Theater, studying with my coach Oscar OnTheWay, and I just finished reading Peter Skagen's insightful book *Screen Acting Trade Secrets*. I'm working hard; enjoying it. Oh, and by the way, I just finished a course in horseback riding, which I know is important for this character."

Now she knows you are working your career and want to be there. She knows you are employable by German guys, that you are gaining an international profile, and that you can also do theater. You study up. You work hard. You like it. You are not a freaky weirdo. You can save them money on stunt riders. You are a pro, a contender who does not stumble.

You may thank me now.

At this point, she will probably say something like, "Good to know. Thank you." You will nod generously, exuding easy confidence.

Then, "Do you have any questions?"

This is the second stock question in audition rooms. It serves several purposes. First of all, if you have no idea what you're doing, then it will become instantly apparent. For example, when you ask, "Is this a western?" you are going to get a gigantic X. Thanks for playing. So, it's a quick way to separate the wheat from the chaff.

Conversely, if you ask a smart little question because you did your homework and the script is not clear on one little point, then she will love you. She will engage you. She will help you. She will look at you with new eyes.

The question also allows you to clarify points of pronunciation. For example: writers love their characters' names. They'll spend weeks coming up with just the right one. You need to say it correctly. You cannot do the scene saying it wrong; it's like a stab in the heart to them every time. If in doubt, ask. Filmmakers also love the names of all the weapons, and places, and stuff in their space movies and TV shows. The fans are fanatical about those names too.

You do not want to say the line: "Set your Fahzers on stun."

The question also allows the casting director the chance to let you in on any secret info she may have up her sleeve, such as, "The director really wants a very real person here."

Beautiful. Score. Inside information.

You may ask, "But Peter, why wouldn't she just tell me that? Why do I have to ask that?"

Because, dear one, she has done so in the past and been sucker-punched by criminal actors so many times that she quit.

You see, actors are rather well known for being childish and full of excuses. For example, one actor (who was going to do a crappy audition anyway) called her agent and said, "Sorry, Marg, I screwed this one up because the damn casting director gave me this ridiculous direction just before I did the scene. Why do they do that?" In the worst-case scenario, Marg calls the casting director to complain, they talk, they shout, everybody gets a black eye, and somebody gets fired.

So, the casting director got fed up helping actors and quit doing it. Unless you ask.

Next to last, it lets you clarify any technical issues that may be important. For example, when you made the scene audition-friendly, you may have brought a prop, or removed a line, or decided you wanted to walk out at the end of the scene. Now is the time to let her know or ask questions if you are unsure. "Do you really want me to jump off the flaming alien cruiser, because I was not planning on doing that."

Lastly, it gives you the option of saying, "Nope." This can be the most powerful answer provided you go on to nail the performance, but only if you go on to nail the performance. When you're gone, she will turn to her cameraman and say, "Wow. A real pro."

Make Them Shut Up and Lean In

Okay. Now it's time to do the deed.

The casting director will probably say one of the following: "Okay." "When you're ready." "Let's put one down." "Rolling." "Action." She's signaling to everybody that the scene is about to happen, so look out. The cameraman will push the record button, the casting director will prepare to read for you, and you will make ready to drop into the scene.

But by far the better way for this to happen is this: you should cue *them*. This is what's called an advanced audition technique. First, you want to be sure you don't cause any explosions in *their* heads. You want to avoid all the land mines. But second, you want to shut *them* up. Anytime *they* have to tell you anything or give you directions of any kind, *they* begin to lose confidence in you. It's subtle, often subconscious, but it happens. You're supposed to be the pro, the sovereign state, the alpha dog who knows what he's doing, right? Take it to the limit by shutting *them* up completely. Take over the room. Take control. Shut *them* up, and show off your chops. Force *them* to quit looking for technical faults and start looking at you and your stellar performance.

Trust me here. *They* want this. This is your job. Be so good with your technique that it ceases to be an issue. Force *them* to watch you. If you can take over in the room and make these tired, irritated, jaded movie people shut up and watch, then you can do the same in the movie. This means you can make millions of tired, irritated, jaded regular theater-goers shut up and watch. This is a good thing. This gives *them* maximum confidence in you. *They* are no longer trying to imagine what you can do, *they* are witnessing what you can do it on set. *They know* the audience will pay attention. *They know they* will succeed, *they* will make money, and *they* will have a chance to make another movie. All this combined will cause *them* to bend over backward, or forward if necessary, to get you in the movie.

Success in the audition room: you shut *them* up and make *them* lean in.

Think about a movie theater. The lights dim, and everyone shuts up and leans forward. They turn off their critical minds, and they open their hearts trusting that you will honestly and kindly tell them a tale. Movie people, real movie people, have giant hearts bursting with the love of movies. That's why *they* do the work. Therefore, *they* have to be extra careful with those hearts. Especially because of this: once *they* got into the biz, *they* found knives, creeps, and knaves everywhere. Everywhere *they* turn, some jerk tries to stab *their* big little hearts. *They* get scarred and scared and jaded and mad. *They* protect *their* big little hearts ferociously by littering the place with land mines and by trying hard not to shut up and lean forward. But still *they* want to. But *they* don't. But *they* really do. Get it? *They* are dying for some gracious actor to come in, take over, and shut *them* up. Thus *they* get to be kids again on a Saturday afternoon in the cinema, and all *their* grown-up work seems worthwhile. *Their* hearts overflow with love for everything and everyone, especially you.

This is a good thing, and it is all due to your hard work, your confidence, and your generous heart.

Once you book the gig and show up on set, you are to do the very same thing. Take over. Shut *them* up. Make *them* watch. Be kind to *their* hearts. Do not be an egotistical prick about it. That's not you. You are a confident alpha dog, in love with everyone. Look around the set and you will see the pros, the working actors, the stars, doing this very same thing. That's why they are pros, working actors, and stars. Usually, the bigger the star, the bigger their aura of shut-up-and-watch. Not shut-up-and-watch cause I'm a huge selfish egomaniac, but shut-up-and-watch as I honestly and kindly relate this tale to your big little heart.

It's a beautiful thing to see.

The Actors are Here

I have made several movies. It's a crap-load of work. You get very tired and discouraged and unhappy and poor. My friend Keith Melton in LA, a director, wants to have a production company called Sisyphus Entertainment, because Sisyphus was the poor dude in Greek mythology who had to push a rock up a hill for all eternity. That's how it feels. Months and years of labor go by with no result and potentially no paycheck at the end of it. Finally, if you're very lucky, then you corral the funding, and finally you set up an office, and finally you start hiring people, and finally you cast it, and *finally* you make it to the first day of the shoot, and guess what? Everybody is nearly dead with exhaustion and anxiety because it could still fall apart at any second. You could cut the air with a knife.

And then, in the midst of all that, something magical happens, something that turns everything around 180 degrees, something that signals to everyone that we are making a movie, that the pain is over and the wonder is about to start. All our suffering has been worth it. The gates of Heaven are opening.

Do you know what that one thing is?

It's the actors. Arriving.

Suddenly everything turns electric, light, and magic. The actors are here, and we are saved. We are making a movie. The magic is going to happen. Right there, those people, those are the actors. Look at them. They look so much like regular people and yet so much like Earthly gods, for they are our salvation. Recording the spark and magic of life they emit is the very essence and reason for our being. And it means the funding is in place and we have a shot. The actors are here. We're shooting. We did it. Joy. Bliss. Magic.

You see? Once the script is perfect and finished, everything revolves around the actors.

You.

And do you know how *they* feel if you show up all scared and shriveled? *They* just want to die. The actor-gods are scared. We are screwed. Somebody kill me.

But if you show up like you're supposed to, confident, alpha doggie, bigger than life, shutting *them* up, making the lean forward: Joy. Bliss. Magic.

The actors are here.

Needless to say, *they* are looking for shades of this joy in the audition room. If you can bring full-blooded joy to the room, then you will be treated like the little god you are and people will throw money at you. You will be astonished at *their* behavior.

But you, you just love the work and want to do it. You will be perplexed. You will sigh. You will forgive *them* and get on with it.

You will do your work as best you can, and then on to the next one that showed up out of nowhere because of the magic you bring, and so on, and so on.

Okay?

So, take over the room. Feel free and encouraged to do this right from the first moment. Don't be a jerk about it. Just shine your light. Show that you know what you're doing.

I like to enter smiling and alpha dogging, hit my mark, nod when I'm ready, speak my speech, say thanks, and leave. Without *them* saying a word. Try it yourself. Let me know how it goes.

Readers

So, at this point—remember, we're back in the room now, about to do the scene—you should nod at the cameraman, focus, connect with the casting director, and begin your reading.

Do not be alarmed if she truly sucks as an actor. You may be tempted to stop and laugh your head off. You may consider it a terrible affront. You may wish to cry. Do none of these things. The fact is, she probably will suck, on purpose, for this is yet another little land mine.

As part of the whole leveling-the-playing-field theory, many casting directors will play the scene with you like low-talking zombies. Their voices will be flat, quiet, and without emotion. They strive hard to give you nothing whatsoever to play off. No reactions. No connection. No nothing. They may even avoid your eyes so you're playing the scene to the tops of their low-talking zombie heads. It happens all the time. For people trained in theater where actors hang on to each other's eyes for dear life, this can be a nightmare.

You must remember that the casting director works for the producers, who expect her to be fair and just across the board. She cannot be accused of favoritism. You must also remember that the producers hear her voice on the tape reading opposite the actors. If she were to engage with the actors and play the scene with them, then she might get tired and start to falter later in the day. She might willingly or unwillingly vary the read based on the actor in question, leading to accusations of favoritism. She might spend too much energy acting and not enough casting. There is also the danger of leading the actors astray. Suppose she, the casting director, believes the scene should go a certain way, but the actor has a different idea. Her reading may not fit with his, and thus the scene is clunky and wrong. Or the actor may start to swerve in her direction—she is the casting director after all—creating an uneven, uncertain performance. Then the actor calls his agent and says, "Sorry Marg, I screwed that one up because the damn casting director was doing this weird read and she threw me off." You know the rest.

In the end, most casting directors take the easy way out and read everything in these ways:
- flat—so it's the same for everybody,

- quiet—so her voice is not too loud on the camera right next to her, and
- without emotion—so she doesn't lead anyone astray.

Another reason is more complicated but nonetheless important and telling. If you haven't worked on set, then you haven't experienced this bit, so it may come as a shock. Hold onto your chair. On many occasions, you, the actor, will be required to do the scene by yourself. The star will have gone back to the hotel do to press interviews, but *they* need to shoot your close up. So, you will do it to nobody, just a bit of empty space next to the camera. Sometimes *they* will be kind enough to tape a little X on a stand or sticking out from the side of the lens. That is the star. Sometimes, being very kind, *they* will scribble a pair of eyes on a piece of paper and tape that up for you. The script supervisor will read the star's lines from somewhere off in a corner. The script supervisor cannot act; her words will come out flat and zombie-like just like the casting director's. You will do the scene. This can be very difficult, especially when the scene is about how your brother slept with your wife and has now come to kill you. Nevertheless, it happens all the time.

A brief example: I was a cranky train engineer in the old west. I blew my train whistle to scare away a herd of horses that the leading men had rounded up. Off the horses ran. In my close up, the director stood on a ladder next to the camera (I was up in the train engine) and wiggled his fingers around like he was playing air-piano. Those were the horses running away.

You can learn more about these crazy actor games in the next section. For now, you can see that a pro actor would have no trouble doing this little trick in the audition, whereas you, the beginner, are likely to go boom on the land mine and give yourself away.

Instead, be ready. Prepare the scene so you can do it to a lamppost. Know it backwards and forwards so you can pick it up anywhere and do it to the end. Rehearse with a boring friend. Exhume an actual low-talking zombie and run it a few times with him. Whatever it takes.

On the other hand, you may come across a casting director who loves actors and acting and really likes to get in there and mix it up with you. Fine for some. If you like what she's doing and where she's taking you, then you're golden. If you don't, then you could have a problem. You have to do the scene to the end and then somehow, politely, confidently, tell the casting director she's doing it wrong and ask her to do it again but right this time. Tricky. Sometimes this is worth it when your version is better. Many times, it's not. My general advice in cases like this is to follow her lead. She knows what she wants and, more importantly, what the director and producers want, and because her voice is on the tape too she cannot knowingly lead you astray. Plus, she will be flattered.

If there is a reader in the room, then all the same applies. Usually, readers are unemployed actors who will try very hard to create the scene with you. But sometimes not. Sometimes they are directed to be zombie-heads.

To sum up: be fully prepared to do it with the zombie head. If you don't like what you're getting from the casting director, then re-cast her in your mind and play the scene the way you know it should go.

Eye Lines

Next, make sure the casting director is giving you a good *eye line*. She should be close to the lens and at roughly the same level.

You see, watching a movie is a lot like voyeurism, as I have mentioned. Pretty much totally voyeurism. It's like peeking through a hole into the girl's change room—exciting, but it's also very informative because you get to see what the girls are really like when no one is looking. How wonderful.

The movies are like looking into the girl's change room times 12 because we can sneak up on a single girl in the change room and look right at her, right into her eyes, from 12 inches away, without her seeing us, while she talks to a friend about a boy she likes. This is called the *close up*. We are eavesdropping from a foot away, right in front of her face, and she has no idea we're there. We get to see into the depths of her soul.

Impossibly, fantastically fun.

Remember, the camera seeks this close up. It's what the audience wants. So, the audition will be done in close up as well, almost looking you right in the eye but not quite. And you have no idea we are there.

If you look right into the camera, then you catch us looking at you, and we feel terrible. If we are on the razor's edge of being caught, then we are frantically delighted.

So, your eye line must be as close to the camera as possible without ever peeking into it. Looking at the camera—known as *spiking the lens*—is a huge kaboom. It means you're aware of the camera, and all our fun is over. End of magical illusion.

If you look at the camera in the audition room, then you will look at the camera on set (or so *they* think), so *they* cannot possibly hire you. Jumbo X all over and around and through your name.

The only times you can peek are:

* during your slate;
* in a commercial when you are addressing the buying public;
* or in rare cases where the script calls for you to look as in the television show *The Office*.

Otherwise, it does not exist for you. You do not see it. You are totally unaware that it is there. But you must look as close to it as possible.

Welcome to the fun world of film acting.

Normally, that sweet spot next to the lens is exactly where you'll find the casting director. Sometimes though, she gets a little tired or she just forgets and drifts off a few feet. This is the time to confidently ask, "Do you want this eye line? Cause I'd prefer to be closer." She will then say, "Yeah, I like this," (some do), or "Oops, right, thank you." And she'll snug up to the camera. Be confident. It's your audition. She will respect you for knowing what you're doing and getting the job done right.

Okay, so this is all fine if you're playing a scene with just one other person, but suppose you are at a poker table with three other *hombres*. Then what? Do you keep the same eye line for all of them?

No.

You must make it audition friendly, remember? You must very carefully establish *specific eye lines* for each separate *hombre*. You will rehearse it this way and be ready to do it in the room. You must use the right eye line for the right *hombre* throughout the scene. You cannot play the whole thing to one guy or lazily pan your eyes around the room and expect the scene to play properly. The eye lines must be exceedingly specific so when *they* are watching it later *they* can clearly see when you are talking to Pedro and when you shift over to Miguel. After all, Pedro may be secretly on your side, whereas Miguel may want you dead. *They* want to see that in your performance.

Problem: you are short on actual *hombres*. Solution: establish imaginary eye lines for each of them.

Place them all close to the camera. Do not place them all over the room like a real poker game. You'd be showing your profile to the camera most of the time, which we have already concluded is a big fat no-no. Put them all close to the camera, but far enough apart so they read as separate, specific eye lines. Eighteen inches, or half a meter apart, are plenty. It is not exactly realistic this way but it will look realistic on camera, okay? Trust me. Put yourself on camera and have a look if you want.

So for the sake of this example, Pedro can be the casting director herself. Miguel will be her shoulder. Lupe will be a short little guy, so he's her elbow. And Don Ricardo will be the doorframe on the other side of the camera (which you will not look at when you are going back and forth). Get it?

Keep your Eyes Open and Slow Down

Next, keep your eyes open and slow down.

It's not fun being a foot away from the girl in the change room if she has her eyes closed. If she blinks all the time, then we get anxious and irritated; she looks like she's lying or avoiding us. But if her eyes are open, then she is alive, dramatic, and fascinating, and we get to merge with her, heart and soul. We are mesmerized. We never want to leave her.

Similarly, if she talks reallyreallyfastlikethiswehavetoworksohard-tounderstand …

See? If you talk too fast it's too much work for us to keep up with you and we quit trying. Who wants to work that hard? And again, you appear to be very unsure of yourself, and therefore uninteresting. One of the classic amateur mistakes is to race through the scene as fast as you can. First, you're nervous. And second, you're terrified that you might forget a word. So, you announce the words as fast as you can all the way to the end. There, I did it.

And another X for you.

Anybody can remember lines. Anybody off the street can do it. It is not impressive. However, if you slow down so *they* can relax, and then you let the scene unfold at its natural pace, *they* will love you.

Acting is an art, not a race, otherwise the fastest actors would be the best ones. Correct? Is there an Oscar for Fastest Actor in a Lead Role?

Think of it like dancing. The idea of dancing is not to get to the other side of the room. It is just to dance to the music. Similarly, in acting, you must let the scene unfold naturally according to its own rhythm. You can't push it along.

If you slow down, even to the point where it feels uncomfortable to you, then *they* will love it. You will appear very sure of yourself. Very compelling and dramatic. *They* will want to hear what you have to say. And *they* will relax. *They* don't have to work. *They* can settle in, relax, and let the story unfold. In theater, actors are constantly reminded to pick up their cues and keep the pace up. In film, we constantly remind ourselves to slow down. The pause is our most powerful weapon.

I want to take a moment to remind you that these are still technical skills. They require no talent. I hear you getting tense. Don't. You simply have to be willing to do the work. Slow down. Play the punctuation. Punctuate the sub-text. One thing at a time.

And don't blink.

Watch any great actor and you'll see they seldom if ever blink, and the longer the speech they have to give the slower they talk. It seems counter-intuitive but it is true and correct. If you slow down and keep your eyes open, then we will stay with you as long as you want. Watch Jack Nicholson in the courtroom scene in *A Few Good Men*. Jack is famous for talking so slowly he almost sings. That is not an accident. He is a BFS who knows what he's doing. Jack is also famous for being still on camera and punctuating his performance. No blurry scenes; he hits each and every nail on the head one by one. Jack is also a champion of keeping his peepers open at all times, which you will see in his several big speeches in that film.

Jaws is quite an old movie now, but if you rent it you'll see one of the great examples of this. Quint, the old boat captain played by

Robert Shaw, has to do a four-minute speech about how his navy ship, *The Indianapolis*, was sunk, and how 700 men were eaten by sharks while they waited for rescue. For four minutes, the camera held him in a *close up* as he told his ancient mariner's tale. Four minutes in a movie is forever. Have you ever gotten a shot of Novocain at the dentist's office? Well, that takes about 20 seconds. We're talking four minutes here, in one of the highest-grossing movies of all time. He had to keep literally millions of people on the edge of their seats for four minutes. How did he do it? He simply sat very still, kept his eyes open, spoke very slowly, and hit each nail on the head one by one. "Japanese submarine slammed two torpedoes into our side, Chief…"

Works every time.

Set the Stage

I like to sing classical music. One of my coaches once told me this: "If you want to be a singer, you have to learn to take up more space." The same goes for you. Take up room. Expand. Amateurs walk into the room shriveled up like calamari. They are so scared they seem to have themselves hidden in some inaccessible corner of their spinal column. Professionals walk in and take up the whole room.

Not only that, professionals turn the whole room into the setting for their scene. If it happens to be a courtroom, then they address the judge of course, but they also occasionally turn to address the jury, which they deeply believe is there. They acknowledge their client next to them. They glance at the opposing attorneys. Somehow these actors even seem to let us know where the doors and windows are and how cramped and stuffy it is.

They do this by expanding into the space and believing in it. The space then naturally shows up in their performance even when they are not actively trying to show it. Their belief somehow communicates directly to the people in the room, creating a mental picture and inducing *them* to believe as well.

That can only be good for you.

You've done the work of analyzing the scene. You should know the space like your own bedroom. Now is the time to visualize it with all your might, and let it expand into the room.

The Moment Before

The scene is about human beings who have lives, not characters in a movie who suddenly appear on screen. Humans are always coming from somewhere and going somewhere else. You need to know all about them and their lives to play them well, and specifically you need to know what happened in the moments *before* the scene you are about to play so that it rings true.

Spend some time figuring this out. Since it's the moment before, it won't be written in the script. It is up to you to know in all detail. Did she run from the bus stop to get here? Did she just witness a murder? Did she just resolve to dump her husband? Did she just learn her mother has cancer? Did she just do her mascara? It makes a difference.

You need to fully understand and visualize the moment before, and then fully inhabit it before the cameras roll. This gives you your foundation of reality, and it sets you on course to get what you want in the coming scene.

Get What You Want

Okay, so, now you're going to do your scene. Your only concern now is to get what you want. You've studied the script, you know the story, you know your dramatic function, you've applied your brand, learned your lines the right way, made it audition-friendly, smiled and alpha-dogged your way in, stepped around a dozen land mines, and made it to the inner sanctum. Honestly, the only thing you have left to do now is get what you, your character, wants. Love? Respect? Validation? Vengeance? Relief? You know what it is. Go and get it. What do you want the other person to understand or do? Love you? Get out of the way? Die? Let everything else go. Forget everything in this whole book. Be present and try everything to get what you want. That is the stuff of drama. It's not about people being nice to each other; it's about people scrapping over love, safety, ego, and money.

Do not attempt to be emotional. Emotions are a by-product. They are what happen when what you want is denied by other people. They help you manipulate others to get what you want.

You can always, in every second, choose whether to be offended by someone's criticism or not. You can accept flattery, or not. You can cry at the funeral, or not. You can swear when you hit yourself in the thumb, or not. It's a choice. Logically then, the emotions that accompany these choices are also choices. Right?

I know you're resisting, but think about this for a minute.

When you are out in the woods by yourself, you do not do a lot of acting out emotionally. There is not a lot of begging, pleading, manipulating, seducing, crying, or screaming. First of all, it's peaceful in the woods, but secondly there is no one standing in your way. There is nobody there trying to influence you. If there are no fish in the creek, then there are simply no fish in the creek. That's it. If you get mad about this and stomp your feet and scream, it will be for one of these reasons:

You are mad at the people who killed all the fish,

You are mad at yourself for picking the wrong creek,

Or you are mad at the creek for being such a jerk.

By screaming at the creek, you endow it with human characteristics that it does not have. You *anthropomorphize* it. You think that, because you screamed at your mother and she gave you milk, the same trick will work on the creek. Unfortunately, the creek has no mind with which to listen. It will not be moved by your pleas and give you fish.

You know this. But it's your last resort. "Maybe if I scream at the creek, it'll feel bad and give me what I want." We humans are famous for this kind of behavior. We pray to the sun god and the rain god, and we sacrifice chickens and goats to get the gods to comply with our wishes. To make them do what we want.

You see?

So in all cases, you are acting out towards people of one kind or another trying to manipulate them into giving you what you want. The various behaviors that accompany this trying-to-get-what-you-want result in physical phenomena called emotions.

Watch a kid. If five minutes of crying don't pay off, then he'll very consciously try five minutes of shouting. If that doesn't work, then he'll try five minutes of the silent treatment. Failing that, he'll move on to violence against inanimate objects. And then it's on to violence against animate objects like mother's shins. He'll continue until he either gets what he wants, finds something else he wants more, forgets about what he wants (if he's young enough), or, worst of all, until he makes a plan for getting it later.

The fact that we make and execute these plans is what is most frightening and fascinating about human beings. Somehow, we bury the desire, subtly act to get closer to it, maybe for decades, and then pounce when the moment finally arrives to get what we want.

The mysterious person is the one with many unfulfilled desires. The evil person is the one with the most strenuously buried desires, which fester and multiply, and which the person seeks to fulfill even at the expense of others.

Unenlightened people cannot separate themselves from these manifold desires, and therefore believe their emotions are inescapable. The enlightened folks, including you now, know that their desires are the cause of all their suffering, and decide always to have a choice.

This is precisely why actors are so scary to the unenlightened. We can choose how to react to life moment by moment. We can choose what we want and therefore choose our emotional state. Because of this, we are unpredictable, influential, and scary to others.

You've read the script. You know what your character wants. Decide to want it desperately, and go get it. If what you're doing is not 'emotional' enough to convey the story, then want it more. Good actors are a willful people. Want it from the depths of your soul. The character does. Then watch as your emotions start to flare up. This is how it is in real life.

Watch people in real life trying desperately to get something they desperately want. A woman begging her husband not to go away, for example. She may be screaming and bawling her head off, but she's only vaguely aware of all that. She's not trying to be 'emotional'; she's trying to get what she wants. The emotions are a by-product of her inner life and outer desire. That's all. Your job is to live in front of the camera, not to 'act like' the woman but to be the woman. You do that by identifying with her inner life and wanting what she wants, to the end of the line.

If you do that, then you can't go wrong.

Next, look out for the ways you try to get what you want. Your tactics. They reveal and define your character.

Do you start out being logical, then attempt to get even more logical, and then go for the silent treatment? Or do you start out with seduction, move on to subtle threats, and then pull a gun? Those are two very different characters. Each change of tactics in a scene is called a *beat*. Make friends with these beats, and use them to get what you want.

Connecting

Now it follows that if you want something so desperately *from* someone, then you will have a strong connection *to* them. You will be interested in them, to say the least. If you want something bad enough, then everything else in the world will disappear from your mind except for them. You will only be aware of your desire and the subject of that desire—in other words, what you want and who you want it from. I remind you that stories are about rape, and murder, and adultery, and hatred, and kidnap, and belonging, and brutality, and jealousy, and power, and drugs, and rejection, and war. Stories are about people who desperately want things from each other, like: "Please don't chop me up with your broadsword." Or even more deadly: "Please love me." In the typical scene, your desire is obstructed by the opposite desire in the other person, as in: "But you're trying to invade my country," or "I can't love you because you are a psychotic child molester."

In the acting world, this deeply intertwined relationship you have with each other is called a *connection*. Doing it is called *connecting*, the hallmark of the good actor. You connect by doing the homework of asking why until there are no more whys and by believing in your world and your desire.

The depth of this believing is what is often known as the talent part.

How to Prep Step By Step

Here's the condensed version of how prepare for your first audition.

Read the script as a member of the audience so you experience the story.

Check out all the details of production. Are you available? Is it a union shoot? Does it shoot in Istanbul? Who else is in it? Who's making it? Do you want to go on this ride?

Ideally: love it and want to do it. At least: commit.

Understand the project details: type, genre, tone, style, etc. If you are very keen (and you *are*), then screen similar movies or watch the TV show to get a feel for it.

Analyze the script based on the section on story and screenwriting along with any other books on the topic.

Analyze the scene based on my method of how to learn lines asking "Why?" and "What's the meaning of this?" until you run out of questions. What's the scene about? Why is she looming? What is the meaning of every single word, every single punctuation mark, and every single blank space? Understand every single detail of the story world and the character world. What's the beginning, middle and end of the scene? What's your emotional journey through the scene? What's the climax of the scene? What is your goal? What are your tactics? Strive to create a definitive understanding of the scene based on the author's intent. In other words, know it better than he does. This will take time and work. This is what you get paid for.

Understanding all this, look for the best ways to communicate the scene. Are there opportunities for action, humor, gesture, or diversion? Are there keys lines of dialogue or bits of business that define the conflict?

Build a picture of the character's life, situation, relationships, starting point and goal(s). Do the same for everybody else in the scene.

Apply your brand, looking for ways to fully express yourself inside the story. Make choices to play the scene your way, not the cliché way, provided it still works for the story.

Make sure you play all the punctuation, written and unwritten, to make your performance sharp, lucid, and editable.

Own the lines. If necessary, say them in your own words and then work back to the lines in the script until you identify with them completely and they belong to you.

Learn your sides (with page turns) so you can refer to them in the room if necessary.

Make the scene audition friendly. How are you going to handle the bit where you jump off the boat and kiss the frog? Is there anything you need to mark or omit or even add to make the scene work as an audition?

Plan and rehearse the necessary choreography. Do you need to enter? Exit? Rifle through your purse? Mark the kiss? Show your red nail polish? Remember the past? See the fire? Stare knives at the judge? Pet the dog? Rehearse until perfect.

Plan your eye lines. Are you talking to one cop, or five Mexican *banditos* around a poker table? You need a specific eye line for everything you look at. Put them all in the neighborhood of the lens so it can see you. Rehearse until blue in the face.

Check your standard American accent. If you happen to be a standard American, lucky for you. Everybody else, check, rehearse, and recheck until you own it.

Be sure you can be understood. This often means slowing down.

Rehearse your eyeballs. The audience (and the producers) want to see your eyes, so know when to keep them open and visible (most all the time) and when to cleverly withhold them (use your artistic judgment).

Rehearse the whole scene again and again until technically perfect.

Plan your wardrobe. Dress in the status and situation of the character, and wherever possible use your own clothes. No costumes. No rented police dogs.

Plan your props. Bring your cell phone for the phone call (but turn off the ringer), and anything else necessary to the scene or to your reality, provided it's not distracting.

In fact, remove all distractions. This includes boobage, noisy jewelry, loud shirts, and tongue studs.

Imagine the space, and set the stage in your mind.

Commit to the moment before.

Connect with your reader, or if necessary, with an imaginary reader.

Make everything else disappear.

Honestly, urgently, and realistically try to get what you want.

Explore the scene. Do not guide it; let it guide you.

Hold back your emotions. It is what real people do and it's much more interesting.

Perform the scene as you would in real life but tend toward the close up, or pillow talk performance, to lure in the camera.

Add some special sauce—a little sparkle of sexiness or charm that does not detract from the scene and the story.

Land the scene. Don't stop prematurely or let it just peter out; make it land or definitively conclude.

Rehearse, rehearse, rehearse. Remember, you will lose up to 80 percent of your brain power when you enter the room. Commit the remaining 20 percent to being present and spontaneous in your performance. Everything else should be automatic.

Be ready for anything. You don't want to be so locked in that you can't be free during the actual audition. Loosen it up again so it can live and breathe and move around if necessary. Give yourself little adjustments or try some improvisations so you remain flexible.

Rehearse until bored and satisfied.

Relax.

Maybe do one final rehearsal before leaving for the audition, and then do not under any circumstances rehearse again, not even lines.

Forget everything.

Bring the stage with you into the room.

Let go and live the scene.

I know it looks and sounds like a huge, intimidating list, but it will get easier and easier over time, and the results will be worth it. If you do it right, then you will knock your competition out of the room, and you will start succeeding beyond your expectations.

Adjustments

Now, the casting director will hopefully be blown away by your work, considering all you've done. But she may wish to give you an *adjustment*. In theater we'd call it a *note*. In other words, she wants you to make a change. It could be entirely subjective. Maybe she thinks the scene plays better with less emotional content. Maybe she thinks it will look better with more movement. Maybe she noticed you peeking at the camera. Maybe she knows exactly what the director wants. The point is, if you've done a good job, then she will be moved to help you fine-tune it.

Examples: She may ask you to move the scene along more quickly to match the pace of the show. She may remind you that you were shot in the leg in a previous scene, so you might want to include the results of that in this scene. She may want to see more of your character's secretive, conflicted nature because it plays an important role in the trial scene they just added. In most cases, adjustments are related to some aspect of the story you didn't understand or didn't hit hard enough.

You will take in that adjustment, accept it totally, commit to it, and adjust your belief and intent accordingly. This ability—to freely and quickly adjust—is necessary to the film actor. It's another one of the hallmarks of the pro. Practice it.

Seeing that you have adjusted for her brilliantly, she will say, "Thank you."

Thank You Means Goodbye

In this case, it also means, "You have done a terrific audition. Let's not spoil it by going on any further."

You will say, "Thank you" and get the heck out of the room.

If you stick around for any reason, then you are *selling past the close*, meaning you have already closed the deal but for some stupid reason you are still there trying to convince her. This is just plain dumb. It confuses and offends people, causing *them* to lose confidence in you, often closely followed by retracting *their* offer. Okay?

So, again, in this case, thank you means, "Sold. Goodbye." Say, "Thank you," do a little bow if you like, make quick eye contact with anyone else in the room, and make a bee-line for the door. Get out.

Throughout this entire process, *they* have been looking for reasons not to hire you. Do not give *them* an extra second to look. Do *not* stop to chat about anything, especially your recent audition, the weather, your prospects for booking the role, or your intent to head straight to the bar. Keep your mouth shut. Ooze easy confidence and land your exit. Do not trip over the chair. Do not bump into the door.

Especially, do not walk into the closet like I did. Yes, I embarrassed myself nearly to death and nearly wrecked a perfect audition for the movie *Resurrecting the Champ*. I mentioned earlier that many big films came to my version of Podunk; I auditioned for three of them, booked one, and would tell you all about it later. This is the one I booked, from the closet. Only a couple of roles were on offer for this flick. One was the rather large role of Rocky Marciano for an actor who was a boxer and looked like Rocky. That's not me. The other two were smaller roles—co-workers of the lead played by Josh Hartnett. I took my own advice, did all my work as outlined in this book, met the director, and knew in the room I'd booked the gig. I heard, "Thank you." I thanked *them* back, turned around, and walked into the closet. I briefly considered staying there for the rest of the day. I thought better of it and turned back around. With a smile I said, "Closet."

I can be forgiven in this case though because it was a room I had never been in before and the two doors were side by side. How could I have known? I don't normally walk into a room and immediately check behind me to see if there's a closet next to the door. I hope they put a big sign up for everyone else on that day: Closet! Don't walk in here like Skagen did. I'm sure they had a big laugh about it, but I booked it anyway. It was one of two times my scene was cut from a film, so if you rent it you won't see me in it. Still, it was a paycheck, a credit, and an opportunity to work with some top-notch people.

One of the movies I didn't book was *The Assassination of Jesse James* with Brad Pitt. I really wanted it, but even though there were aggravating circumstances, I have to blame myself for this one. After the first audition, I happened to bump into the casting director who said, "They love you for the marshal." I'm sending you on to meet the director next week." "Should I change anything?" "They love it." "Okay."

Next week arrives. *They* call me into the room where I am suddenly overwhelmed by a massive wave of negative vibrations. The energy of the room was horribly tense and uncomfortable. It had nothing to do with me, of course. Somebody in there didn't like somebody else. *They* were fighting for some reason unknown to me. The trouble was that I let this negative energy affect me. I did my work (negatively), left mad, and didn't book it. This kind of thing happens. The lesson is to be careful, stay focused on your job, and don't pick up the bad energy of the room and its occupants.

The third movie was a little thing called *Brokeback Mountain.* I was called in to read for two different roles. Lovely. But in this case, I got sucker-punched by plain bad luck. I arrived early, about 30 minutes before my time. The green room was empty. Hmm. I signed in and sat down to crank up my alpha doggieness. The casting director came out and said, "Oh, Peter, you're here. Great. We had a lot of no-shows. Come on in. Oh, and by the way, we want you to read for *this* part."

She handed me new sides.

As we were walking into the room.

To meet Ang Lee.

He was wonderful and welcoming. He stood up to shake my hand. I hit my mark and did a good read considering it was the first time I had ever seen the lines. He thanked me graciously.

I didn't book it.

The lesson here is simply that stuff happens. You can't win them all. You can only do your best and get out of the room while they still love you.

The Top One Percent

You've heard the President speak about taxing the top one percent in his State of the Union Address, right? The reason is this: about one percent of Americans have about 90 percent of the wealth in the USA. I'm embellishing a little bit, but no matter. You should think of it that way: a tiny fraction of people get most of the goodies. A tiny fraction of students get to go to Ivy League schools. A tiny fraction of pitchers get to play pro baseball. A tiny fraction of singers get record deals. A tiny fraction of actors get to be movie stars. And a tiny fraction of auditionees—one or two percent—book the gig on the first take, work a lot, and become contenders.

I want you to be one of them.

What it takes is total commitment. You have to want it. You study this book and other books, you take classes, you practice, you relax and have confidence, you make sure you get it, and you apply your brand.

If you do this, then the casting director will love what you did and put you on the USB stick for the director. The director will love you too and forward the USB to the producers. *They* will love you deeply and forward the USB to the studio, network, investors, whomever. *They* will agree that you are smashing. *They* will notify the casting director. She will notify your agent, and your agent will notify you.

In some cases, you will get the call the next day. Often, it will take a week or two. Sometimes, you get a call two months later saying you booked it, production had been delayed, and you start in two weeks. It all depends on the city, the project, and a dozen other things.

What happens if you didn't book it?

The Silence

Nothing.

Zip. Nada. Bupkis.

You will hear nothing from anyone. The whole thing will just fade away like an old soldier. You will not be dismayed. You will remind yourself that this is how it is for everyone, that you can't book 'em all, that you made a good investment in your future, and that you are one step closer to booking the next one. You will revisit the audition in your mind and look for ways to improve. You will not criticize yourself.

You will quickly reread this entire book.

The Callback

If *they* are not sure about you, then *they* will *call you back.* A great many actors brag about getting callbacks for projects not realizing that a callback usually means you blew it.

It means you had *them* interested in you in the first audition, but you let *them* off the hook somehow. You weren't focused, you made a few technical mistakes, or you didn't commit all the way. You should have booked it right there and then, but instead you were only *mostly good*, leaving *them* unsure. So what *they're* going to do is pick a few more guys *they* weren't sure about, call you all back in, and make it harder.

You will get a phone call from your agent telling you there will be callbacks next Wednesday at three. Secretly, you will say, "Damn." Outwardly, you will say, "Perfect. Who is going to be in the room?" She should know and be able to tell you. If she doesn't know, then ask her to find out. This is critical information. You see, in the callback you will not only face the casting director and cameraman, but also you will meet the director, the producer(s), and sometimes the BFS. Sometimes, the BFS is also the director or one of the producers and sometimes the writer. So, already it's harder for you. Now you have to do it for Mr. Costner. You might even have to do it *with* Mr. Costner if he decides to get up and work with you. Harder. Since it's a callback, you know you blew it somehow but frequently not exactly how. This adds to your anxiety and makes it harder still.

Quickly look everyone up on IMDB, as I have already discussed, looking for photos where possible, putting faces to names, and remembering important accomplishments in their careers. Look for things to talk about. Review the first audition in your mind looking for ways to improve. Sometimes the path is clear; you know that you stumbled through the middle of the scene and made a mess of your eye lines. You will correct those mistakes. You will then go through the entire process again. Review the script. Analyze the story. Re-learn your lines. Everything. You will then carefully consider the ways in which *they* might want to make it harder and prepare for them. You'll see what I mean in a minute.

On the day, you will do everything the same as before with one exception: you will not bring headshots and resumes. *They* already have them. You will start from the car, revamp and relearn your monologue, and enter the green room with easy confidence. Be extra wary of the stink-eye because all the guys there are vying for the same job, and they all have a shot. Sign in, and then get present and alpha dog. Make sure you wear *exactly the same clothes* and in all other ways *look exactly the same* as you did the first audition. You want *them* to recognize you when you walk through the door and be reminded of why *they* liked you.

It is even more important this time that you take over the room. Give *them* the confidence *they* didn't feel the first time. Fill the space with your fascinating vibe, smile easily and confidently, and make eye contact. Do not shake hands unless *they* make the first move. *They* will be sitting behind a long table with a monitor on top. *They* will probably be eating lunch and talking on their phones. *They* will be tired and jaded. Do not be alarmed. *They* are run off their feet, but *they* are also desperate to cast the movie and *they* hope to cast you. *They* really do. *They* do not want to have to go back to LA to get somebody or to do another round of auditions, which costs money and takes time. *They* want to cast you. Let *them*. Give *them* no choice.

Normally, the casting director will introduce you to everyone, "Everybody, this is Sarah GonnaBee. Sarah, this is Mr. Costner, Mr. Smith and Ms. Jones, our producers. And you remember Scotty the cameraman? And today, you'll be reading with Leslie."

Yes, yet another little land mine just cropped up. Now you have a reader to work with, so you can't count on the same read you got from the casting director. She will stand off to one side so she can manage her clients.

Do not pick up *their* energy. Be prepared for it to be, in fact, a bit creepy or uncomfortable. Often, this is the first or second time the casting director has met *them*, so *they* are all still getting to know each other. Plus there is a Big Fat Star in the room so everyone will be tiptoeing around. Add to this the huge and insoluble production problems that always exist, and the fact that *they* are still not cast, and you can get an anxious, if not creepy, vibe. Pay no attention. It is not about you. It's about *them*.

Believe in and commit totally to the following: what *they'd* really love right about now is for an interesting actor to come in, shut *them* up, and make *them* lean forward. Even the BFS will love this because it means there is yet another pro in the movie, someone he can work with and rely upon, another good actor to help the picture. Any BFS worth his salt wants all the good actors he can get because the better the movie is, the better he looks, and at the end of the day he somehow gets all the credit for the acting in the film.

Hit your mark, look at the casting director, and say, "Same thing?" Normally, *they* want to see your first read again as a starting point. Being a pro you know this and you beat *them* to the punch. She will nod or she will give you an adjustment right away. "We're looking for more energy." Whenever you hear the word energy come out of a casting director's mouth, it usually means commitment. More urgency of commitment. In other words, want it more and try harder to get it. It doesn't mean *they* want you to shout and run around the room energetically. It means to switch on your insides. Broadcast your fascinating vibe. Commit. You will say, "Fine, thank you."

Connect with your reader, wait for the casting director to call *rolling* or *action*, and do the scene again with more urgent commitment. The callback tends to be a little more formal in this way because the casting director is trying to make herself look good in the eyes of her employers, so she books another job in the future. The rest of *them* will watch you on the monitor. When you're done, the casting director will probably also call *cut* to end the scene. Sometimes the director will call cut. Sometimes nobody will.

Now, there will be an awkward little silence.

What's happening? The director is evaluating what he just saw, and he is considering an adjustment. *They* weren't sure about you, remember? So now he is probably going to challenge you. The casting director is waiting for him to decide exactly how.

If he just nods, or says thank you, then you are done. Get out of the room. Do not stay behind to argue your case. Do not feel slighted. Do not ask Mr. Costner for an autograph, and then say, "By the way, what was with *Waterworld?*" Get out of the room. You may have just nailed it. You may soon be working on a Kevin Costner film.

On the other hand, the director may have decided that you don't have the right quality he needs for the scene.

On the other other hand, maybe you just nailed it but the producer recently gave the part to his nephew. Or the part was cut from the script an hour ago because it was too expensive to shoot.

You cannot do anything about any of this.

Get out of the room.

But more than likely, the director is going to challenge you somehow because it's the callback and he really wants to be sure about his choice.

Usually, the reason they called you back was because you failed to *get* it somehow. You didn't quite get the story, and the scene, therefore the performance wasn't on the money. The director will try to enlighten you. You will try to understand the fullness of his words. If you don't understand, then you will discuss it in an easy, confident way until you get it.

Get it?

Then you will instantly nod to the casting director and the camera-man, and then do it again *informed by the adjustment.* You will make *them* lean forward. When you are done, feel free to say something like, "Yes, that felt better. Thank you."

What you just did was reassure *them* that you are professional. You were able to have a working discussion with a BFS without freaking out, you were able to take an adjustment without taking it person-ally, and you were able to perform that adjustment under the gun. You should therefore be able to do the same on the set. Excellent.

Now, try to get a read on *them*. If the director shifts a bit in his chair, for example, then maybe he'd like to see more. Feel free to invite more adjustments. Do not overdo it. Do not sell past the close. This is tricky, advanced audition technique, which is why I wanted you to nail it in the first audition.

You may discuss it some more and do it again. You may not. He may at this time say, "Thank you."

Get out of the room.

At this time he may engage you in conversation to get a feel for you personally. Feel free to use the revised monologue you rehearsed in the car, and where possible, work in the background information you looked up on the Internet, and perhaps, just perhaps, a little flattery. Do not over do it and become a fan. He's checking that you give *them* confidence, and that *they* like you.

If he asks about any of the special skills listed at the bottom of your resume, then demonstrate them immediately wherever possible. Are you a singer? Sing instantly. Dancer? Lay down some moves. Martial artist? Bring out that spinning hook kick. Do not overdo it. You don't have to sing all of *Evita.* Demonstrate briefly. If the skill can-not be demonstrated, then do a brief monologue about it. For example: "Yes, I do ride horses. I just finished a series of 12 classes with Sandy Palomino at the Westside Training Center, so I'm a capable beginner, and I really like it." Do not lie. He is checking to see if you can actually do the skill (amazingly, some people lie) and how good you are because he might want to use it in the movie. In other words, he's checking that you can help make *them* money by saving on stunt riders.

And now for the boobage. If the part requires nudity, then it will be noted in the first breakdown for all to see. Accepting the first audition means you accept the nudity, and you will perform it should you be hired. Do not accept the first audition on a wait-and-see-if-I-chicken-out basis. You will almost certainly chicken out, irritating yet another casting director and adding yet another brick to the already heavy load carried by your fellow, responsible actors. Since you accepted the first audition knowing about the nudity, you will not be asked to disrobe at that time. You will be asked to perform the scene demonstrating that you can act. Only when everything else is in order will they want to do the *boob-check* or the *butt-check* in the callback. Often, the boob-check is done as a subsequent callback for that purpose only. In most places, a local union representative will be present in the room at that time to ensure everyone's safety. Double check with your agent. You will either come prepared to do a quick reveal at the time of the callback, or you will slip into a change room and pop back out again.

There are reasons for the boob check.

It validates your willingness to do it.

It foreshadows your comfort level on the set.

It shows them exactly what they are buying.

Like it or not, boobs and buns sell tickets, but not just any old boobs and buns. First of all, amazingly, some actors lie about their proportions. Some neglect to mention their tattoos. Some boobs don't match. Some point in different directions. Some are obviously plastic. Some buns are wrinkly.

Heroes need heroic buns, so some body parts simply aren't right for the part.

So-called boob casting often turns out to be challenging because the boobs are a role of their own. As I mentioned above, they compete with the actor who owns them and all other actors in the scene. Casting them is like casting Siamese triplets; all three individuals have to be right for the part.

I advise all my actors to give the question "To boob; or not to boob?" a lot of thought. I agree with the many actors and coaches who maintain that the body is just another tool in the actor's kit, and that many benefit from getting their kit off as soon as possible to let go of self-conscious attachments. But that applies to your training and live performance situations. To boob on camera means to be recorded for all time; therefore their first appearance is the important one. Their debut must be carefully considered. Producers know that while boobs sell tickets, star boobs sell a lot of tickets. The most valuable of all therefore are previously unseen star boobs. Your best choices then are: get them out early to get them out of your way, keep them under wraps to extract their full value when you become a BFS, or keep them to yourself.

Okay.

Back to your callback, for now it is danger time. Anything can happen at this point. Be alert and aware and hold on.

In one callback, the director asked me to do the scene for him, watched, and nodded. Then he said, "Now, I'll shoot it." I said, "Oh, you didn't shoot that one?" He said, "No, no, I mean this." And he produced a pocket video camera, which he waved around in my face as I did the scene again for the main camera. I mean he walked around in front of me, with the camera literally inches from my face. To this day, I have no idea what he was doing. Testing my concentration? Maybe. Taping me himself to save time? Possibly. Falling in love with me? Not likely. I just stayed focused, did my job, and booked the gig. Ours is not to reason why.

In another one, the director started improvising with me from across the room while I was doing the scene with the casting director. He was an actor himself and apparently felt that all good actors should be present enough and free enough and sharp enough to go wherever the scene takes them. I happen to agree. I bantered with him a bit and then turned back to the casting director and finished the scene. He announced, "Yes! Thank you. You're not right for the priest, but I'm going to find a place for you in the picture." And he did.

Once I forgot to turn off my cell phone and of course it rang as I was doing my scene. There was no pretending it wasn't happening. If I ignored it, then nobody would be watching my audition; *they'd* all be wondering who was calling. I had no choice but to answer it, *in character*, say I was busy, hang up and finish the scene. The director smiled broadly at my cheeky improvisation skills and gave me the job.

This is yet another reason why I want you to book it in the first audition. You never know what kind of curveballs are headed your way in the callback. The whole thing is fraught with danger.

Normally at this time there will be a little pause where some decision is silently made. The director will then nod to the casting director who will nod to you and say, "Thank you."

Get out of the room.

Say thank you, make eye contact, nod, bow, whatever, but do it fast and confidently and get out of the room. Your fate is sealed.

Now comes the debate. This is yet another thing working against you in callbacks. You see, in the first round of auditions, all *they* had to do was put a checkmark beside your name. It was relatively easy for you to book the gig. Now though, *they* have to talk it over. And *they* are going to raise every possible objection to hiring you including your height, your complete history, and the little zit on your chin. *They* are going to carefully go down the list of why *they* shouldn't hire you. *You* made *them* do this by screwing up your first audition. And *they* will be comparing you directly to the five other guys *they've* already seen. This makes the process even more subjective, combative, and unpredictable. In my experience of callbacks, usually the best actor does not book the gig.

Suppose you're the best actor. Four out of five of *them* love you and want you. But that old number five doesn't agree. He thinks you're too old or too young or too quirky, or you just rub him the wrong way. *They* argue, fuss, and fight. Old number five won't budge.

Eventually, *they* settle on the tall guy.

If *they* do settle on you, then congratulations. You beat the odds.

If *they* didn't, then turn to the Appendix. You'll find a list of the 50 major mistakes you could have made in the audition room. Some we have covered; some we have not. Being thus instructed, you will not make any of them.

There should be one reason, and only one, why you don't get the part: you just weren't right for it. Turns out the director wanted someone shorter, or blonder, or older, or Korean, or an expert in kung fu, or bilingual, or a stand-up comic, or whatever, and you just weren't right for it, that's all.

Let *them* remember your terrific audition. Let *them* call you a few months later for a part that is right for you. Book it. Work. Build. Succeed. Become a BFS.

Write me a nice thank-you note.

Oh, but first you're going to have to do the job.

YOUR FIRST DAY ON SET

Think what you've accomplished thus far. You've resolved to be a film actor, you've cracked open the Hollywood safe (even if only slightly), you've discovered what the hell *they* are looking for, you've polished your brand, set up your business, taken some good classes, got a head-shot, found an agent, promoted yourself, understood screenwriting, suffered through a lot of auditions, figured out I was right, perfected the art of the audition, mastered the craft of learning lines, and a whole lot more.

Now it's time to work. You've booked a job. You *booked*! You've done it. You did a competent audition, you were right for the part, and you got the gig. Now what? Countless students come to me with this very same plea. "I worked so hard to get the job, I never thought I'd actually have to do it! Now that I've got it, I have no clue what to do. What do I do now? I've never worked on a real set! What do I do? Did *they* make a mistake? *They* know I have no experience, right? Am I going to get fired? Oh my God, what do I do?"

Do not panic.

There are only really three or four capital mistakes you can make on the set and one of them is panicking. Much of your job on set is to strangle the urge to panic, to remain calm, and to manage your nerves. Working actors will tell you it's what they get paid for.

The other biggies are being an egoist, being unprepared, and stopping a take. Running away is also not so good. More on these later. Pretty much everything else can be dealt with, provided you don't panic.

Let me help you by explaining *everything*.

Sit back. Sip your latte. Everything will be revealed. Comfort yourself with the knowledge that you actually have surprisingly little responsibility on set. Extremely little, in fact.

Here it is:

Don't do those four things I just mentioned.

Deliver the story and the spark of life between the words "action" and "cut."

Easy.

Getting the Call

Very often, you'll be driving when your cell phone rings. It's your agent saying something like this: "*They* want to book you on *Angry Blood Two*. It's two days at scale. Your outside dates are June 6 and June 10. Okay? Congrats."

And that's it. You just got hired. You'll be on set for two days. You're getting paid scale, meaning minimum wage under the actors' guild agreement. Your two days fall somewhere between June 6th and 10th, and you are committed to being there.

Wow. You are a bit stunned. You nearly veer off the road but you get it together. At this point, you let out some kind of scream, or yelp, or holler. And you feel vindicated. You did it. This is closely followed by heart palpitations and panic as you wonder about a million things, such as "Now what?" and "What if I die of a stroke on the set?" You've spent so much time trying to book the gig that you forgot about actually having to do the gig, and you realize it might end badly.

Wanting to avoid that reality for a few more minutes or hours, you push it out of your mind. *They* want you. You've done it. You've booked it. You are a Big Fat Star. Sort of.

In a few minutes, you're going to want to tell someone that you are a BFS. Hopefully, you have hands-free dialing. There will be more yelling and screaming, some congratulatory talk, some expressions of disbelief, and then the bomb will drop. Your friend or family member will say something like:

"Oh My God, you're going to meet Johnny Depp. Will he be there? He'll be there, right? You're going to meet JOHNNY DEPP OH MY GOD! I'D FREAK OUT!!!"

You pretend to be cool about the whole meeting Johnny Depp thing because you are a cool, modern, real, live, verifiable, serious movie actor and *so there*, and you rather quickly hang up. And then you really start to panic. Because not only are you going to meet Johnny Depp, but you are in a scene with Johnny Depp where you have to ask Johnny Depp if he'd like some cream to go with that coffee, and suddenly you feel your face going all hot and clammy and you realize you have *flop sweat* (nervous perspiration) a full three weeks before you have to do the scene. Your friend's anxiety went straight into your heart where it will stay until the very moment you ask Johnny Depp about the cream. Soon after this, if you have any instinct for self-preservation at all, then you will stop calling friends, enemies, and family members to brag about getting hired. It only hurts you.

But now, wait a minute, you say. What the hell is the point of being a real, live, verifiable, serious movie actor and *so there* if I can't brag about it?

Go back and read the bit about how you had better love the work. The work itself has to sustain you because all the rest of it is a pain in the ass.

Do you need me to repeat that? Because I will. No? Got it?

Okay, so now what?

Nothing.

Nothing happens on average for about a week. Sometimes more. Sometimes less. It depends on the project. Television tends to happen faster, movies slower, and commercials at the speed of light.

During this time, you frantically try to defuse that friend's anxiety-bomb ticking away in your heart. You remind yourself that Johnny Depp puts his pants on one leg at a time, whatever the hell that means, and he's probably cool, and that there is no need to have a heart attack at this particular juncture. You reassure yourself that all will be well, that you are enough, that they really want you, and that you won't shrivel up and die, and so on. And you wait. And nothing happens until one day when you've forgotten about it for a moment or two and the phone rings.

The Wardrobe Fitting

"Hi, it's Marjorie from wardrobe on *Angry Blood Two*. I just want to confirm your sizes."

For a moment, you'll be clueless. Then it dawns on you that it's Marjorie from wardrobe on *Angry Blood Two* phoning you about your sizes. And you'll tell her. And more than anything else, you'll be honest because Marjorie is going shopping for you, or even worse, she's going to start constructing the wardrobe for you herself, and the only person who is going to look stupid when it doesn't fit is you. This all goes back to the Resume section on page 72 where I told you not to lie on your resume. If you said you weigh 108 pounds like all other actresses in the world, then you will be tempted to further the lie to Marjorie. And then you're screwed one way or the other, because if you stick with 108 your butt won't fit the skirt, and you can bet that Marjorie is going to have to explain this to the director, whereas if you decide to tell the truth of the matter, which is that you are really 122, well closer to 143 actually, Marjorie will have a better chance. She still might have to tell the director that they have another fibber on their hands, but at least the skirt will fit.

This does not bode well for you, dear actress. There is enough pain and sorrow involved in making a movie, a forest of insurmountable obstacles, and then you come along with your petty vanity adding to the pile. (Do not talk back. If you want the skinny butt, then get the skinny butt. That's your job. Do not lie and blame other people.)

After giving Marjorie your sizes honestly, you wait some more. A few days later she calls back inviting you in for a fitting. She gives you the address of the production office—probably in the back of some warehouse—and in you go. It will feel weird walking in. Lots of people working frantically, and no one paying you any mind. Flag down someone and say, "Hi, I'm Ashley, the waitress in the cream scene. Which way to wardrobe?" They will tell you and then vanish down a hallway.

Find Marjorie. Say "Hi." Thank her for doing your wardrobe. Hope *they* have forgiven you for lying, if you did, and that *they* haven't decided to hire someone else, which *they* could.

Marjorie will be nice. All wardrobe people appear to be cut from nice cloth. She will lead you through the wardrobe room. You will pass the wall of fame: the wall upon which they have affixed the headshots of all the actors on the picture. You will see yourself hanging there, looking out across the room. *They* do this to make an overall wardrobe plan, to remind themselves who is who, and to call you by name when you arrive.

Realize that *they* really want to look after you. *They* know that acting is hard and dangerous and nerve racking and that *they* themselves couldn't do it. They know that everything hinges upon a good performance. Everything that everyone does on the set is about helping you give the best possible performance and about shooting it in the best possible way. But the performance is first. Nobody cares about beautifully photographed bad acting.

Be gracious. Let *them* help you. Help *them*. We have a chance.

Marjorie will take you to a change room where you will find a selection of wardrobe to try on. Try it on and discuss it with her. She wants to help you, but she also has to mind the director's wishes. Do not be an idiot and say you think the waitress is wearing diamonds and a little black dress. Do not make it about you. It's about the story. Go back and read the chapter on Story and Screenwriting (page 87) and why we are all gathered together. Care, but not about yourself. Get the wardrobe that's right for the waitress, not for you. Except when it comes to shoes. Get comfortable shoes. You'll be standing in them for two days, and there's nothing worse than doing that in new shoes that don't fit.

Marjorie will take a picture of you in your wardrobe to show the director. Before she takes it, she will say: "Flashing." This is a little warning of the flash of light to come.

Thank Marjorie again and then get changed. Then ask Marjorie where to ask for a script, a day-out-of-days, and a call sheet. Collect these and go to your car. I'll wait.

Okay. I'll explain.

The Script

The script has most likely changed since you did your audition. Your scene might be totally different. Maybe now you ask Johnny if he's ever been to Memphis. Different. Maybe now you get stabbed. Very different. Maybe now you run away with Johnny and have a torrid affair in Florence. Really very different.

Why? What's going on?

Once *they* go into production, the team will have daily meetings on all aspects of the shoot. Issues are going to come up. Maybe *they* can no longer afford the museum location, so *they* have to shoot that scene in somebody's office. The writer will cringe and then go off and revise the scene. So that everyone knows it has been revised, he'll print it up on yellow paper and stick it in the script. The next day *they* make another change. Johnny Depp doesn't want to order coffee; he prefers mineral water. That revision goes on green paper so *they* know it was changed on a different day. Pretty soon the script is 300 pages thick with all the colors of the rainbow. There is actually a standard sequence of colors to follow, and all the changes with their accompanying dates will be listed on the cover page. Being an actor, you are expected to keep up.

An example: *Hell On Wheels*. When I did my audition, there was no mention of my character Burly getting shot in the episode. When I picked up the script after my wardrobe fitting, Burly was robbing the train office and getting shot in the gut by Durant. A later revision sent by e-mail had Burly getting shot through a window by Elam. On the day of the shoot, Burly shot Nell the whore, and then got gunned down by the Irish Boys. See? You need to keep up and adapt as necessary. You often have very little time. You just have to do it. This is one reason *they* press you so hard to adjust in the room—you are going to have to adjust a lot, and sometimes very quickly, as the shoot progresses. I have never been on a shoot where *something* didn't come up.

I hope there is no need to say this next bit: don't post the script on the Internet.

I will personally hunt you down and kill you. The Production will then sue your dead body. Get it into your head that you have to stop being a fan and start being a filmmaker. Stop trying to get attention for yourself, and start trying to help the movie get made. This will entertain and instruct the audience, lift the spirits of the world, and provide you with a career.

Okay?

Read the entire script again. Figure out why you are in it, and what you can do as a performer to help. Re-read the section on *Little Dragons*.

Do your homework. Everything you need is in the script. Find it. *Get it.* That's your job.

Every actor's process is different of course, but by way of guidance, I'll tell you a few things I like to do to get ready. After I get it and learn my lines according to the section on how to learn lines, I like to do the scene over and over again in my own words. This helps me connect with it on a personal level. Then I like to keep an eye out for situations in my real life that are similar to the scenes I have to play. I take note of how I feel and what I tend to do in those situations. I observe other people in similar situations. Given the chance, I will actually play the scene in some form. If it happens to be a waiter scene for example, then I might actually pick up a coffee pot at my local diner and pour a few cups for strangers making sure to offer them cream with that. Get it? Be a creative problem solver. Find your way to a better performance, whatever it takes. That's also your job.

The Day Out of Days

This little baby is the schedule. It lists all the shooting days, what's to be shot on each day, who needs to be there, where *they're* shooting, and so on. You can check to see which two days exactly you will be required on set. Do not take this as gospel. Take it as a good *guesstimate.* Things change on a movie daily, as I just mentioned. These are your most likely days. Probably, but not necessarily, that's when you'll be shooting. Johnny's plane might be delayed, and *they'll* have to shift one of your days to accommodate. Maybe the weather has messed up the schedule. Who knows? You were given outside dates. You must be available for all those dates just in case, so don't go planning a trip to Spain based on the day out of days. Use it as a reference for when you'll most likely be working.

The Call Sheet

This is normally generated the day before your shoot day, so you might not be able to get it just yet. The call sheet is the schedule for one particular day of filming. It lists all the scenes in order of shooting, the provisional order in case it rains, all the actors who will be there including which ones are new to the show etc., *the call time* (what time you need to be there), the weather forecast, the address of the location, sometimes a map, an advance look at what's to be shot the following day, what time the sun sets, and more. Every tiny bit of info pertinent to that day of shooting is cleverly squeezed onto two sides of a legal-size piece of paper.

You should commit this entire page of information to memory if you can. If you can't, then focus on these three things: your call time, the shooting schedule, and the important names to remember.

First, your call time. You must not be late under any circumstances. No excuses are acceptable unless you have been hit by a bus, in which case you still won't be able to make an excuse because you'll be dead. That's the only acceptable excuse. As everybody knows, the first rule of show business is show up. And do not be late. Do not even be on time. Thirty minutes early is on time. On time is late. Thirty minutes late might get you fired on the spot. I showed up exactly 60 seconds late to a set once because my car broke down, and I got the evil eye so many times I thought I was going to turn into a zombie. I might have gotten fired. Do not be late. Once you're a BFS, go ahead and be late if you want. That will hasten your fall and make more room for the rest of us.

The next thing to commit to memory: the day's shooting schedule. Have a look at the sample call sheet on the next page. Near the top of the page you will find a grid listing the scenes to be shot by scene number. (Flip open your script. You will see that each and every scene has a number ascribed to it.) Next, you'll see a brief description of that scene. Then there's a list of which actors appear in that scene, whether it's day or night, how many pages long the scene is, and where it is to be shot. Note that in the movie biz scenes are counted by eighths of a page. The scene isn't half a page long, it's four-eighths. This is a standardized system that helps everyone along the line keep track of everything. If there are any *company moves* (the whole cast and crew moving to a different location), then they will also be listed. For example, at noon we move from the house to the diner.

Below this schedule is the cast list. You will see your name there. You will smile. You'll see that you are cast number eight, and you will check which scenes you appear in. In this case, it's only one: in the diner. You'll see that the diner scene is up fifth, giving you lots of time to prepare and wait around.

You will see Johnny Depp's name. You will smile again. You will not be nervous. You will manage your energy.

Next to your name you will see these symbols: SWF. This means that you (S)tart work, you (W)ork, and you (F)inish work all on the same day. Johnny would have (S)tarted weeks ago, today he (W)orks, and sometime later he (F)inishes.

The One Where Biff meets Anita   Super Double Happiness Productions   Thursday, Sept 25, '14   Day 10 of 29

Exec. Producer	Philip D Bag	(333) 310-0738
Producer	Lee Price	(555) 486-1424
Producer	Rusty Pipes	(555) 892-8800
Director	Mel D'Dramatic	(333) 370-1634
Line Producer	Phil Isty	(565) 944-0892
Prod Manager	Rema Szkberg	(565) 483-0734

The Munch Bunch

CALL 9 AM

BREAKFAST	8:00 AM	CRAFT SERVICES	
LUNCH	1:00 PM	Cobo Guy	(333) 899-0032
SUNRISE		SUNSET	
6:15 AM		7:50 PM	
WEATHER	70° AM	80° NOON	72° PM
Humidity	10%	Mostly Sunny	

Production Office   [555] 673-8978
301 S Hubert Lane
Los Gatos, CO, 80535

LOCATION: John Oak School 4114 Elm Road, Exeter, Virginia

Crew Park: East Parking lot
Travel time from Prod. Office – 40 minutes

Note: Questions? Call Rema Szkberg - Please be very detailed
Note 2 Closed Set, no posting to social media

Note 1: Walkie Assignments (5)
Note 4: Walkie Units: 5

Nearest Hospital   [555] 966-7432
Holly Heart
3000 Zombie St, Los Gatos, CO, 80535

Contraction: 1/2 hour on call
Electrics: 1 hour on call

SCENES	SET AND DESCRIPTION	CHARACTER #	D/N	PAGES	LOCATION/NOTES
45A	Detention Classroom	1, 2	D	67-68	John Oak School - smoke machines.
	The fire alarm is set off by Biff's hair				
31B	Library	1, 2, 27, 28	D	48-50	John Oak School - slime buckets
	The kids get slimed				
		TOTAL PAGES			

#	CAST	CHARACTER	SW/SF	MU	SET	MINOR?	SPECIAL INSTRUCTIONS
1	Lou Kahnis	Biff Wellington	W	830	900	N	Best Inn Town Hotel
2	Dee Vah	Anita Knapp	W	800	900	N	
3	Eileen Dover	Kitty Katz	H			N	
27	Bill Board	Beau Tie	SWF W	1300	1300	N	
28	Manny Kin	Ken Doki	SW	1300	1330	Y	

STAND-INS / ATMOSPHERE		PRODUCTION NOTES	
STAND-INS	REPORT AT:	PROPS:	sc. 1 books
1 S-I (Fine)	10:00 AM		sc. 2 books and rope
2 S-I (Stephanie)	10:00 AM		sc. 3 car keys
3 S-I (Vanessa)	10:05 AM	LOCATION:	1 Site rep, 1 PSG, 1 Officer
		GRIP:	sc. 1 Wheelchair dolly
		ADDL LABOR:	Studio teacher
		WARD:	sc. 2 Janitor's uniforms
	SAG	MAKEUP:	sc. 4 Biff's facial scar
	AFTRA	CAMERA:	sc. 5 PRE-rig GOD to Prop Cam
	NON-UNION	NOTES:	

ADVANCE SHOOTING SCHEDULE					
SCENES	SET AND DESCRIPTION	CHARACTER #	D/N	PAGES	LOCATION/NOTES
22C	Cafeteria	1, 2, 3, 4, 5			
	Biff gets hit in face with spaghetti				
33	Girl's Bathroom	3, 5			
	Anita and Kitty talk about The new Podcast				
		TOTAL PAGES			

Nameless Productions

[Episode #75/The Bad Tater Salad]

CALL SHEET BACK

Director: Mel O'Dramatic

(4/25/2014)

CREW CALL: 7:00 AM

Realize that your call time is not your work time. You will typically be called to set about three hours before you are expected to shoot. This gives *them* time to prep you, dress you, do your hair, and so on, and gives you time to calm down and get oriented. If your scene is first up, then you may be called at 8 a.m. and be shooting by 8:30 a.m. It does happen. Once, I was called at 8 a.m. and was shooting at 3 a.m. the next day. Also happens. But the rule of thumb is about three hours.

Knowing all this will help orient you to the day so you can prepare and conserve your energy. If you're sitting around all day with your nerves running rampant, then you won't have anything left for the take. This is one of your major jobs on set: manage your energy. Save it for the camera.

Next up is everybody's names. Your fellow actors are listed on the front. The entire back of the Call Sheet is devoted to listing every other person on the movie along with their jobs. Want to know who the props master is? It's listed. Since you're going to be working with all these people, and since *they* all know who you are, it's a very good idea to know who *they* are. If nothing else, it eases stress.

Now... you're still sitting in your car at this time... put the papers down, take a deep breath, be cool, and drive home.

Later: examine, learn, prepare.

Okay, now what happens?

Nothing.

For another few days, or sometimes weeks, nothing.

Then, the day before you think you're supposed to be shooting, you start to get worried.

"Did they replace me? I thought I was supposed to be making a movie tomorrow."

Your Day Begins

At about 11:30 p.m. the phone rings. It's Grant, the 3rd AD (assistant director), with a frantic message: "Hi, it's Grant, I'm the third on the show. Your call time is 8:30 a.m., and I can e-mail you a map and a call sheet."

What happened? They just wrapped up shooting for the day, figured out what they need to do for tomorrow based on the fact that everything is always changing, came up with a plan, and now they're telling everyone about the plan.

You say, "Cool."

Grant e-mails the material. You look it over and see what might have changed. You memorize some more and set your alarm. Do not drink wine to calm down. Trust me, you don't want to be hungover on your first day. Go to bed. If you are like me, then you won't sleep too well.

Get up with plenty of time to spare. Don't worry about eating as there's food on the set (unless it's a very low budget movie). Don't worry about anything. Manage your energy.

Take a shower. Throw on some clothes. Do not do your makeup or hair. Just get cleaned up. Put together a little care package to take with you: cell phone, MP3 player, books or crossword puzzles, the script, the call sheet, any little stand-in props from your scene so you can practice in your trailer, a little toiletry kit in case you want to trim your nails or pluck a nose hair, your lucky crystal, business cards, air freshener (trust me on this one), medication, or a lift for your right shoe, and anything else you would normally take to stay sane if you had to spend a day in jail. That's often what it feels like. I like to bring a folding chair. I can't stand sitting on the padded bench they provide in most little dressing rooms, and sometimes I like to sit outside and catch some rays of sunshine. If you're a guy, then I suggest you bring baby wipes so you can take off your makeup at the end of day. Ladies, the makeup people will normally do it for you.

What *not* to bring: *a camera.* Most productions forbid the use of cameras on set other than the ones making the movie. An *autograph book.* I will kill you and hit your dead body with a stick. You are *not a fan,* remember? You are part of the process, part of the crew. You will not see *them* getting each other's autographs. Do not bring a *friend.* No, you cannot bring your friend, Amy. Sorry.

Booze, drugs, guns, and chainsaws are also frowned upon.

Print out the map. Get in your car and go.

If you're on a bigger movie, then *they* will pick you up (maybe in a helicopter) to take you to the top of the mountain where Brad Pitt will be waiting to do the love scene with you. This will have been negotiated and arranged by your agent in advance. If you're just starting out in Podunk, then you'll often be required to drive yourself. Depends on where you're working, what guild you belong to, the budget of the film, etc. Most likely, you are driving. If you do not drive, then arrange for a cab or a friend or a mom.

Give yourself plenty of time. Allow for traffic and car trouble. The reason I was 60 seconds late that day was because I had to abandon my clunker and pay a passing motorist 60 bucks to take me to set. Car trouble is not an excuse. I didn't allow enough time.

Follow the map. Sometimes you are heading to a downtown street corner, sometimes to a barn in the country, and sometimes to a studio somewhere. No matter. Follow the map. Everything will be clearly written out for you. When you get close to the set you'll start seeing large fluorescent arrows taped to lampposts. Follow these arrows. They are directing you to the set. You will only see arrows, not arrows with signs saying This Way to the New Johnny Depp Movie, for obvious reasons.

Arriving on Set

When you get close, you'll see a collection of tents and trailers. This is called the circus, also for obvious reasons. You'll be met by somebody in an orange traffic vest. Say: "Hi, I'm Ashley, the waitress." He will welcome you and show you where to park. Then he will get on his walkie-talkie and announce your arrival. Just about everyone on the crew is on *walkies*, so everyone now knows you have arrived and that your name is Ashley. Grab your stuff and walk to the circus.

You'll be met by the same AD who called you the night before. If you're not met, then ask anyone where the AD trailer is, and go knock on the door. But most likely, Grant will meet you. The conversation will go something like this:

"So, you're our waitress today, how wonderful, so nice of you to join us, if you could just follow me I'll *travel* you to your trailer."

Most of them speak in this kind of jaded sardonic tone because they are very tired and especially tired of dealing with *talent* (actors). But *they* have to be nice.

The lingo is *travel* because it includes walk, drive, fly and snowshoe. There's lots of lingo on the set; somebody should write a book. Hmmmm.

For now, keep your ears peeled and learn as you go.

Grant will show you to your trailer. Now, if you're just starting out, and you're just a *day player*, meaning you have a small scene that shoots for a day or two as in "Hey Johnny, do you want cream with that?" then you'll be shown to a *honeywagon*. Imagine a semi-trailer with six or eight little staircases on its side leading to six or eight little doors leading to six or eight little tiny dressing rooms built into the one trailer. That's a honeywagon. One of those little rooms will be for you. The word *waitress* will be taped to the door.

"If you could just get into your *wardrobe*, I'll travel you to *hair and makeup.*"

Right. Will do. In you go.

Inside, you'll find a very uncomfortable padded bench to sit on, probably a CD player, a little shelf, a minuscule bathroom with a tiny sink and toilet, and your wardrobe hanging up on a hook. On the bench you will typically find your contract, which you'll typically be asked to sign. Usually there are four copies: one for you and three for them. Sign. In other cases, your agent will have done this for you in advance.

Next to your contract, you will find your *mini call sheet and script.* For convenience, the ADs provide you with the call sheet and today's pages from the script in a little booklet form. Put this in your pocket for reference during the day but not before double-checking your scene. It may have changed again overnight. If it has, then start analyzing as you change into your wardrobe.

Five minutes later, the AD will come a-knocking on your door asking if you're ready. He'll then travel you to hair and makeup. All of these different places are trailers in the circus with steps up to the door. It's common practice on set to call out *stepping* before you actually mount the steps, so that the makeup artists inside don't poke someone in the eye when the trailer moves.

Hair and Makeup

Enter the trailer and say, "Hello, I'm Ashley the waitress." They will be wonderful to you, sit you down, and start in on you. Hair does everything above the sideburns. Makeup does everything else. They do not mix.

Rule one about makeup and hair: keep your ideas to yourself. Do not start in on what you think you should look like, or how you like your eye shadow, or anything else along these lines. These people are professionals. They've had meetings with the director about your look. They have considered what's right for the story, the lighting, the camera, and how you'll look next to Johnny. They will take one look at you and know all your flaws and how to deal with them. They are professionals. We are making a movie, not doing a photo shoot for the cover of Vogue. You must accept this totally, and let them do what they do; it's what they can earn an Oscar for.

A special note: do not under any circumstances go back to your trailer and change your hair and makeup later, you vain moron. I would kill you for the fourth time today, but they will do it first. You have no idea what they're doing or what looks good on film. Leave it alone, or perish.

Rule Two: find a convenient moment to ask the secret question. The secret question is: "Sooooo, how's it going?" No one on Earth loves to talk more than hair and makeup. So, invite them to talk about the production.

"Soooo, how's it going?"

They will spill. They will tell you that it's been wonderful, the director's a saint, the cast is lovely, we're ahead of schedule, it's great. Or … It's *shite*, the second leading man is jerk, we call him the Prince of Darkness, but Johnny is wonderful, but there's tension, and we're behind, and the director has been yelling a bit, but it's just because of the schedule, and so on.

See? You'll get the lay of the land. If you don't ask the secret question, then they might not spill. So, ask, and use it to your advantage.

Your job at this point, aside from managing your energy, is to manage your nerves, and try to be part of the solution around here. Try to fit into the flow, join the party seamlessly, and do your acting bit efficiently. Believe me, being a day player is the hardest job in the business because of this. You have to parachute in on a picture that's already running, fit in comfortably, meet Johnny, and do your scene in one or two takes because they're behind, do it all with ease and grace, make everybody look good, and then go home. It's somewhat like being suddenly transported into a battle zone in World War II with bullets zipping over your head, being asked to run into no-man's land and take out a tank, and then just as suddenly being transported back to your couch. Shocking. This is also partly why it is so dang hard to get hired for these roles. You'd think, oh, it's just a one liner, not a big deal. Actually, it is a very big deal.

More on this in a minute. For now, do everything you can to get acclimatized, manage your energy, and manage your nerves.

Note: there may be stars in the trailer. You may be right next to a BFS getting her hair done. More likely, it'll be a minor BFS getting her hair done. The major BFSs typically have their own trailer somewhere and often their own personal makeup artist who is part of the entourage. If you do happen to sit next to one, then smile and say something like, "Hi. I'm Ashley, the Waitress. Nice to meet you." Then take it from there. Some will chat with you happily; some will sigh wondering how their lives came to this. Don't let it get to you. Mega Stars tend to have Mega Problems, so let it be. Manage your nerves.

When they are done with you, say thank you and go.

The Important Names

Walk back to your trailer. On the way back, make sure you tell your AD where he can find you. Keep him apprised of your whereabouts all day long. Most of the time you won't be needed, but when you are, you are.

You: "I'll be in my trailer."

Grant: "Thank you."

Sit on your uncomfortable bench, learn your new lines, learn some names, rehearse, and relax.

Here is the list of people whose names you need to know. Connect the names with the faces as soon as you can.

The director: in charge of all things creative. You may have met him in the audition.

His department of ADs: the assistant directors run the set and the actors.

The First AD in particular: he or she is the general on the field of battle who moves the army of things and people around so the director can get his shots and make his day.

The Second AD: generates the call sheets, and does all the paperwork and whatever else the First asks.

The Third: runs the circus, preps, travels, and manages the actors. In this case, Grant.

The TAD or trainee assistant director: typically manages actors, helps with extra or background performers, and relays information around the set.

The writer: probably won't be there, but if he is, say hello. Maybe have a chat about the scene, his vision for it, etc. It can't hurt.

The continuity supervisor: in the olden days, this job was known as script girl, largely because it seems that only females are capable of doing this demanding job. I have personally never seen a man in the job. The job: in the crazy panic of the set, keep track of *everything*—what was shot, when, what camera was used, what angle, what size shot, who was in the shot, what they said in the shot, what were they wearing, how far behind schedule they are, what shots will cut with what other shots, which *takes* the director likes, notes to the editor, notes to the producer, notes on the budget, and more. She is the set historian. The job requires a keen eye, a big brain, a powerful ability to multi-task, fantastic interpersonal skills, and a profound knowledge of the filmmaking process. Her notes go directly to the editor who refers to them throughout the editing process. Copies also go to the producers. She is also the person who will throw lines to you if you forget during your scene, so it's good to get acquainted.

The producers: the CEOs of the movie. They are in charge of everything, including the director. These are the people who pay you and who have risked a lot of money making this movie. *They* want you to help *them* make that money back.

The executive producer: the entrepreneur who (often) decided to make the movie, found the money for it, and gave it all to the producers to make the film.

The other actors: for obvious reasons.

The DOP or DP (director of photography): in charge of how the film is photographed. This person makes you look pretty, so be nice.

The camera operator: this is the guy actually running the camera. The DOP doesn't have time for that.

Hair and makeup: for obvious reasons.

Wardrobe: for obvious reasons.

The props master: he or she will be around you all day filling your coffee pot, or providing you with new cigars, or plates of roast beef, or whatever.

The sound mixer: he is in charge of recording your voice as you work, so it pays to be nice to him. He will also be in charge of threading a wireless microphone through your underwear to your collar, so it pays to be acquainted.

Anyone key to your day: The wranglers if you're riding horses; the fight coordinator if you're getting punched in the nose; the special effects guy if you're getting shot in the back; the dialogue coach if you're doing an accent; and the medical expert if you're doing a hospital drama and need to know how to say *streptococcus pyogenes.*

Then get to know as many other people as you can.

The Big Wait

And now… nothing.

You wait.

Use your three hours to get acclimatized. Everyone is different so do what works best for you. Some actors hang out in the trailer the whole time, rehearsing and relaxing. Some find it better to get out of there and socialize. Being an actor, you are a demi-god on set, and thus you are are welcome anywhere and at any time. So wander around if you like; strike up a conversation. The teamsters (truckers) are usually hanging around with nothing to do because they did their work early in the morning. Chat with them. If you spot a fellow actor, then go chat, but beware of the pecking order. If it's Johnny you see standing over there, then it's perfectly fine to say "Hello Johnny, I'm Ashley, I'll be your waitress today, nice to meet you." Then gauge his reaction. He may be chatty and welcoming. He may not. Take a hint. Beware also that actors are kind of bizarre to the outside world. You know this. Some of them wander around deep in thought trying to get into character. Don't bug them. Some of them are nerve-wracked to the point of collapse. Don't bug them. There is nothing you can do to help. Some love to gab and share wisdom and stories. Let them, as long as it doesn't interfere with your process. Some are all about the work. Some are just plain insane. Take a hint.

Example: I played a mountain man in a mini-series. The scene was about a lovely Native woman—played wonderfully by the leading lady—being sold into slavery to a terrible man. The leading lady wanted to be in tears for her scene so she got busy and cried all day. Whenever I saw her—having tea, talking to the director, or just waiting—she was bawling her head off so that when the cameras rolled she was already into it and looked like she'd been crying all day. That's her process. Figure out yours.

If you can, go to the set where your upcoming scene is to be shot. In your case, go into the café and check it out. Wander around. This is your place. You've worked here for years. You should know where everything is, how to grab the coffee pot without looking, how to order food, how to make change, where the dirty dishes go, etc. So get busy and learn all this stuff. Get used to your place. Make it second nature. Rehearse your scene. Manage your nerves. Manage your energy. Visualize working the scene with Johnny. Calm down.

Nobody's going to come to you saying, "would you like to go into the café to get used to your coffee pot?" This is your job. Do it.

A Word on Continuity

This is also a very good time to practice your *continuity*. We've all seen movies where the continuity is all wrong—the cowboy has the gun in one hand in the first shot, then somehow it jumps into his other hand in the next shot, and then in the next shot it's somehow back in his holster. That's just really bad filmmaking, and it's basically the actor's fault. In your case, you might want to plan how you're going to deal with the coffee pot. When and how are you going to pick it up, how are you going to hold it, when are you going to pour the coffee, and so on? Because in each take, you have to do it exactly the same way every time. I mean exactly and to the letter. Was your left hand on the counter when you poured the coffee? Did you pour it before you said the word coffee, or after? It has to be exactly the same every time you do it. Otherwise, when they cut the shots together later, the shots won't match.

What's so bad about that? Well, if you're the star, then *they* might have to re-shoot the whole scene. If you're the waitress, then *they'll* simply cut around you. Did you hear that? *They* will *cut*, around you. Meaning *they* will stay on Johnny. Your stuff didn't *cut*, so it hits the cutting room floor. Meaning it is possible you could be cut right out of the movie except for your hand and your voice saying the bit about the coffee.

Even more of a warning: editors love to *cut on the action*. Example: the camera sees you behind the counter, asking if Johnny would like coffee. He nods. You lift the coffee pot, step toward him, and… CUT TO: a close shot of Johnny and the counter as your pot enters the frame filling his cup. The action is a natural cutting point because it mimics where you would be looking if you were standing there watching the scene unfold. It gives the movie energy, and makes the cuts seem to disappear. Get it? So your move with the coffee has to happen at exactly the same time and in exactly the same way in every take so that no matter which one the editor uses, it matches.

Yes, there is a person on set who is watching out for this kind of boo-boo—the script supervisor—but ultimately it's your responsibility. It's part of your job. And doing it right is a good way to ensure you get a lot of screen time. Give the editor good continuity so he or she can cut to you without the coffee pot jumping around or disappearing altogether.

Realize that your p*erformance* and your *continuity* are separate things. Don't get stuck doing the same performance every time. You must be free to be alive and react second by second in each take. But your continuity must be the same. So, if you have to do things like pull a gun or answer the phone, then plan it, rehearse it, and lock it in. And there's no better place to do that than on the actual set.

So, work your scene until it's all second nature, until your continuity is locked in and your performance is ready but flexible. Build your confidence. Manage your energy. Breathe. Relax.

Now, wander down to the working set—wherever they are currently shooting—and watch. Maybe they're shooting the parking lot stuff with Johnny before moving into the café. Find a corner out of the way and watch. Or just go sit in the chairs marked *cast*. That's you. Have a seat. If it's a very thoughtful set, then there will be a chair marked *Ashley*. That's really you. Most of the time there will be a monitor, a live feed, for you to watch everything they are shooting as they shoot it. You and your fellow actors can sit around and chat openly and watch what they're shooting on the screen.

Or, if you like, walk right up to *video village* and hang out there.

Video village is the bank of large monitors showing what's being shot for the benefit of the big-wigs. The director, the producers, the DOP, and the script supervisor all will be found here watching each take go by, chatting, making adjustments, feeling proud of themselves, or terrified, or whatever. Often the actors in the shot will be found here between takes having a look at what they just did on the playback. It's the central hub of the shoot, and it's a great place to get a feel for it all, to put faces to names, to introduce yourself, and to watch the other actors at work. You might learn a few things.

Three basic rules must be observed at video village: do not be a chatty pest, do not start trying to direct the movie, and shut up and sit quietly during takes. The microphones are highly sensitive. You don't want to ruin one of Johnny's takes because you squeaked your chair.

Watch the recurring process that happens from shot to shot, try to relax, manage your nerves, manage your energy, and slip into the happening. Stay there all day if you want. Or go back to your trailer and rehearse some more, or go back to your diner, or go have a bite to eat.

There are two places to eat on set. The *crafts' service table*—also known as *crafty*—will be located in a safe place away from the set, and features all kinds of goodies for your use: snacks, coffee, candy, pain killers, throat lozenges, granola bars, fruit, green tea, and more. Have at it. Also, somewhere in the circus, a catering truck serves hot meals. In your case, since you're shooting in the morning, the AD might have invited you to have some breakfast. Just wander up to the truck, have a look at the menu scribbled on the outside wall, and order up. Breakfast burritos seem to be featured on every set in the world. At lunch, same thing. You will be given several menu options. There will be a room or tent set up nearby full of picnic tables, and even more food—salads, coffee, desserts—where you can eat and socialize if you choose. Or you can take your plate back to your trailer to keep rehearsing. It's up to you.

When on set, I'm kind of a gregarious recluse. Half the time you can find me in my trailer working my scene while listening to music. The other half of the time, you'll find me mingling. A few laughs always calm me down. Plus, there's the potential to learn a few things and meet new friends. Try it. You might also catch the director when he has a second and maybe find out why he hired you or what he's thinking about your scene. You might want to say "Thank you." Keep your eyes and ears open. Remember the pecking order. Do not be a fan. Do not be a jerk.

Do not under any circumstances ask for Johnny's autograph. Do not ask for a photo. Do not use your cell phone to secretly snap a photo. Moron.

Imagine for a second that you are a house painter. You hire a nice young fellow to be your assistant, mix your paint, and hand you brushes. The first morning, he arrives like a little puppy and stares at you in awe. Then he says you are the most amazing house painter he's ever seen.

Then he asks for your autograph.

Then he says he loves you.

How do you feel?

Creeped out?

Maybe just a little?

Wanna keep working with this guy?

Or do you want him gone?

This is precisely how BFS's feel if you do something similar. They want to work with other pros who are there to get the job done. Who care. Who are not fans, but actors making a movie together. Sure, the BFS is making 5000 times more money than you and he's famous all over the world, but so what? That's the biz. If you're lucky, then you'll be earning that one day yourself. If not, then you keep going because you love and value the work and because you are a pro and not a fan.

Right?

If you are stupid enough to ask for an autograph, then the star will most likely oblige or perhaps agree to do it for you after lunch. A few minutes will pass. One of the ADs will come along to tell you that you're *wrapped*. Meaning done. Meaning finished. Meaning fired. Meaning embarrassed and humiliated. Meaning probably dropped by your agent. Meaning back to your job at the sewer supply company.

No matter how tempting it is, do not be a fan.

Blocking

Usually, it happens when you have to pee. You're on the way to your trailer. Your trusty AD runs up to you saying, "Ashley, we need to travel you to set." You indicate that you really need to pee. He indicates that you really need to travel to set.

Ah, the joys of showbiz.

My advice at this point is to pee fast and then get your butt to the set. The crew has just finished the last shot in the parking lot, and they're even now marching into the diner for your scene. And they need you. They can't do anything at all until you get there.

Your AD will probably pass you off to the first. This guy (almost always a guy) is the set general. The fist of the director. Think of him as a cattle driver with a whip and hemorrhoids. His job is to *get the day*, meaning to move this army sideshow along so the director can shoot everything he needs to shoot on that day to finish the movie on time. Sometimes they have to shoot seven pages of script a day, which is clearly impossible, but they have to do it. The budget only allows 15 days to shoot, total. Must make seven pages per day, with all the dialogue, all the scene changes, all the action sequences, the car crash and the love scene. And that's just today! The first AD has to make that happen.

Some big time movie directors will take years to make a film. In that case, getting the day involves doing one shot of a woman screaming behind a closed window. That's it. That's the day. You'd think this would be easy for the AD. A vacation. Not so. Every movie has the potential to be a joy or a nightmare, and no matter what, that poor guy has to organize it all, plan it all, allow for it all, and somehow drive it all home.

To help everyone, long before they started shooting, he made up a plan called a production board. He took everything into consideration. The starlette can only be here for five days, so we have to do all her stuff in a row. The leading man is only here on two of the same days, so all their combined stuff goes there. We only have the crane for a week, so one of those days has to be devoted to the driving off the cliff sequence. The zoo is only available at night, so we have to shoot the love scene in the polar bear enclosure at 3 a.m. on Tuesday, and we have to get it all that night—no second chances. If it rains, then we'll have to shoot the love scene in the studio and somehow find a way to go back to the zoo later and shoot some long shots with body doubles so it looks like the stars. Then we have to fly to China by Friday. I think I'm going to kill myself.

It can take months to figure out this giant three-dimensional puzzle, and usually it involves a lot of suffering and shuffling of people and things and places. Sometimes, you lose the star. Just can't make it work. Sometimes, you find out the movie just can't be done, and you shut it all down. But you want it to work, damn it. Hence the inestimable value of the first ADs. They earn their wage. By skill, and experience, and force of will, they hammer the schedule into place and are subsequently responsible for making it happen, day by day. They *must* get the day.

You'll see him surgically attached to his walkie, issuing a constant stream of marching orders, such as: "Okay, we're on the move. The diner scene, number 43, is next. Let's wrap the parking lot. *Strike* (get rid of) the cars. Lunch is in 45 minutes. Let's get the waitress down here instantly. We need to rehearse. Let's get the props in. Bobby, are you ready to set the house on fire after lunch? What's the ETA on the fire crew? Where's my waitress, dammit? We have three more pages to do by 7 p.m., and we have to be back on set by 4:30 a.m. to get the sunrise shot. Let's move it. WHERE'S MY WAITRESS?"

And then you walk in.

And he'll say, "Hi Ashley, I'm Dave, the first. So nice to meet you."

Remember, everyone will know your name. And you learned theirs right? So you can say, "Hi Dave. Pleasure. Where do you want me?"

Dave will show you to your counter and your coffee pot.

You will find yourself facing about 50 people. This is your first big challenge. They will be staring right at you rather critically.

Surveying you.

Judging you?

You will be tempted to freak out.

Do not.

This is the whole production crew: the DOP, the operator, all the camera assistants, the sound crew, the lighting team, the grip crew, the set decorators, the makeup artists, the props master, everyone. They just stand there, eyeing you, as you wait, befuddled, behind the counter.

They are not judging you; they are doing their jobs. Waiting for God, er, I mean the director, to *block* the scene.

Blocking, as in theater, simply means working out the movements of the scene—what is going to happen where, and how. Start here, move there, play the fight over by the door, run behind the bar to get the gun, play the dialogue while loading your gun, shoot the guy coming down the stairs and then exit out the window. Obviously, you need to know this stuff. But so does the crew. They are waiting for this to be revealed to them, just like you are, so they know where to set the lights and cameras. That's why they are watching so intently. You have to act the scene, but they have to shoot the scene. To shoot it, they have to know what the scene is. So they stand there watching and waiting for you and the director and Johnny to figure that out.

Okay? Calm down. It's all good. They're just waiting for blocking, just like you.

If you happen to look around at this time, wondering where the director is, then you'll probably spot him off in a corner somewhere talking intently with a very handsome man. Then you realize the handsome man is Johnny Depp, and no wonder he's handsome. He's Johnny Depp. He's talking to the director. This is your second big challenge. It's Johnny Depp!! It really is!! You will be tempted to panic. Do not. They are not talking about you. No one is against you. Everyone loves you, in fact, because here you are at your counter helping *them* make *their* movie. *They* chose you from 1000s. *They* want and need and love you. The director just has to talk to Johnny right now. Maybe they're talking about the scene, or maybe they're talking about the Dallas Cowboys. When you are a BFS, you will find out.

A hint: most likely *they* are talking about the upcoming scene, and how they'd like it to go so it best tells the story. Johnny is responsible for carrying the movie on his shoulders all the way to box office success, so it's kind of important to him. The director is responsible for carrying the movie on his shoulders all the way to box office success, so it's kind of important to him, too. Sometimes this results in a constant hellish battle; sometimes it's bliss. Whatever. Not your problem. Not your job. Your job is to do your best to help *them* make the movie by performing your role as the diner waitress and asking if he'd like cream with that coffee, so that he can say no, so that in the clear coffee he can see the reflection of the bad guy behind him so that he can beat him to the punch so that he can frisk him so that he can find out he works for Big Pauly. That's your job. To accomplish that job, you need to know the blocking. And so, along with the crew, you wait.

Sooner or later, the director will arrive. He may shake your hand. He may be an ass. He may be an idiot. He may be a she. She may be an idiot. She may be royal bitch. She may be the definition of grace and brilliance. *They* come in all shapes and sizes and colors and backgrounds. You have no control over this. Not your job. Just let it be, and do your best with what you have. Just so you know, most of them are pretty nice although frazzled to within an inch of *their* lives.

Do not pick up this frazzled energy. Stay calm. Manage your stress. Wait for the blocking to begin.

At this time, Johnny is likely to appear. (Dear Johnny: I am just using you as an example because I like your work. I am taking a lot of liberties. I hope you don't mind.) Okay, Johnny appears, and takes your hand, and says something like: "Hi. I'm Johnny." Third challenge. Johnny is touching you. You will be tempted to freak out. Do not. Say: "Hi. Ashley. Really great to meet you."

Done.

Most probably, that's it for introductions, small talk, and conversations.

Use all your grit at this point to stay calm, manage your nerves, and manage your energy.

Every director is different and every blocking is different, but typically it will start with a line reading.

Director: "Okay, diner scene, let's hear it."

You and Johnny will recite the scene for him. Don't go acting. Don't pour the coffee. Just recite the scene. The director just wants to be reminded and to get an initial feel for what it looks like and sounds like coming out of your mouths. He may wish to make some changes as a result.

Director: "Just say 'cream'? Okay, Ashley? 'Do you want some cream with that?' is just too long. Doesn't sound realistic. Just say: 'Cream?' "

You say, "Okay." And, of course, you remember that, and do that.

It bears repeating that film acting is largely about your ability to stay cool under pressure and roll with the punches. More than acting classes, what you mostly need to learn is staying cool under pressure. Jim Carrey puts it this way: "It's not enough to be able to do the scene. You need to be able to do the scene with people throwing tennis balls at your head." That's the feeling on set. It's chaotic. It's panicky. It's constantly changing. You got hired because you look the part and can deal with it all. You are a film actor. That's what film actors do.

I have seen directors change the entire scene before blocking, as in "Let's shoot this in the kitchen instead, and forget the coffee." *They* rather regularly change lines, delete lines, give your lines to Johnny, or Johnny's to you. *They* are fond of blocking the scene so it's awkward for you but good for the camera. Sometimes it's about style, or timing, or feel, or mood, or other things of concern to him and unknown to you. Try to follow along. Try to contribute. Otherwise, keep your mouth shut. Do not expect every little thing to be explained to you. This is not your personal film school. Help as best you can, keep your eyes and ears open, learn as you go, and roll with the punches. If you feel you need to understand something to do your job, then ask. Of course, ask. But don't be an idiot.

Here is you being an idiot:

Director: "And Ashley, if you could pour the coffee really slowly, please? Don't splash it. And look at Johnny while you're doing it. Okay?"

You: "Why?" (This question is okay but only just okay.)

Director: "It's a mood thing." (This is where you should stop.)

You: "I don't get it. Waitresses work fast." (Oh, no.)

Director: "Just do it for me, please?" (He is not going to explain his entire vision for the movie, you dope. Help him get the shot he wants. Pour slowly.)

You: "But, what do you mean 'mood thing'? I think she'd be really running." (Shit. Now it's getting awkward, and there might be trouble.

You're making it about you. You clearly don't understand filmmaking. You're overstepping. Wasting time.)

Director: "I'm building intrigue. Everyone needs to look suspicious. Okay?" (He's a nice guy. But this is your last chance.)

You: "Oh, so intrigue! Cool. Right! Intrigue. So, I should, like, look at him kind of out of the corner of my eye? Or play it really innocent, as a diversion? Or, I could pour with my LEFT HAND? Subliminally sinister. Actually, *sinister* is Italian for left-handed. Did you know that?" (Oh, God. See, this is exactly what he wanted to avoid. He doesn't want you *playing* anything. He wants you to pour slowly. That's all.)

Director: "Right. Just pour it slowly. Okay? Don't do anything else? Okay?" (Please, God.)

You: "I know! We could do it like three or four different ways!" (Somebody fire this girl!)

Get it? Trust the director. Do your job. When you are Johnny Depp, you can have deep discussions about sinister things, but by then you will know what you're doing. For now, listen and do. Help them get the movie made. Make it about that and not you.

The director, or sometimes Johnny, will either discuss the blocking with you, or, more likely, tell you what the blocking is going to be. "Ashley, you'll start out in the kitchen. Enter when Johnny passes the cash register. As he sits, pour him some coffee without being asked, and hand him a menu." (The "hand him a menu" part is not in the script. Do not be an idiot. Hand him the menu as instructed. Things change, remember?) "Hover over him until he furtively glances out the window, and then ask if he'd like cream with that. When he says no, go clean up the dishes from the booth over there. Okay?"

You say, "Okay. Should I ask about the cream when he's looking out the window or when he comes back to the coffee?"

Johnny: "Just whatever, baby. Flow with it."

Great.

So, you flow. And you remember the flow scrupulously so you can blend it with the continuity you practiced and match it take by take. Sometimes, all the continuity you practiced has to go. Fine. Concentrate, memorize, flow.

And whatever you do, you will not start directing the scene yourself. Right? Not your job. Contribute. Co-operate. Be assertive about what you think is right for the character and the story, but also be collaborative. Defer to the star. Defer to the director. But also try to be an equal partner in the process.

Hey, you're the one who wanted to be a film actor.

Sometimes, directors are very hands-on. Example: I was playing a prosecutor in a made-for-TV movie. Scene: in my office, talking to the investigating cop. Director: "Okay, Peter, we're going to start on your briefcase, so put the papers in, snap it shut quickly as the camera tilts up to your face, and then do your first set of lines, then grab your coat on the way out as you do your second set of lines. We will follow you with the hand-held camera. Exit through that door, come down this hall as the cop badgers you, spin around here in the foyer and do your last set of lines on this mark here. Then exit *camera right*. Okay?" (Camera right simply means to the camera's right as it looks at you. If you were facing the camera, then you'd have to move to your left to go camera right.)

I bravely said, "Okay," quickly practiced it a few times while they set up, and luckily got it on the first take. Later, I realized how much I liked the complicated blocking. Why? The part of my brain that is usually criticizing my performance as I do it was busy trying to snap shut the briefcase. The other part of my brain was just doing the scene. Result: a scene I was proud to watch when the movie aired. Now, I pray for complicated blocking.

Sometimes, directors are very hands off. Example: a western TV series. Scene: the leading man comes to me for a horse. The director didn't block anything; he just motioned for us to figure something out. The leading man looked at me for guidance.

Huh?

Whattaya lookin' at me for? I'm just the day player!

But he kept looking. So, I got busy and blocked the scene. "How about I start in the corral over here. When I see you coming, I'll lead the horse out, close the gate, and we can play the scene here on the street. Then I'll hand you the reins and go back inside. What do you think?" He nodded, and before I knew it, the crew was setting up the shot. I think we did two takes. Done. That was my whole day.

No, I did not get a director bonus.

Some directors are very collaborative. Example: a cop show. The director asked us to work out the scene to our satisfaction first, and then he made adjustments for the camera and story to his satisfaction.

Nice.

As you are all walking and talking through the blocking, a person scurries around at your feet. Do not be alarmed. She is in the camera department. She puts little bits of tape down on the ground to remind you where to stand, or sit, or lean as you proceed through the scene. You've heard of *hitting your* marks? These are your *marks*. Suppose you start the scene in the kitchen where the camera can't see you. This is called your *first position*. You don't need a mark for it. Then you enter and hit your mark in front of the coffee maker. This is called *second position*. And so on. Easy. If the director says, "Okay, let's take it back to firsts," then you know what he's talking about.

Notice that your marks are red, whereas Johnny's are blue. Under stress it's easy to forget this and hit the blue ones.

If your scene happens outside or on some uneven surface, then the bits of tape will become tiny sand bags the size of your thumb. Same thing goes for the colors.

If you are doing a long shot in which the camera sees your feet, then they will try to put a little stone down for you, or a leaf, or maybe nothing. You'll just have to remember.

More about your marks in a minute.

Rehearsing

Once you have blocked the scene, you may be asked to rehearse it. Maybe. Mostly not. But if it does happen, it will happen like this:

Director: "Let's run it."

First AD: "REHEARSING!"

Everyone will shut up and watch.

The first will call: "First positions, please. And... Action on rehearsal." You rehearse it. You do not go full blast with your performance. Just walk through the scene at more or less half power while still keeping the proper pace of the scene. The rehearsal is not really for your benefit; it's for theirs. It gives them a better look at how the scene is actually going to play out so they can make last minute changes to the lights, the coffee, the marks, etc.

If it's an action scene, then do it at one quarter power and in slow motion so everyone can clearly see what's going to happen and so no one gets hurt. When the cameras roll, you go full blast hoping to get it on the first take.

Many directors choose not to rehearse at all, thinking it might diminish the final product. Film acting is about danger and improvisation because that's how life is. In life, we don't rehearse; we just do. We have an intent, of course, but we fumble along as best we can. That's what looks real on camera. Being a film actor, you know this, you love this, and you embrace this. You use the rehearsal to work out little technical things for yourself, such as where to wipe the counter and how not to trip over the furniture.

A note: some directors want you to actually rehearse it full blast. Some of these directors are the best on Earth.

Sorry about that.

Best course of action: stay on your toes and do as the star does.

And then you will be dismissed.

The first AD will call out the words: *second team*. That's not you. You are *first team*. You are a demi-god actor.

The Second Team

The second team is made up of actors who wanted your job but didn't get it. They are also called *stand-ins*. Their job is to stand in for you, to literally stand on your marks so the crew can use them for reference as they set up the lights, the dolly track, the boom location, and so on. They are human mannequins. Sometimes these mannequins are asked to replay the scene for everyone's reference as they go along, but mostly they just stand there. The DOP needs to see how his lighting will look on a face, and so on. You get the idea.

There are two basic kinds of *stand-in*. *Star stand-ins* look like the star. It's easier for camera and light if the stand-in is the same height, has the same coloring, and so on. Very often, the stars bring their own, believe it or not. Somewhere along the line they met somebody they liked, and they now insist on having him along on every shoot. That guy's job is to be fun for the star to have around, to be one of the entourage, a kind-of sort-of confidante, someone to play gin rummy with, or to score chicks, or whatever, to travel with the star, to drink with the star, to protect the star, to be a tall Mini Me, to be paid stupid amounts of money, and to have no responsibility whatsoever except to stand around when asked.

Utility stand-ins—usually one or two males and one or two females—are hired on every shoot to stand-in for everyone else.

One fine day, you'll arrive on set to find that the girl who always beat you out for parts in the past is now your stand-in on this job. You will feel glorious and vindicated. Until next week when you're standing in for her.

The bottom line is: you, the demi-god, are far too exalted to do any standing around yourself. Plus, it's more practical. You can go get your makeup fixed if necessary. Learn how to shoot your gun. Check your wardrobe. Learn your lines. Rehearse. Calm down.

How do you get a stand-in job? Tell your agent you'd like to be a stand-in. It might work. The stand-in job though is seen as a step or two down from acting, so your agent might not want to bother. If you're just starting out, then it's a great way to get some experience and make some connections, so she might bother.

The better way is to find out who hires stand-ins in your neck of the woods—usually a *background* casting director—and submit your stuff directly to her. Background casting directors cast the background performers, also known as extras or *atmosphere*. In this case, she would have provided all the patrons in the café scene and maybe a cook or two. Very often, she also handles the stand-ins. She probably has favorite people she hires all the time, so you may need to be persistent. If you are very ambitious and kind of creepy, then you'll *accidentally* bump into her at the gym, take her to lunch, and then casually slip into the conversation that you might like to stand-in one of these days.

Okay, back to the set with Johnny.

For the next half-hour or so, the crew sets up the shot the director has chosen. The camera is readied, the lights are lit, the coffee is boiled, and the counter is cleaned. If it's an action movie, then this set up can take two days. Everything the crew is doing is based on the blocking. The marks. That's where they set up the light so it is perfect for you. That's where the microphone is waiting to pick up your immortal lines. That is where you will be in brilliant focus.

When you go back to the set to shoot the scene, you must hit these marks perfectly. And did I mention you have to do it without looking? Yes, you will see bad actors looking down for their marks. But that will not be you; you will be a pro. In real life, people do not look down for their marks. You are playing a real waitress who doesn't have marks.

How to Hit your Marks (Without Looking)

Especially in low light, movie cameras have a very shallow zone of focus. It's like a slice of air. Take a step too close or too far back and you're out of focus. This zone is called the *depth of field*. Filmmakers love depth of field because it gives them more power to select what the audience looks at. If the teardrop is the important part, then the cinematographer can make sure just the teardrop is in focus, so the audience has no choice but to look at it. Maybe—such as in a tight close up in low light—your eyes will be sharp and your ears will be out of focus. Beautiful. On your road to becoming a BFS you must master slipping into this zone with professional precision. Yes, there is a guy on the camera crew—the *focus puller*—who will try to keep you sharp, but without an actress who can hit her marks with accuracy as she walks through the scene, production stops being about capturing the spark of life and starts being about just getting something in focus. So, consider this as part of your job. Hit your marks.

Here are a few ways to do that.

Moonwalk: Stand on your mark. Walk backwards three steps or so out of the shot. When you walk three steps forward, you should be on your mark.

Parallax: stand on your mark. Line up several objects in your eye line so that "When I'm standing here that guy's elbow covers the doorknob behind him." When they call action, walk in until those things line up again. As long as the guy with the elbow hasn't moved, you should be on your mark.

Peripheral vision: see the mark and any other handy reference points as you walk in using only your peripheral vision. No peeking.

Practical marks: sometimes you can use things in the shot to help you. Put a glass on the counter, for example, and remember where it needs to be in relation to you when you arrive. You should be on your mark.

Magic touch: every now and then you can use your body to feel your way onto your mark. Maybe you can feel a certain rock under your foot, or put your hand down on the hood of the car, or lean against a desk just so.

Use the set: sometimes you can just feel where you need to be in the room, i.e. about three feet in front of the Captain's desk or right in the middle of the elevator.

Find your Light: if you are a very savvy actor, then you will be skilled in just feeling the light on your face. When it feels perfect, you stop. You should be on your mark.

Lean on your scene partner: trust the other actor to hit his mark and just follow him. It's cheating, but it works in a pinch.

Use the Camera: if you are in a close up, then you might be two feet away from the camera doing your lines to a little X taped to the lens. You should be able to feel it when you're right in the perfect zone.

Use the crew: I once had to march out of a building spouting a bunch of lines and stop on a particular spot in the parking lot where they couldn't put down a mark. The camera crew marched along in front of me with the camera looking back. When they started slowing down, I just slowed with them until we all stopped together in the right place.

These are the basic techniques. Memorize them all. Then develop more of your own.

The Little Wait

You now have somewhere between 20 minutes and 20 hours to wait before you go back on set to shoot the scene.

What to do?

How about rehearse?

I like to rehearse until I am blue in the face because when the camera starts to roll, and Johnny looks me in the eye, I know I'm going to lose 20 IQ points. I can't help it because the tension is too great, especially for a day player. Know your part—and everyone else's too—

inside and out. You'll feel enormous confidence that you can deal with whatever may happen. Often the director will want to pick up a scene in the middle, for example. Be ready. Free up mental space for confidence by knowing your lines, your blocking, your continuity, your dramatic function, your motivation, and the story, inside and out.

Potentially rehearse with Johnny.

Not like this is going to happen in real life, but it's fun to imagine.

Why doesn't it happen? Most stars are far too 'important.' They are 'busy.' Usually, they are terribly nervous themselves and don't want to show it. Often, they are desperately rehearsing in their spacious trailer hoping against hope to be better than you are, and deserving of their ten million bucks. Occasionally, they are getting a 'massage,' or drinking 'soda with Himalayan berry juice,' or talking with their 'advisors.' Once in a while, they are seriously working through their own process, and they find it easier that way. Many times, they don't need to rehearse; they've seen it all and done it all so many times that this is nothing to them. Now and then, they are legendary geniuses who never rehearse; they don't know what it's for. More than you can imagine, they don't want to be reminded that they were once as nervous as you are. Frequently, they are idiots who have no clue about what they are doing, and they will lean on you and the director and everybody else when the cameras roll to make them look good. If you're lucky, then they are magnificent and powerful and generous beings who would in fact rehearse with you if only you would ask.

If you are in the same general pay scale as the star, meaning you are a lead or supporting actor yourself, then you don't need my advice. Go ask him. Rehearse if you want. Whatever.

Otherwise, my advice is: do what they do, which is simply learn how to prepare on your own.

Why?

You are the only constant that will go with you from set to set. You have to do a great performance no matter who you're working with. We're making a movie, not a play. We don't have time. You are doing this scene once and only once, ever. There will be no matinee. We don't have time. Film acting is about danger, so you want to keep it fresh and unprepared. It's what you get paid for.

Next, work on your continuity. Now that you know exactly how the scene is going to go, perfect your bits of business so you can reproduce them take after take, each time as though it was the first time.

Calm down. Do yoga. T'ai Chi. Meditate. Talk to your angels. Auto-suggest. Go chat with friends, or make new friends. Do some sit-ups. Do the Sudoku puzzle. Manage your nerves. Manage your energy. Go back to the set and mingle—without getting in the way—and get used to the space, the buzz, and the people. Watch them set up your scene. Read your old acting books. Read this book. Call your therapist. Kiss your girlfriend if you're lucky enough to have her along. Breathe deeply. Remember that in the great expanse of eternity, nothing you do today matters one bit. Recall that Johnny puts his pants on one leg at a time, whatever that means. Visualize your future success. See it. Taste it. Count backwards from 20. Do anything to prop up your confidence. Rehearse again.

My 'A' number one, top of the heap, best of the best, super secret tip to relax is to laugh your head off. Laughing releases that furious ball of nervous energy in your stomach, circulates it, and makes it accessible to you in your performance. It oxygenates your blood, bringing the color back to your face and the life back into your eyes. It forces you back into the present moment. It reminds you that acting is supposed to be fun and that everything is kind of a big joke that shouldn't be taken seriously. I like to find a private place and just go for it, forcing my nervous self to laugh. I realize how ridiculous I am, forcing myself to laugh in a *port-a-potty* on a movie set. I laugh at my sorry self. I mean, why not?! Nobody's shooting at me—it is not my execution day. The fate of the free world is not on the line. We're just a bunch of kids playing make believe on a planet spinning around a star in the middle of nowhere. What's to be nervous about? I laugh for real. I shake my head in wonderment, look to the Heavens with a big sigh, and walk back out set with a little twinkle in my eye. Works every time.

Things not to do: kiss somebody else's girlfriend. Pull out your secret stash of 'medication.' Brag to your friends on the cell phone. Hyperventilate. Drink coffee (it just makes your nerves that much worse). Bombard yourself with negative self-talk. Let others get to you, interrupt your positive vibe, or psych you out. Spill food on your costume. Barf on your shoes.

And now for some Positive News and Reassurance

Remember, it's not all about you. Quite a number of things help you out. See below. You are not responsible for any of them. They all make your job easier. Some say yours is the easiest job on the planet. Katharine Hepburn—who has more Best Actress Oscars than anyone—said that acting was a silly profession that could be easily mastered by a four-year-old. So take heart. Here's what you have working for you.

They Already Believe

This is one of my favorites. Pick up David Mamet's great book *True and False: Heresy and Common Sense for the Actor.* In it he gives us a little analogy, which I'm going to paraphrase here. He says, roughly, that if you go to a party and someone points out a woman across the room and says "See her? She's worth a billion bucks," you would believe him and keep believing him until you got significant information to the contrary. You see? She may only be worth $2.95. Doesn't matter. You believe she's the billion dollar dame. Even if she spills dip on her dress you think, "So that's how a billionaire spills dip." You have been predisposed to believe. And so it goes with the audience and your character. If another character says "Here comes Doctor Brown," and then you show up, you are Doctor Brown. That's it. You have done nothing but show up. And you are Doctor Brown, and you will continue to be Doctor Brown to the end of the movie, provided you don't try to do something stupid like *act like* Doctor Brown. It's not necessary. The audience will actually hate you for it because they already believe, so why are you rubbing their noses in it? They would much rather that you got on with the actions that constitute the story, thank you.

The Story

Oh, right, we're telling a story. Riiiiight. That's why we're all gathered here together. Because of the story. Not you. Not your acting.

The story.

You've sat in a darkened theater watching a great movie and had to pee, right? And when you got back what did you say to your date? You said, "What happened?" Not, "How was the acting by that waitress with the cream line? Was she believable?" Why didn't you ask about the waitress? Because you don't care. You care about the movement of the story. You care that the alien burst out of a guy's chest and is now running loose on the ship. That's what you care about.

So when you, the waitress, actually arrive on the scene, the audience already believes you are the waitress, and all they want from you is the next story point which will be some kind of action or revelation that has already been invented and written down by *the writer.*

The Writer

This person spent months and years studying story and mulling over every detail of this one. Then he or she meticulously blueprinted it. And *that* is the thing. That is the heart of the matter, the reason we are all here, and the reason the audience is all here. Already blueprinted. Already done. No help from you required. Everything you need to do and say is written down for you. We only ask that you don't screw it up.

How easy is that? Walk in, pour the coffee, and ask if he wants cream. Nothing to it. Why then do so many actors have self-induced strokes over it? Just do what's on the page, please. The writer has figured it all out. Your job is just to do it. Easy.

Your Sell/Brand/Hit/Power Zone

You walk around broadcasting something all the time whether you like it or not. Whether you are acting or not. You broadcast a message. It's that message that the filmmakers saw and wanted when *they* hired you. *They* wanted your brand of waitress. It works for the story. No acting is required. You are already broadcasting it. There's no need to act like you. Just do what's in the script.

Scared you won't be able to do it? Lucky for you there are *other actors*.

The Other Actors

They will be hanging on to you with their eyes, believing that you are the waitress, treating you just like the waitress, talking to you about coffee, feeding you cue lines, doing what they need to do according to the script, leading you through the scene, and generally propping you up as much as they can knowing that you, in turn, will prop them up.

If you ask, then they might even give you helpful advice and encouragement.

So easy anyone could do it.

How much luckier you are that you have an entire group of filmmakers working for you.

The Crew

These people are doing everything in their power to make your job easier. Worried about your face? Makeup. Worried about your protruding arse? Wardrobe. Worried that you don't look any good on film? Director of photography. Worried that they won't catch your fabulous performance? Focus puller. Worried that you'll forget your lines? Script supervisor. Worried that the coffee won't look real? Props master. Worried that you're wrong for the part? Casting director. Worried that they won't hear your tiny voice? Boom operator. Hungry? Caterer.

Thirsty? Production assistant. Worried that you can't speak English? Dialogue coach. Worried that you can't stand up for all 20 minutes of your scene? A grip will bring you a chair. Worried that you look terrified? A camera operator once told me that in a case like this he'll zoom in a little closer on you, making you appear bigger in the frame and thus more confident. Everybody is there to help you.

So, what are you worried about? That your performance is off-key? Lucky for you there's a *director.*

The Director

The director's job, and deepest interest, is to help you deliver the story as blueprinted in the script according to his vision. If something is not working, then he will let you know. Usually, he will take you aside (to avoid possible embarrassment) and prompt you toward a better delivery: "The coffee comes sooner; she's a good waitress."

Easy.

Man, this job is looking more and more like a piece of cake. How much more lucky can you get? Oh, wait, I forgot about the *editor.*

The Editor

Worried that your performance was uneven? You've still got the editor. He or she is going to labor over the footage for eternity, snipping your best bits from each take and weaving them into one performance. The performance you gave on set is not your final performance. The editor *builds your performance* later using all your good stuff. How great is that?

You theater actors out there must be shaking your heads in astonishment right now. Imagine for a minute that somehow someone could take your best reading of each line from every show in your run and magically stitch them all together into one show. And *that's* the show that went on tour. The best of everything you ever did. Wow.

It's beginning to look like you barely need to be there at all. But wait, there's more.

The Music

Another friend is the music. All the elements of the sound track are also carrying you along. Little did you know that when you pick up the coffee, music begins, foreshadowing the importance of your line: "Would you like cream with that?" You could have said it in pig-latin and the audience would still be on the edge of their seats.

Oh, then there's the *prequel.*

The Prequel

Often you are doing an episode of a beloved TV series or a sequel to a beloved franchise like Bond or Batman. You could stumble through your entire performance sometimes (remember Mr. Freeze?) and the audience won't care. Not a bit. They came to see Batman and express their love and support of the franchise.

And don't forget the *event.*

The Event

This is also working in your favor. If you're in a movie, then there will be a premiere and a big box office release. Well, people love big box office releases. They get all dressed up and want to cheer for something. Plus, there is the *audience.*

The Audience

Right there with them are several hundred other people who got dressed up and came out to the theater. This also works in your favor. Comedies are funnier when others are laughing.

You see? You are not doing it all by yourself. You have enormous help from all directions. Easiest job in the world. No wonder so many so-called stars can't act to save their lives. They are standing on so many hundreds of shoulders. So, take heart. Ease your mind. Be calm, be confident, and be technically schooled. Go out there and deliver the story as blueprinted in the script. There is nothing but help for you everywhere you look.

First Team

Okay, now that you're all pumped up with confidence, here's what happens next. Your faithful AD will arrive and say something like, "We need you on set." Or if you are close by already, then you might hear the first AD call for the first team. That's you, remember? Time to go to work. Time to lay down your 12 seconds of the movie.

Here's what happens now.

You walk to your first mark and prepare yourself by recalling why you are in the movie, what your dramatic function is, what your scene is about, and what you need to do. You make the crew disappear and believe you are the waitress. Your job is to sell the story by selling the waitress, by pouring the coffee and delivering the line "Would you like cream with that?" You rev your engines. You are on the start line waiting for the green light. All the other actors will do the same thing.

You will hear someone, probably the first, call out for *finals*. What he means is *final touches*. While you stand there revving your engines, you will be suddenly surrounded by people touching you. No, not fans. They will be members of the crew doing final touches on your makeup, hair, and other elements so that your take is as perfect as it can be.

These are the folks who might be touching you.

Makeup.

Hair.

Wardrobe.

Sound. To make sure the mic they pinned on you is hidden.

Props. To make sure you have a fresh pot of coffee with exactly the same amount in it every time.

Focus puller. Won't be actually touching you, but might have a tape measure held up to your nose making sure you will be in focus.

Camera assistant. Again, not touching you, but potentially correcting the marks at your feet.

Production assistant. If you have been busy smoking one last cigarette or drinking a last gulp of water or frantically reviewing your script, then the *PA* will be there to take these things from you while you work.

Set decorator. Not touching but close by, making sure the coffee cup is in the right place for every take.

While you are being so touched, you may also be getting last-minute instructions or information.

The director might give you a last bit of encouragement or direction: "Remember, she's a good waitress. Have fun."

The camera operator might give you a bit of direction from his department: "If you could please remember to lean a bit to your right when you are at the counter so we can see your face? Thanks."

Johnny might have something to say about the scene that he neglected to say before. "I'm going to take a big pause before I sit down. Okay, baby?"

Roger that.

Part of your brain is recording all this info while at the same time ignoring the final touches while at the same time remembering what you are doing while at the same time believing you are the waitress while at the same time revving your engine while at the same time remaining calm.

Any second now they are going to *call the roll*, and you will be in the movies.

Rehearsing Again

Or maybe not.

Some directors like to rehearse again now, immediately before they shoot. But in my experience on about 30 movie sets, I have rarely seen rehearsals. And if they did call for one, then it was for a technical reason rather than to help the actors find their footing. Say there is a small fight in the middle of the scene. They might rehearse that just to refine the blocking so no one gets hurt and so the camera crew gets a chance to practice following it.

Again, save your big sloppy kisses and big acting guns for the take. I have heard many stories of actors who shot all their guns in the rehearsal and had nothing left for the take. You become so keyed up on a movie set that this is entirely possible and easier than you think. So in general, walk through it saving your big guns for the take. If Johnny, or the director, wants a full-on rehearsal, then do that, but guard your energy. That's your responsibility: to give your best when the cameras roll.

You might run into a perfectionist director who wants to rehearse it 90 times looking for *bits of gold*, as they say. Then *they* shoot it 90 times. Stanley Kubrick had this reputation. Enjoy—or grit your teeth—and do your best.

You wanted to be a film actor.

With rehearsals done, it's time for action.

Calling the Roll

You know: roll camera, sound, speed, all that stuff.

Calling the roll is what happens immediately before the director calls ACTION and you go to work. You don't need to know everything they're talking about during the call, but I think it helps. I think it pays to know everything that's going on and why. The call varies from place to place and crew to crew and sometimes even from day to day. Shooting is impossibly tiring and frustrating and sometimes a crew will change up the lingo just to have a little fun. But typically it goes like this.

> First AD:— "PICTURE IS UP!" I capitalize this and everything that follows because it is normally shouted across the whole set so there is no confusion about what's happening. In fact, others in the AD department will relay the shout to the farthest reaches of the circus so everyone knows. We are going for a *take*. "PICTURE IS UP."
>
> First AD:— "WAITING ON CAMERA." Sometimes the first AD likes to let everyone know what the holdup is and to encourage everyone to move it along. In this case, the camera crew needs another moment to make final adjustments.
>
> Camera Operator:— "READY."
>
> First AD:— "FIRST POSITIONS PLEASE." or "BACK TO ONES." That's for you. Get on your first mark and get revving.
>
> First AD:—"FINALS" (or touches or last looks or checks). Final touches if necessary.
>
> First AD:— "QUIET PLEASE." Sometimes people forget.
>
> First AD:— "READY?" Or sometimes, "IS ANYBODY NOT READY?"
>
> First AD:— "ROLL CAMERA." This is the instruction for the camera operator to turn the camera on.
>
> Camera operator:— "SPEED!" In the olden days, the camera took a few seconds to crank up to full operating speed, so the operator lets the AD know when he's ready.
>
> First AD:— "SOUND!" The camera is just shooting the pictures. The sound is recorded by another group of people who have gear of their own.
>
> Sound Mixer:— "SPEED." Same thing as the camera business. It means he's running and ready.
>
> Camera Operator:— "MARK IT." On this command, a camera assistant, usually the 2nd AC (or clapper/loader) will put the famous clapperboard, or slate, up in front of the camera and clap its little arms together. The slate identifies the movie, the director, the director of photography, the scene, the camera angle, and the take numbers so the editor knows what he's looking at later on. Scene one, Charlie (for C, as in third angle), take five. Again, there are different slating conventions in different areas, but this is the basic American style. The

clapping business is done so the editor can put the sound and the picture in sync with each other; he can see when the arms collide on the film and hear them collide on the sound track. All he has to do is line these up in the editing room and everything is in sync.

Clapper/Loader:— "SCENE 5, APPLE, TAKE ONE." He verbally identifies the take to eliminate confusion, then claps the sticks together, and then gets out of the way.

Camera Operator:— "FRAME." Usually, the camera operator has to reframe on the actors after shooting the slate, so he's telling everyone he has done that and is ready to go.

First AD or 2nd AD or director: —"BACKGROUND ACTION." This is not your cue. Repeat, this is not your cue to go. This is the cue to the background performers to start mingling and drinking coffee and looking at menus, because obviously they have to be going before you enter.

Director or sometimes first AD:— "ACTION" (or go or run it or let's begin). This is your cue. Start now, and don't stop until you hear:

Director:— "CUT."

You're done.

Warnings and More Encouragement

As we have seen, the traveling circus/army that is a film crew can handle virtually anything you can throw at them. Even your bad acting is no problem. The director has seen worse and has a million little tricks up his sleeve to help you improve your performance. If worse comes to worst, then they'll just cut around you or have another actress come in later and *dub* over your voice. In other words, she will rerecord all your lines in sync with your lips to improve your bad line delivery. It's a pain, but they'll do it. And it won't necessarily work against you. All actors have to start somewhere, everyone has a bad day now and then, and everyone has been dubbed once in their acting lives. It's part of paying your dues. And, especially when you're just starting out, it's not a problem. I wish I could drill this into your head.

In fact, you have seen movies in which the leading man was a ghastly actor. Terrible. But you still enjoyed the film and it still made money. Not that I want you to be crappy, but let that be a lesson to you.

I once worked on a TV movie with an elderly actor who couldn't remember his three lines. At all. But he was a pro who kept trying. He kept *picking up his lines,* he *kept calling for lines* (more on these in the chapter on Stopping on page 281), he kept checking his script between takes, he kept cool, he kept working, and he kept a happy heart. It took an hour to get those three lines, but guess what? Nobody had a problem with that. At all. I'm not suggesting to come to set unprepared; I'm suggesting there are few problems the crew can't deal with, provided you stay calm and confident and keep at it.

However, there are four problems the crew can't handle: being unprepared, ego, nerves, and stopping.

Being Unprepared

They can't really shoot if you don't know your lines. It's tough to make the movie that way.

An example: a Movie of the Week. I was playing a cop (again). The leading man was there, waiting with me. Everybody was waiting. Two hours later, the leading lady showed up saying, "Oh, I had the most wonderful sleep! I feel so good. What are we doing?" She didn't know the scene, didn't know her lines, and didn't even seem to know what planet she was on. We blocked the scene, and then we waited another hour and a half while she went to makeup and tried to learn her lines. There was nothing to be shot in the meantime; she was the whole day. I saw the director silently plotting her murder. The producers frantically tried to rescue the budget. The first AD hated his life and all actors. The rest of us sat around awkwardly. And nothing could be done about it except to wait. And maybe to suggest that she try sleeping on her own time.

Don't be her.

Read and apply this whole book and show up prepared. Do something to rescue the reputation of actors the world over. Help your career. Help the film. Be prepared. Or do us all a favor and quit.

Ego

That actress was just dumb. But she wasn't the much more terrifying incarnation of the actress: the egomaniac diva.

The egomaniac diva is a weak, terrified child with an armor-plated and completely fake image of herself who will let others die to preserve this fake image. She is not interested in the story, the production, the whole war on Mars, the director, her fellow actors, or the lives of others. She only wants desperately to avoid facing the truth. She is the worst kind of person and death to a movie.

She and the filmmakers have completely different and mutually exclusive goals, you see. Picture a supermodel on a soccer pitch. What's worse is that she insists on pretending to play soccer, she insists that everyone else pretend with her, she insists they make her look good, she insists they do all the soccer playing, and she insists they give her credit for scoring all the goals.

Things are not going to go well for the team.

Without a doubt, the egomaniac will be a shitty actress. She will be full of excuses. She will blame others. She will waste time. She will be impossible to talk to or direct. She will disparage and outrage the other actors. She will lord over the crew. She will be a general and constant pain in the ass. If confronted, then she will fly into a rage and disappear into her trailer. Then she will ask for more money. If 'she' happens to be a 'he,' add an overdose of testosterone to the mix and watch the fireworks.

The director and crew can do nothing except grin and bear it. Hope. Hate their jobs. Hate all actors. Die a little bit. Hope the problem leaves soon.

What you, the egoist, haven't realized is this: your days are numbered. Your future is grim. I'm looking for you even now.

Nerves

If you are nervous to the point of shaking, then there is nothing they can do for you. Nothing. Except hope that it doesn't get worse.

I was once directing a commercial for a big oil company. We had shut down a working service station for a day to shoot this spot. The man I cast as the station manager had done a terrific audition; he was calm, confident, and perfect for the part. Great. Cut to the day of the shoot. The whole crew is there ready to go. The station is shut down completely, costing the company bags of money. My actor arrives on time, but he's shaking and dry in the mouth. He asks for a little time. I'm more than happy to oblige him. We shoot some other stuff for an hour. Then we need him. No options. I call him and ask him how he's doing. He's even shakier and drier. I ask if there's anything I can do to help. He says: "I can't do this."

And he gets in his car and drives away.

Now *that's* an example of an actor problem that we cannot solve.

We are now screwed. Tens of thousands of dollars of crew and equipment and station-closing and no actor. And of course the client is staring knives at me. My career is threatened. I want that actor dead.

I don't care what you do or how you do it; just find a way to deal with your nerves. Go laugh your head off as I do. Hypnotize yourself. Practice yoga. Do zen. Remind yourself that there is no need to be nervous. Sing the *Galaxy Song* by Eric Idle of *Monty Python*. Some like to shake hands with every single person working on the film in any capacity and get to know them. Some do the opposite and want to float in and do their work without knowing anyone. Some like to stay in character at all times throughout the shoot. Some swear by acupuncture or auto-suggestion or ayurveda.

I find that auto-suggestion, or self-hypnosis, works wonders for me. But I've always been very suggestible as I found out at age 12 when a hypnotist—The Man They Call Raveen—came to town.

Poke around, experiment, and find out what works for you. Staying calm under pressure is at least half of what you get paid for. You must be completely relaxed to be able to access your imagination and do your work. Any amount of nerves and the camera will see it. You will infect people around you and it will spiral out of control.

For some—the very young and beautiful who don't know any better—it might be easy to remain calm and confident. For others, it seems a monumental challenge.

Because I am Merlin and I care, here's a short list of things to think about if you're nervous and floundering on the set. It's kind of a list of golf tips. Try them. See if they work for you.

Psst: they will also help your acting.

Golf Tips

TREAT IT AS A JOB

What did I do about the runaway actor?

I looked around the set at all the faces turned anxiously toward me, picked out a guy who looked like a station manager (because he happened to be one) and said, "How'd you like a job?" He shrugged, and said, "Sure, if you want." The money sounded good, and he was there anyway.

To make a long story short, he worked out great. Way better than the other guy would have been.

Why was he so great?

He didn't care about the 'acting.' He didn't understand the acting. He put no pressure on himself to perform or live up to any expectations, especially his own. He had none. He had no acting coach in his head judging him. He had no vain desire to be famous or important or loved. For him it was just a very well paid regular day, pumping gas, chatting with customers, and cleaning windows. Stuff he did all the time. All he had to do was wait around while we set things up and then ignore the camera. Nothing to it.

Then he got to pick up a big, fat paycheck.

Most of the BFSs I see on set? Same thing. They show up to work. No big deal. Today, they're pumping gas. Tomorrow they are suits. Next day they are soldiers. Whatever. They're just being themselves doing these different jobs. How much fun is that? If they feel awkward or fake about pumping gas, then they do what they call research. They hang around a pump jockey for a couple of hours, watch him work, and ask a few questions. Simple job-shadowing. Just training for the new job. When they feel confident, they go ahead and do the job, ignoring the fact that the camera is there. Then they pick up their big fat paychecks. Basically, that's it. If you can do that, then you can be a working actor. Add to that some basic film acting technique—like hitting your marks—and a clear understanding of story and script and the audience, some clever self-promotion and business development, and you too have a chance to be a working actor.

Throw in a little talent and sex appeal and you can watch your star rise.

By the way, my replacement station manager liked the work so much he went on to become a working actor in town. He never took it too seriously—he actually kind of laughed at how easy it all was—and just did his work and collected his pay like anyone else. He just happened to do it where the camera could see him.

I admit that my station manager had a little help on this occasion. He was working in his actual environment, the gas station. He wasn't asked to imagine the gas station or imagine bullets zipping over his head on Omaha Beach. He did his regular job in his regular workplace. And when doing that, it's easy to tune out your surroundings. He tuned out the surroundings all the time in real life. He became so focused on his job that he didn't hear the traffic and the sirens, and he didn't notice the security camera that watched his every move. So he found it easy to lump our camera into that group of things he would normally ignore. He had no time to pay attention to such things. He had stuff to do, a job to do.

That, right there, is the basic skill of the movie actor, and it's the best way on Earth to control your nerves. You have a job to do. The job is urgent and fascinating. There is no one watching. There is no reason to be nervous.

Be the Guy

As previously mentioned, Hollywood doesn't really want actors. It wants the *guy* from the story to walk in the door, being the *guy*, saying what the *guy* says, doing what the *guy* does, willing and able to do it for the camera at a later date.

Do that.

How?

That's why you're an actor. You are able to disregard everything life has told you about who you are and choose instead to have a different present moment. You free yourself from all your conditioned reactions. You become liberated and free to choose. You understand that the past isn't the present. The past is like the wake of a ship—as philosopher Alan Watts was fond of saying—that shows where the ship has been but does not drive the ship and has no power over where the ship will go the future. It can be disregarded. New choices can be made in every moment. You know that.

An entirely new past can even be chosen—that of the guy—and used to inform the choices of the present. Therefore you must know the guy. Therefore you must study the script like hell and use your imagination like even more hell. Knowing the past of the guy and choosing that past, you become the guy in the present.

Simple.

Tell the Truth—I mean Lie

Having chosen that new past, you commit to it totally so that you become it, and therefore you are only able to tell the truth of it. Everything you say, every move you make, is the truth. Totally honest. Just based on an imaginary past. So, kind of like lying. But you're being absolutely honest about it. Except that you still know in the back of your mind that you are an actor who must hit marks in an imaginary circumstance. So, that's sort of like lying again. But you're doing that to tell the truth. I mean, you are not the Prince of Denmark. Clearly. You are only acting like the Prince. So in that regard you are lying. But to make the audience believe you are the Prince—and they deeply want to—you must believe you are the Prince and honestly communicate that in every possible way. So, you're telling the truth. Strict, absolute honesty. And the more you can fake that, the better.

Make it Real

If you are struggling with being the guy, then the least you can do is be yourself.

Struggling actors tend to 'act,' or resort to a cliché of some kind, or lie unconvincingly, or tell the truth unconvincingly, or flop right out of the scene. Please don't do any of that. Look for the truth of the situation, the real human behavior. It's likely you have been in a situation similar to your character's. Remember it. And do it. As you. Do it as you would do it in that same situation. Try to accomplish the goal in your own way. Be you. Rely on your own history, your brand, and your own personal instincts. Oh, and the writer. And the director. And the editor. Okay? Go with your own reality, and let the audience apply the character in their minds.

Now is Good

No matter what you do, you have to get into the present.

If you look around you right this second, then you will see and hear dozens of things you didn't even know were there, including, probably, a camera. You tuned them out because you were so interested in the job at hand: reading this book and becoming a BFS. You let the job consume you to the exclusion of those distractions. The next time you are hired to play a girl reading a book in a café, you'll know what to do: exactly what you're doing now. You just lump the camera crew in with those dozens of ignored things and get on with the job at hand. If the waitress happens to come over, same thing. Just let that be part of your job for the moment, order your muffin, and go back to the book.

Easy, isn't it?

If that isn't easy, it's because you are overly focused on something more important to you, like whether or not you look good, whether or not you're are doing things 'right,' or will get approval or love or whatever else. These are all vain and selfish pursuits that have no place in your working life as a generous actor trying to help tell a story to a paying audience. Give up these pursuits and get on with eating your muffin, or stabbing your boyfriend, or robbing a bank. Whatever the story calls for.

You've heard of actors having 'presence.' This is it. They are perfectly present, doing what they're doing. They're not worried about what they did yesterday or how they're going to be received tomorrow. So focus. Be present. Accomplish your goal. Now is all you ever have anyway, so love it and remain with it.

Talk to Yourself, I mean the Other Guy

This is a little trick I use in my classes all the time. If an actor is struggling, then I'll just say, "Talk to yourself, please."

"What?"

"Just do the scene to yourself."

Usually, he wrinkles his brow skeptically. Then he tries it. And then the scene starts to work because he is no longer trying to push it on anybody. Obviously trying to push the scene revolts the camera. Living the scene on your own terms lures the camera in. It gives the scene the unwatched quality that marks all good film acting.

The danger is in disconnecting from the other people and things in the scene. Once the actor is really connecting with himself and living the scene on his own terms—looking for his own approval and nobody else's— I encourage him to also connect just as strongly with his scene partner.

Bada-boom. Bada-bing.

That deep connectedness, going in both directions at once, is perfect film acting, and it's dazzling to watch.

Keep your Eyes Open

I use this one all the time. If I focus on the technical requirements of film acting, then I quit worrying.

Two examples:

As I mentioned, I love directors who give me a lot of blocking and business to do in a scene. The part of my brain normally reserved for self-judgment is busy trying to pick up the umbrella, freeing the creative side to do the scene. Try it for yourself. If the director is not playing along, then give yourself a list of tasks to do and watch your nerves diminish and your performance rise.

I mentioned before that you must cultivate the skill of keeping your eyes open at all times while on camera. It makes you powerful and mesmerizing. I also asked you to speak slowly so that the audience can relax into the story without having to work too hard, and so you sound powerful and mesmerizing. If all else fails, then I simply focus on these two things with all my might. Again, this shuts up the judgmental brain and lets me get on with the work.

You Can't Win 'Em All

I will now relate my Elvis story.

I was once hired to be the singer in a pretty famous Off-Broadway show in my hometown. I had never sung before in public, but the director knew I could sing and wanted me in the show. I am grateful to her to this day, because otherwise I'd still be singing for my shampoo bottle. But at the time I was so nervous I could barely walk. I spent the next six weeks drinking gallons of beer and singing in karaoke bars, trying not to die. I didn't make as much headway as I had hoped for. Rehearsals began. The girl singer was nice and affirming, and we worked out some nice arrangements of the big opening song. But because of poor planning or a low budget, we never had a rehearsal microphone and sound system. See, this was a live, interactive show, and I was supposed to be a schmaltzy wedding singer at an actual wedding. As it turned out, I didn't get the mic and sound system until opening night. If you're a singer, then you know that singing on a mic is a tricky bit of business. You need to know what you're doing. It's also completely terrifying if you've never really done it before. You make a little noise and hear it booming all over the room. So here I am, opening night, having never sung in a show before, having never used a mic before outside of a karaoke bar, and I have to open the show with a big song, a ballad, in Italian, for a crowd of people at the Italian Club!

A million on the stress scale.

Lucky for me, I mentioned Elvis in the dressing room. I don't remember exactly what I said, but it was probably something like, "I wonder if Elvis got this nervous?"

One of the young actresses in the room said, and I quote: "Elvis. Yech."

Shocked me.

I was a big Elvis fan. How could anybody not like the King?

Thinking about it, I eventually had to admit there were people—even women!—who didn't like Elvis. Obviously so. Now, Elvis was handsome, talented, sexy, the King of rock and roll, one of the richest and most famous individuals to ever have lived on Earth, the cream of the crop, the top of the heap, and this young thing turned up her nose at him. Some women don't really care for Brad Pitt. Some men don't care for Angelina.

Hmmm.

What a relief.

Stupid, but what a relief.

Because what I realized was this: you could be the best singer or actor in the world, have all that other stuff, and some people aren't going to like you. You can't win them all, no matter what you do, no matter who you are. Some people just aren't going to like your song. You're only going to have a certain fan base, and only if you quit thinking about yourself and focus on the job. Give it your all, and let others judge whether they like it or not. Let it go.

If Elvis only had, say, 80 percent of my Italian audience, then I figured I'd be lucky to get 40 percent of them. And even if I sucked badly, I'd probably still win over some of them. My actual thinking that night wasn't as coherent as this, but just knowing that *for sure* some people weren't going to like me and my song, and *for sure* some of them would, diminished my anxiety.

I was definitely going to fail.

And I was definitely going to succeed.

Both.

Always.

Simple as that. No need to worry about it. I went out there and gave it everything I had and made myself proud. Most of the crowd liked it. The rest never would. What a relief.

Yes, there are better singers than me, but I was the singer that night, I had the guts to get up and do it, and I had the common sense not to make it all about me. I gave them the song that opened the show as best as I could. And that's what you, dear actor, need to do too, by realizing you can't win them all. You are going to win and lose every time, and there's nothing you can do about it.

So get busy winning the ones you can by giving them what they want and paid for, not your vanity and self-doubt.

Imagine

What about the whole bullets-flying-over-your-head scene? How do you accomplish that while making the world go away?

Use the magic *what if?* "What if I were a soldier in battle? What would that be like? How would it feel? How would I react?" Use your imagination to visualize the scene as intensely as possible, and then just let your body act it out.

If you want to see the 'what if' in action, watch a kid playing with soldiers. What do you notice? The rest of the 'real world' doesn't exist for him. He has tuned it out to focus on the vital business at hand. Next, you will notice no trace of ego involvement—he's not doing it to look good or be important. Third, you will notice that he freely travels the landscape of his imagination, inventing that which he has no direct experience of, and believing in it totally. Fourth, you will notice that his body freely and automatically acts out the events of his imaginings without him consciously trying to be an 'actor.' And fifth, you will notice that he's having a hell of a good time.

Do that.

Give Up

This is a powerful golf/acting tip.

Just let go of everything and float off with the current. Don't try to control anything. Don't try to do anything. Just let go. Give it up. Let the cookie crumble.

Works for me all the time, and it will for you too, provided you do all the technical work first. You can't just pick up a saxophone having never seen one before, let go, and expect to play. You have to do the work first. Then you let yourself go.

Remember that all bad acting has one thing in common: the actor is watching himself, trying to control the scene, and trying to force it on us. As a former tennis pro, I can tell you that watching yourself and trying to control your swing are death to your game. You have to let go. It's like splashing around in the water trying to save yourself. You're likely to drown that way. But if you let go, then you'll notice the water holds you up and you can float there as long as you want.

In acting, it means giving up the illusion that you are in control of everything, dropping your vanity, and having the courage to rely on your work and your talent to face the unknown. Not only is this courage universally admired, but also it is fabulous to watch on screen.

Another singing example: I was lucky enough to see Frank Sinatra in concert way back in the '80s. Frank was the original teen idol, an Oscar winner, and for my money the best pop singer of all time. Here's why: for the first few bars of a song you would hear his great voice, and then something magical happened. You stopped hearing his voice. It disappeared. The voice vanished and was replaced by something better: the story. You'd fall into the story of the song, mesmerized, discovering it, and feeling it along with Frank. The worst singers are the ones who force you to listen to their voices. Boring and vain. The best singers have the courage to make their voices disappear in favor of the tale they are telling. They have the guts to let themselves go into the story and to bring you along with them. The great actors do the same thing.

Show Off

This is another great technique you used as a kid. "Look Mom!" Once everybody was watching, you went off the high diving board grinning from ear to ear. What a thrill it was. Remember? Showing off what you could do. Getting the applause. Wanting to do it again. I remember that no matter how good I was on my own, I was always better with people watching. I rose to the occasion. So did you.

Just access that feeling again—you're an actor, right?—and show them how good you can play the queen or the gambler or the ghost. Soak up that limelight. Ask if you can do it again.

Do Bradley

Students are always asking me, "Yes, but how do you appear to be someone else? How do you create a character?" First of all, the character has already been created by the writer. You don't have to create anything; you just have to embody it. Literally, be the body that does the actions and says the lines. "Make the *word* flesh," said Peter O'Toole. And remember there is no single right way to do that, provided you understand the story and what the character is after.

For example: I recently saw Christopher Plummer playing Caesar on stage. When you think of the cliché of Caesar, you think of a man who is powerful and commanding and fierce and self-indulgent and impossibly cruel. Plummer didn't do any of that. He was garrulous, and fatherly, and funny, and charming, and just plain cool. Did it work? Of course it worked. It was magnificent. The counterpoint—the king of the civilized world as a cool dude—was a fascinating way to give the story a depth and complexity it wouldn't otherwise have had. There have been countless Romeos and no two the same. Every single one is valid.

Back to Bradley and how to appear to be someone else. You do this all the time. You have been in a bar, or at the dinner table, or in the cafeteria at school, where you said something like this: "Did you see Bradley in the cafeteria yesterday? Incredible! He was all like …" And then you did your impersonation of Bradley. Your voice changed, your cadence and mannerisms became just like Bradley's, and you even thought like Bradley. In a very real sense, you became Bradley for those moments.

Recognizing Bradley, everyone watching laughed uproariously.

You just did a brilliant 'character.' I put that in quotes because you are still very clearly you, but you allowed yourself to channel Bradley's mannerisms for a few moments by visualizing him in that comical situation and letting your body act it out. Your visualization was a kind of program you fed into your hard drive; your body then ran the program.

You do this all the time, not just in the cafeteria. If you walk into a fancy restaurant and see everyone acting in certain way, then you will tend to imitate them. You can learn complex skills, such as a tennis serve, just by watching somebody else do it. It's how you learned to talk. It's basic to humans.

To play Captain Hook in *Hook*, Dustin Hoffman said he based the character on three different people. He imitated all three at once, and voila, the Captain came to life.

Anthony Hopkins used reptiles when coming up with Hannibal Lecter.

Do that.

If it makes you feel better, or more like an actor, then imitate another actor. Just do it like Marlon Brando or George Clooney. This will help you access that skill and get you going in the right direction.

Explore

Whenever I get a bit lost in my acting and start thinking or worrying too much, I remind myself to explore the scene. It's closely related to letting go, but it is more active and brings a greater sense of urgency to a scene.

Bad actors are obviously acting. They are 'performing' the scene. It doesn't look real. It looks self-conscious, carefully rehearsed, and stiffly delivered. We don't see a person in a situation; we see an actor doing a scene for an audience.

I don't know about you but bad acting makes me mad. It offends me. One of the worst feelings I have in life is when the curtain opens and bad acting begins. It's like getting seasick. I know there are two excruciating hours ahead, and there is nothing I can do. I'm trapped in my seat being abused by the 'actors.' I hate it.

Especially because it's so easy *not* to do.

The basic reason is the same in all cases: the actor is aware of what he's going to do next. His mind is out in front of the scene, watching it, judging it, and controlling it. He's reciting the scene instead of living the scene.

The cure is simple if you have the courage to do it. Just get your mind behind the scene. You've heard a million times that great acting is reacting. This is how you do it. Let the scene happen, just let it happen without guiding it or controlling it or fearing it. Just watch it happening; explore it, wonder about it, and see what it makes you want to do next, second by second. If you've studied the story and know what's going on, then your actions will just happen, and your lines will just fall out of your mouth. When you get really good at it, they tumble out before you have a chance to stop them. You will actually be trying very hard not to say anything. The lines force their way out, organically. They just happen, like the rest of the scene, and become part of your exploration. "Holy cow, I can't believe I just said that. Now what's going to happen?"

This state of exploration is also closely linked to *making the world go away* because you get intensely focused on what's happening, it's wonderfully dangerous and thrilling, and you don't have enough brain power to pay attention to anything else. Your reactions are pure and new. You become that person in that situation. It's very interesting to do. It's completely compelling to watch. And it wins Oscars.

Throughout the rest of your career, I'm begging you, stop performing and start exploring.

Just Do It

Nobody cares what you're thinking or feeling. The audience doesn't care. They only care about what *they* think and feel. The only way you can communicate with them is through actions. By doing things. By acting, but not 'acting.' Get it? They cannot see what you feel; they can only see what you do. So if you are stuck or lost or scared, then just do the scene. Recall this point from the section called That you can Act for the Camera on page 48: a technically correct scene can be 90 percent of a perfect scene. Just do it without any planning, judging, controlling, or acting—act without 'acting'—and the audience will love you.

Why? 'Cause you're being. You are being the guy. That's all that's necessary, and it's one of the hardest lessons to learn.

An example: I once asked a famous actor about one of his famous roles. How did he make the character so creepy? What he said was basically this: "I was scared out of my mind through the whole thing. Terrified. No idea what I was doing. I just did the lines, did the scenes, hoping not to get fired."

You see? To him, it was terror. To you, it was spooky CIA guy. But only because he had the courage to just get on with it.

Make it Sexy

There are teachers in LA that use this as their basic technique. "I don't care if you're playing the janitor, make it sexy!"

Why? Because sexy is the opposite of nervous. Sexy is confident, and open, and free, and loose, and charming, and present, and juicy, and interesting, and alive, and attractive, and powerful. Sexy is alpha dog territory. Dominant. Free to explore the scene. Careless of consequences.

Sexy is also the best way to define your brand, because your kind of sexy is totally different from everybody else's kind.

Sexy also happens to be the best way on Earth to rope in an audience. Everybody, and I mean *everybody*, loves to look at a sexy person. It's fabulous and contagious and life-giving. And there's nothing, and I mean *nothing*, that people like to feel more than sexy.

If there's one thing on Earth that all the BFSs have in common it's this: they're sexy. They light up the room or the screen with it. Everybody wants to share in it. You yourself have a list of movie stars you'd cheat on your spouse with if given the chance.

Yes, it's probably pretty easy to feel sexy all the time when you are a mega-rich BFS. The trick is to do it now. Forget acting school. Start doing sexy school.

Live It

Why wait around to get hired? Why not start being a Big Fat Star right now? In other words, make your life one long movie performance. Make everything you do dramatic and urgent and sexy whether there's a camera around or not. Thus you are always practicing. Thus you are always ready when the cameras roll. Thus everyone around you will recognize your star quality and open doors.

Train

Or maybe don't.

Or do.

Okay, go to school if you want. Practice and good training isn't going to hurt.

Bad training?

Hurts.

So be careful here.

There are sadly a lot of 'coaches' out there who fall into the failed-actor category, the bitter-actor category, the just-trying-to-make-a-buck category, or the total-rip-off category. Any one of these can damage you quite seriously if you're not careful.

I once had a student come to the first night of class shaking like a leaf. I asked her what was wrong. She said that her last coach told her she was too short, too old, too ugly, too untalented, and too worthless ever to be an actor and she had no business trying. When I asked her when this happened she said, "20 years ago."

Wow.

This woman had been savagely brutalized by a bitter-actor and had lost two decades of her acting life because of it. Shameful. Of course she wasn't terrible and all those other things. She was in fact wonderful, with a face the camera loved; and I got her working again. More than likely her 'teacher' was in the same age group and wanted to trim down the competition by destroying this woman's confidence. Sadly, this kind of thing happens all the time all over the world. Others will soak you for money and teach you nothing. Others are just trying to pick up chicks. Others are egoists who want to feel important. They will pontificate and claim to be the holy font of knowledge. It's usually best to tell all these people to go get stuffed.

If you find one who wants to, "break you down to build you up again," then tell him to go get stuffed as well and find a coach who will be affirming and supportive. We all know the business of acting can be downright dirty and full of rejection, but that's the business. The acting needs to come from confidence and affirmation. I've never seen shouting and emotional violence make anyone better, so don't let anyone do it to you. Especially in the name of acting, which is first of all an art, and second of all a talent we are each born with. Imagine shouting at Picasso to make him paint better. Ridiculous.

What we need is a safe place to learn the craft and to access our inborn abilities, and we need a carefully measured push now and then when we're ready for it.

Good acting teachers are like good parents. They don't make up ridiculous rules. They don't punish you for ridiculous reasons. They don't hurt you "like they've been hurt." They don't try to live through you. They don't use you for their own gratification. They don't shame you to get even with the world. They don't try to make you into little clones of themselves. They don't force you to go to law school when you really want to go to art school.

They see who you are, accept and love you, and then help you become the best you you can be. They illuminate the path. They help you find your obstacles and then invite you to jump over them. They are forgiving. They are knowledgeable. They are disciplined. They teach you the craft while at the same time inviting you to do things your own way, expand the craft, or even break the rules altogether. They are affirming. If they're tough on you, then it's because they know that's what you need at that moment. They know they can't get a bird to fly by beating it over the head. Above all, they have a good eye. They know good work when they see it. They point it out for you. They try to make you independent of them, not dependent on them. When you blossom, they applaud. And they don't take credit for you.

Seek out these coaches. Be careful. Ask around. Sit in on a class. If they won't let you, then go elsewhere. Interview them. Find out if they've ever worked as an actor before. Watch their work. Get a feel for them. There are wonderful, generous, teachers out there who genuinely want to help, love teaching, and can help you grow.

You will occasionally even find actual movie stars teaching classes because they love it so much, and they want to share their knowledge, be around it, and keep their chops up. Jason Alexander from *Seinfeld* did—and maybe still does—master classes in LA. (Teaching is a great way to learn. I often hear myself say things in class that are news to even me.) So, if you can find a home base like this—a class, a theater company, a comedy troupe—then it can be as helpful as the other kind is harmful.

So, train, practice, and grow as much as you can. The good actors really work at it, whereas far too many actors take a couple classes and then sit around for months and years waiting for the phone to ring. If you love acting and want it as a career, then you should be working on it all the time, every day, like a singer or an athlete. Then, when the opportunity arises, you'll be ready and confident, and your nerves won't get the best of you.

Find Your Own Way

This is the ultimate goal. You're the expert.

Example: Jack Nicolson. Do you think anybody tells him how to play a scene?

You hire him, and you get out of his way.

And then you say thank you.

And then you pay him.

He knows the biz and what works best for him in all situations.

Do that.

I use sports analogies a lot because I think they are instructive. Here's another example: kung fu. There are many different styles: flowing styles, tricky styles, and aggressive styles. There is even a drunken style. As a practitioner, you need to find the one that suits your ability, your body, and your nature. One style or method does not fit all.

I think something similar applies in acting. Spend time finding and honing your particular style of acting kung fu. Don't let anyone try to make you a tiger when you know you're a white crane. Do this by studying the actors you deeply relate to; they'll probably have the same basic nature as you. Watch and learn. Modify. Mix with your sell. Make it your own.

Somebody should open the Beverly Hills Academy of Drunken Acting.

Insert your own joke here.

Anyway. You know what I mean.

Add to these suggestions anything else that works for you personally.

I know it was more than a few pages ago, but we were talking about the four sins on a film set, the four things you should never do. So far, we have only covered three. The fourth is stopping.

Stopping

As I mentioned, don't ever stop a scene in the audition room. There are a million reasons why not to, but simply put, you're shooting yourself in the foot. You can expect your headshot and resume to wind up underneath tomorrow's coffee grinds.

But what about stopping a scene on the set?

Worse.

Here are a handful of reasons for you.

Pros Do Not Stop

One of the hallmarks of professional film actors is that they don't stop. They keep going, no matter what, knowing that that is their job. They work between action and cut. That's the job. Once you hear action you act, and you keep acting, no matter what, until you hear cut. Got it? I don't care if you forget the lines; keep going. I don't care that you tripped over the carpet; keep going. I worked with an actress who broke her leg in a chase scene. Actually broke her leg. Guess what she did? Lying there, she finished the scene, then calmly said, "Guys, I broke my leg."

Another example: *Hell On Wheels*. I'm shooting bullets at the leading man as he gallops by. I run along the boardwalk to get a better shot. I trip. I stumble into the street, arms flailing, trying not to fall. I fall, on my face, in the mud. What do I do? I get up. I look around for the guy on the horse hoping he hasn't circled back on me when I was on the ground. I point my gun, I tell the guys in the saloon to get back inside and climb back on the boardwalk. I keep going, like a real cowboy would in this circumstance. Eventually, I hear "Cut!" I'm a bit embarrassed but I don't apologize. I grin and bear it. It's my job. The director embraces me and thanks me. The other actors pat me on the back.

That's how you do it.

Once you are a BFS, go ahead and stop all you want and talk things over with Marty, the director. Have at it. That will be your hard-won right as a BFS—to make a mess of everything and impose on everyone for your own sake. Maybe you have a legitimate reason to stop, which will result in an infinitely better movie. Whatever. You are a BFS and can get away with it if you want. All the best to you. I just don't recommend it to anyone else because I have never seen an actual BFS actually stop on an actual set. (Yes, there are several ways to not stop—coming up presently.)

First, here are more reasons you should never stop.

Directors Call Cut

Not actors.

That is their power and authority and right. Not yours or anyone else's for that matter. I was once waiting on my mark for the start of a complicated shot. The shot started. I headed outside. Someone called "cut." I stopped. It was not the director but the camera operator. He had failed to get the framing the director had asked for, so he called "cut." The whole place went quiet. I heard him say, "I missed the frame." I heard the director say, "It was a better frame." Then the director took him aside for a little chat. The camera operator came back white as a ghost, and needless to say, he never called cut ever again while I was there.

It Takes Time

We are on a schedule. We need to make our day. Every time you stop, we have to reset everything from the top. Maybe it takes ten minutes or maybe it takes ten hours. We cannot afford it. We are scheduled down to the minute. We have obligations. Please help us make our day.

It Costs Money

Say you are one of the guys in a battle scene in a giant war movie, and the camera has followed you from the boat up to the beach where the Nazis are pounding you with hell-fire, and you forget your lines and call cut. Just imagine. Think about it for a second. Everything stops. The scene can't continue with you standing there, looking at the camera shouting "Can we stop?" So, it all stops. And we have to reset the shot. For you.

It will take 14 hours.

It will cost $750,000.

Thanks a lot.

Next time, if you've forgotten to say: "We're outnumbered!" maybe you could just say "There's too many of them!" And just keep going. That would be good.

There is Such a Thing as Editing

See, if you went ahead and just said, "There's too many of them," then we could just cut it out. We keep going, we get the rest of the shot with the planes and the bombs and the flame throwers, and we save 14 hours and $750,000, and we replace your bad line with one of your good ones from an earlier take. If we didn't do an earlier take, then we can just do a *pick up*, meaning, we'll just shoot a close up of you delivering the right line and cut that in later. Boom. Everybody's happy.

Which *they* won't be if you stopped.

The Other Actors Will Kill You

"Who do you think you are stopping my great performance? I ought to kill you. I think I will."

It's not all about you, remember? There are other people fighting their way up the beach, other people with lines, parts, talent, hearts, and fists. The camera may not even be on you! It might be on the other guys. And then you stop? Death to you. What the camera is shooting is not your freaking job, okay? Neither is calling cut or asking to stop. Support your fellow actors, and do your job the best you can between action and cut. That's your job.

You're Going to Suck Even More

As with the audition, so it goes on the set. If you stop, then you curse yourself. When you start up again, half your mind will be on the fact that you stopped and on trying to remember your lines so you don't stop again, which inevitably means you stop again. You won't have enough brain. Then what happens is terrible to see. You start to melt down like the Wicked Witch of the West. Your confidence spirals down the drain, and you are sunk. No way to get you back. And we're all screwed.

So, don't stop.

How Not to Stop

There are four ways not to stop. Pro actors do these four things all the time. Why don't you do them too?

Pick up your lines

When you forget your lines, just pause, stay in the scene, go back a couple of spots, er … just go back a couple lines to some place where you were going good, and pick it up from there. Get it? Just overlap your bad lines with the good ones. Repeat yourself. Back up a few lines, or a paragraph if you want, start again, and keep going to the end of the scene. You don't stop. You don't freak out. You stay in character and in the scene, you just back up a few lines and pick it up from there. Two seconds of editing and your little boo-boo vanishes. You will see actual pros on actual sets doing this constantly. They are professionals. Professionals forget their lines all the time. They just pick them up. Hopefully, one day, you will join their ranks.

Similarly, a director might talk to you during the scene. As you are doing the scene and the scene is being shot, he will direct you, saying "Now go for the gun" or "This is where you hear the scream" or "Hold the card up higher so we can see it. Pick it up."

And when he says "pick it up" he does not mean pick up the card or pick up the pace. He means pick up your lines: back up a little bit and repeat the last part that didn't go well. The director is aware of a thing called editing, you see. He knows that with a little snip his voice can be removed. If only you would join him in the awareness of editing and learn to pick up your lines. That would be good.

Call For a Line

What if you forget your lines completely?

Stop?

If you want to die by lethal injection, then yes.

If you want to live to see another acting day, then stay in the scene and call for a line. You do know what I mean by staying in the scene, don't you? I mean you stay connected with your scene partner, hold onto that reality, continue with your desire to reach your goal, whatever it is, and keep playing the scene. You just don't happen to know what to say at the moment. In that quiet space where you wonder what to say, you simply ask in a quiet voice: "Line?" From inside the scene, you're letting the crew know you've forgotten your lines. In about two seconds, you will hear the voice of the script supervisor from the back of the room reading the line for you: "I know you have been unfaithful. But, darling, I still love you."

Thus reminded, you proceed with the scene.

Because this one is a rather important line, you may also at this time wish to back up a few lines to get a running start at it. So, in this case, you would have both called for a line and picked up your lines. Get it?

You keep playing the scene. You just don't happen to know what to say at the moment. As you keep playing the scene not knowing what to say, you call out in a small voice: "Line?" I'm repeating myself so you understand. You do not stop, roll your eyes, judge yourself, swear, apologize, and ask for your line. That is what you do not do. Your job is to work between action and cut no matter what. Okay? Play the scene. Stand there for 20 minutes, as the character, trying to find your way back into the scene, back to your lines. Whatever it takes. Just do not stop or drop out of the scene, until you hear "cut."

Do not worry that this makes you somehow bad or wrong or lame or amateur. Actors, all actors, forget their lines. Boys do it, girls do it, and stars in all acting worlds do it. You can do it, too. What matters— as in life—is not what happens but how you deal with what happens.

Say "Okay." Let me know you understand this.

Another example. A friend booked a funny commercial. She was playing an airline agent at the airport, checking somebody's bags. They gave her the two or three funny things they wanted her to say and do, and they started the shot. She did them but she had to call for a line. They tossed it in. She continued seamlessly to the end. She did not hear "cut" so she kept going, making up funny bits and funny lines of her own. It went on. And on. And on. For what felt like eternity, she kept going, struggling to find the next new funny bit. Eventually, the cut came. The crew burst out in laughter. The director hugged her deeply and thanked her from the bottom of his heart. He thanked her for being a pro. He thanked her for making his job easier. He thanked her for saving time and money. He thanked her for making him look good to his clients. He thanked her for making the scene funnier than it was going to be. He thanked her for the very awkward, very real, very un-acted, very funny stuff she invented. He thanked her for inspiring the other actors to be better. He thanked her for entertaining the crew and lightening the mood.

Get it? Not only did she call for a line, she did the third thing you do when you don't hear "cut." You make it up.

Make It Up

If all else fails, then just get on with the scene as best you can. Make it up. If you have done all the homework mentioned thus far, then this should be no problem. You get the story, you know why you are in the story, you know your dramatic function, you know where the scene basically starts and ends, what you're trying to accomplish, where you are, and so on. Just make it up and try to either get to the end or find your way back into the scene as written. Continue until "cut." This is particularly useful when you are doing a scene inside a car, for example, where no one on the outside can hear you call for a line or when something unplanned interrupts the scene, as in the *Mystic River* story. I am relating this story second-hand so I'm not sure it is exactly true. But that doesn't matter. Act as if it was.

Kevin Bacon, Sean Penn, and Laura Linney sit at a table talking about Sean's character's time in jail. Sean is wildly upset about the questions and why the cops aren't doing their job. He pounds the table, spilling the coffee. A bad actor would stumble and fall and call out "Can we stop? I spilled the coffee." To which most directors would say something like, "Goddammit."

A director would have no choice but to stop. You see? You have insulted him and his vision and his authority. You have made yourself the director. This is not your job. Your job is to play the scene between action and cut no matter what. I'm not suggesting you should risk your life for the scene, but you should have that kind of attitude. The show must go on. So you spilled the coffee. So what? People spill coffee all the time. You, your character, just spilled the coffee like real people do all the time. Real people don't say: "Can we stop?" Why should you?

Obviously, as we have already discussed, you think you are not doing it 'right.' Which is wrong. Real people do not stop after spilling the coffee. They have no choice but to go on. So they get on with it. They clean up and resume the discussion, which is what Kevin and Sean and Laura did. They cleaned up, they resumed, they found their way back into the dialogue as written and finished the scene. And guess what? That's the scene that's in the movie.

This kind of thing happens all the time. Why? Because when you start fumbling, you get very real and very present. You get fascinating. You get the unwatched quality that marks all good acting.

Look at your script

If you are in an audition situation, then you can use any of the above techniques or you can just look at the script in your hand as described in the audition section.

Okay, you've done it. You got through one whole shot on set without dying of a stroke. You stayed calm, you rolled with the punches, you met Johnny and did a scene with Johnny, and you even picked up your lines at one point like a real pro. You kept going until the director called "cut."

Now what?

First of all, you're not going to get any applause. Just forget about that. Your fellow actor might say something like, "Good one." But that, too, is rare. Instead, you are probably going to hear one of three things: *going again*, *circle that one*, or *moving on*.

Going Again

This means that for some reason *they* didn't get it on that one. Either the director wants you to take another crack at it, or the camera operator screwed up, or somebody's chair creaked during the take, or whatever. Do not take it personally. Just get ready to do it again. Probably 80 percent of the time it's a technical problem of some kind. Even if it's an acting problem, it's usually a technical acting problem, as in: "Could you hit your marks?" or "Could you not step on Johnny's line?"

or "Could you not look at Johnny until you say the word cream?" If it is a performance problem, then the director will usually whisper it in your ear: "I think you can do more with that line," or "This is the point in the movie where we see that you love her even though you're firing her." Usually, that's about it. Do your best to give him what he asked for. In most cases, one or two more takes should do it. Sometimes you go for 20. Don't take it personally, just do it. There are countless reasons why a director may want this many takes, and most of them are not about you. There are technical reasons, budget reasons, schedule reasons, political reasons, story reasons, personal reasons, mood reasons, and pacing reasons.

An example: pacing. It's not always clear how fast your scene should happen. Suppose it is in the middle of an action sequence. Everything around your scene is happening fast, and then you come on screen happening slowly. No good. So the director may shoot your scene four or five times to have pacing options in the editing room. He may ask you to go faster or slower. He may not. He may have asked the camera to dolly faster with each take making it visually faster while your performance remains the same. None of this is your damn business. Don't expect him to explain. Don't take it personally. Do the work. He's trying to help you and the movie, and you, in turn, need to help him.

Circle That One

Or sometimes: "Check the gate." Or both.

This means they like the take. *Circle that one* means that the script supervisor is literally going to circle the take in her notes, letting the editor know it's a good one. It speeds up editing.

The *gate* they're going to *check* is inside the camera. Film cameras work by stopping the film 24 times per second behind the lens so that each frame can be clearly exposed to the light emanating off your lovely face. That mechanism is called the gate. They open the camera and have a look to make sure the film is okay, not scratched or otherwise damaged, and that they got the shot.

If the gate is good, and all the right notes are circled, and they don't need to go again, then you will hear *"moving on."*

Moving On

This means moving on to the next thing, whatever that happens to be. Could be your close up or the scene where Johnny shoots Big Pauly. Whatever is next on the AD's list is what's next.

But, most likely, it will be *coverage*.

Coverage

We talked about what major sins you need to avoid. The director's major sin is not getting enough *coverage*, meaning not shooting enough of the scene from enough angles so they can be edited together. With enough coverage and a good editor, all manner of other sins can be erased. An editor can speed up the scene, for example, or slow it down. He can create just the right dramatic pacing to suit the story or even the music they have. He can *build a performance*, meaning he can mix and match just your good moments from all 25 takes so the final performance is actually substantially better than you were on the day. He can search through all the footage of you when you weren't even acting—maybe you were waiting for the take to start—to find authentic little reaction shots. He can completely reconstruct the scene in a different way based on some brainwave the director had after the fact.

And he has *insurance*.

Suppose, in editing, the director says, "Jeez, it would be great if we had more of Johnny walking through the restaurant." Well, if he shot enough coverage—in this case, a number of different angles of Johnny walking and patrons reacting to him walk for example—the editor might be able to give him what he wants. But only if there's coverage.

The standard way to get this coverage is to first shoot a *master shot*. This will usually be a fairly wide shot showing the whole scene, everybody in it, and all of the action, from start to finish. Imagine shooting a scene of a stage play from the audience; you see the whole stage and the whole scene. It is the *master*, or reference shot, into which all the other coverage will be edited. In many cases, the master doesn't even appear in the final cut because the editor chose to use all the coverage shots. No matter. Not your job. The *master* is the master around which everyone is working.

They do this for several reasons. It gives the actors a chance to kind of relax, to run through the whole thing to get used to it, to get a feel for the scene as a whole, to establish their timing and rhythm, and work on their lines, their blocking, and so on. Since it's a long shot, little mistakes aren't so visible. Since it's a master, big mistakes will be cut out during editing. It gives the crew the same sorts of benefits. It gives the editor a starting point. It gives everybody a sense of security: if all else fails, *they* can use only the master shot and the movie still works.

As the camera moves closer and closer on subsequent shots, everyone pulls together to make the work more and more refined technically and artistically. And as the director calls for shorter shots and out-of-sequence shots, everybody stays on track. For example, he may shoot all of Johnny's stuff first, and then eventually get back around to your close ups from the top of the scene. Since you shot a master, you should easily remember what you did, and where and how, and be able to recreate it for the camera even though five hours have passed.

This master shot is probably what you just finished shooting in your café scene. It is the master reference that all the other coverage is meant to complete. That means all the other coverage must match it. Remember all the scolding I did about matching your continuity? This is why. If you poured the coffee at a certain point in the master, then you must do it exactly the same in all the coverage or it won't be usable in the editing room, meaning your shot hits the trash. If there are any such problems, then they are not going to cut out Johnny; they're going to cut out you. You lose screen time, you don't help the movie, and you don't help your career. So make the master your master. Follow its orders throughout the rest of the coverage.

You'll have plenty of time to practice because you are most likely going back to your trailer at this point. The first AD will call for the second team, and someone will invite you to relax for a while. That's because the next step in doing typical coverage is to *punch in* (move closer) on a key aspect of the scene. Translation: Johnny's shots. The director may want to do a *Johnny master*, for example, which is a mini-master inside the master-master for Johnny's reference and for even more security. If all else fails, then *they* can open on the master to set the scene, and then use all of Johnny's master for the rest, and *they* are covered. This means *they* have to reset the lights to help tell the story and sometimes to make the movie star look like a movie star. They will have to move the camera. They may have to rig up some dolly track, or a crane, or cut a hole in the ceiling for a light, or who knows what, to get the shot the director wants. Makeup might want to go to work on the star. Set decoration might want to redress a few things. The fight coordinator might want to revise the fight. This will all take time.

Go back to your trailer, congratulate yourself for getting this far, relax, manage your energy, manage your nerves, and rehearse your continuity. Think of ways you can improve your performance. Stay focused. Do not call your boyfriend. This is good general advice, but you might have gathered by now that everyone has a different way of coping. As you go along, you will find yours.

Eventually, *they* will call you back to set where you will find that everything in the room has changed position and that a camera stands where you are supposed to stand. Do not be alarmed. They are doing Johnny's shots remember? Johnny's shots will most likely be done from behind you looking at Johnny over your shoulder (an *over-the-shoulder*, or OTS shot) or from your point of view (a *POV* shot) as if the audience were looking out through your eyes. Therefore, the camera will be placed either fairly close behind you or exactly where you were standing and at exactly the same height. You are now the *off actor*, meaning we will not be seeing your face in these shots or indeed any part of you in the case of a *POV*. But we must still hear your voice, and Johnny must still be looking at you; therefore, you will be required to stand as close to the lens as possible without crashing into things. You are giving Johnny his eye line and the other side of the scene even though you are not being seen.

Let's say the director wants to do a Johnny master that picks up Johnny as he enters the place trying to look inconspicuous, and it follows him to his seat, which lands him in an over-the-shoulder shot with you (where he will play the dialogue) and then follows him as he beats up the bad guy at the next table. Your job now is to replay your side of the master as best you can, given that there is a camera in the way. Do everything the same as much as you can to help you and everyone else with their blocking, their sense of reality, etc. Land on your mark exactly at the right time, pour the coffee, and do the lines as before. It's the same thing but adjusted to meet the needs of the shot. Movies are constructed, remember? You need to be able to act for the camera, remember?

Yes, there's a camera in the way. But maybe the camera can see Johnny's coffee cup. Therefore, you need to pour the coffee. But you can't reach. Somehow you have to pour that coffee. Maybe you wind up crouching between the camera operator and the tripod. Maybe you stand on a box. Whatever. You pour, in the same way and at the same time as in the master. You also do your lines, and everything else. You will feel like a circus performer.

If the camera does not see Johnny's cup, then you can fake the pour from a distance, again faking it in the same way and with the same timing to match the master. Johnny will know what you're doing.

What if Johnny then needs to pick up the coffee where the camera can see it? Don't worry. The props crew will recognize this and will have filled the cup in advance. Therefore, you will fake-pour the coffee even though the cup is already full. Thus you help Johnny with his sense of the reality of the scene and the timing, and the coffee is ready when the camera needs to see it.

I cannot possibly give examples for every eventuality. You're just going to have to learn as you go or take a good film production class or make a little movie on your own for the experience.

Next, the camera is likely to *punch in* (move closer) even more. The director might call for a tighter *OTS* shot, for example, from when Johnny sits to when he gets up. So, now we are into coverage: smaller, tighter bits of the scene. They will probably tell you what bit they are shooting, but sometimes they forget. A smart actor pays attention at all times so she knows what's up and helps the process. This time you just need to play your part from when Johnny sits until he stands. Simple. You are still the off actor in an *OTS* (over-the-shoulder shot), so hitting your mark is paramount—only a tiny bit of your back and your shoulder will be in the shot. Half a baby-step too far to one side, and you're blocking the star. Half a step the other way and you are not in the shot. Pay close attention to your technique. You are as much a part of the crew now as the cast. And pay even closer attention to your performance. Your job is to help Johnny as much as you possibly can: match the master, hit your marks, do the blocking, pour the coffee, nail all your lines, give him your reactions, connect with all your might, and believe with all your heart. And be prepared to follow him, no matter what. Johnny might pick up his lines several times. Be ready for that. He might restart the whole scene right in the middle of the take. Go with him. He might improvise. Play along. Whatever you do, do not stop. Do whatever you can to help. Keep going until you hear cut, circle that one, going again or moving on. Most likely you will hear going again a couple of times. Then the director will probably punch in again to a true close up (*CU*), meaning just Johnny without you in it. You may have to wait a few minutes while they tweak a few things, and then picture is up. You go again. It's the same basic thing but you don't have to worry about your shoulder this time.

Then it's on to more coverage. The director will want to cover the walk in, the fight, the reactions of the patrons, and so on. This will take hours. Fights can take forever. Plus, they have to get the close ups of the bad guy and maybe another close up or two of Johnny during and after the fight. They all need lighting and camera set-ups, props, makeup, fake blood, etc. You may or may not be in these shots. They won't need you for the fight scene, perhaps, but they will need to see you in the background as Johnny walks in. The ADs will keep you informed as to what's being shot and when they need you.

Again, you simply do the same thing as in the master as best you can, and you help out wherever you can. If in doubt, then ask.

Next, the director will probably want to do some *inserts*. These are tight shots of important *things* as opposed to people. In this case, he might want a close up of the coffee splashing into the cup. He will definitely want to see the reflection of the bad guy in the clear coffee. They'll shoot an insert of that. Maybe the bad guy pulls a gun. They will want a tight shot of that too. Maybe Johnny takes the guy's wallet out of his jacket pocket and reads his name. They may want a shot of his driver's license. Again, lights, cameras, people, discussion, and time.

Each time they move the camera or significantly change the shot from the existing location, it is called a *set-up*. How many set-ups a crew can do in a day is an indication of their overall efficiency, and it impacts the budget and schedule. When *they're* shooting television— which needs to move fast—they might do 30 or 40 set-ups a day. That's a lot. That's 14 hours of hard work. You can count on an average of half an hour per set-up. A movie shoot might be significantly slower.

Okay, it is now six hours later and you see Johnny leaving. *They shot Johnny out*, meaning *they* did all his stuff so he could go home. And now (maybe 12 hours after your call time) *they* are turning all the lights and cameras around to look at you. Your turn. All your shots are coming up. Or, more likely, all your shot. It's been a long day, and unfortunately you are the day player, whom *they* love, but who is there to help Johnny with the coffee thing and that's all. So the director will most likely call for a combo master/close up of you in a single shot. Did you remember to manage your energy? This is where it pays off. Otherwise, you're liable to be a limp dishrag after all the stress and strain of the day. And now it's time for your close up. Yippee.

We've all been there. It's not fun. You wanted to be an actor. Welcome to the show.

Your job now is to follow the master yet again, but this time it's on you. Time to live the story and help your career. Quickly re-read this entire book. Then gird your loins and do your best. Remember to keep your eyes open and speak slowly. When people are nervous they tend to rattle off lines like an auctioneer, so speaking slowly enough to match your work of the morning will probably feel weird. Calm down. Take it easy.

Doing It to the Wall

Oh, and did I mention Johnny went home? Meaning he is not there for you in the way you were there for him. Instead, you will be playing the scene with the script supervisor, a non-actor, who will most likely be avoiding your gaze out of embarrassment, or lack of training, or nervousness, or simply because she has to read the lines. So, you're playing the scene to the top of her head. Sometimes she's way in a back corner and you are playing the scene to the director, or one of the stand-ins, or to somebody's palm, or a little piece of tape stuck to the side of the camera. And you alone have to recreate the whole mood and pace of the scene to match what Johnny did six hours earlier, and you have to match your continuity, knowing that if you don't, you won't make it into the movie. This again is called acting *for* the camera. This again is why your technique and overall knowledge of the game is so important. You knew this was going to happen and you prepared for it.

An example: I once played a baseball coach in a wonderful TV movie. They wanted to shoot my close up reaction as the worst player on my team stepped up to the plate, missed a couple pitches, then got his first ever hit, then ran the bases, then made a mistake at third, and then got tagged out a home plate. But *they* had already sent both teams home. There were no players, no crowd, no noise, no nothing except for me and a small camera crew on an empty baseball diamond. I had to recall what it looked like and felt like and sounded like earlier in the day, and I had to recreate my genuine reactions using only my imagination. I'm not telling you this to scare you but to inform you. It's par for the course and happens all the time.

The legendary Henry Fonda apparently used to do all his close ups looking directly into a little light called an *Inky*. He didn't use people at all. This gave him a certain consistency that he could rely on, and a lovely little glint in his eye. Orson Welles reportedly used nothing. He wanted the whole area next to the camera completely empty, and no one reading the lines. He would hear the other people's lines in his head, and he would create all the correct eye lines and pacing and all the right reactions and continuity out of his prodigious imagination.

Remember the audition? You had to do the scene with a casting director who read the lines flat as a pancake and never once looked at you? Now you know why.

The Unfortunate Games People Play

Since you are in show business, you will be familiar with certain juvenile games that actors play on each other to get more glory for themselves; they are the classic *up-stagers*. Well, it can be worse in film. Some low-minded actors will pull subtle tricks on you to mess you up and get more screen time for themselves. Usually, these games are pulled when you are on camera and they are not, which might be yet another reason why Henry and Orson did what they did. Here's a little sample:

The Energy Game

As the off actors, they will intentionally play the scene with very low energy levels. Thinking they are good and kind and know what they are doing, you will tend to match that level to create a coherent scene. That's just what they were counting on. When the camera then turns around on them, they suddenly pump the energy up knowing the editor will tend to choose the higher energy version and cut you out. Dastardly, but true.

The Lines Game

Again, when off camera, they will suddenly come down with a case of can't-remember-the-lines, causing you to stumble, bumble, and crumble.

The Psych-Out Game

Before your takes, they will insert into your mind some doubts to erode your confidence. Even something as seemingly supportive as "Wow, you're doing great" can have the desired evil consequence because it gets you thinking about how you're doing great. Then you watch yourself. You doubt yourself. You judge yourself. And then you are doomed.

The Sneaky Laughter Game

Some passive-aggressive cowardly types will try to crack you up and get you into hysterics under the guise of having a good old time together shooting a movie. Funny, but when the camera is on them, they're all business.

The Appearing or Disappearing Act

These types will appear or disappear as the off actor depending on which way freaks you out the most.

There are certainly many other such games. Beware. Hang onto yourself. Manage your confidence. Be your own person. A sovereign state. An alpha dog.

There is no doubt these games contribute to the fact that so many film actors seem very aloof, and defensive, and self-reliant, if not self-involved, if not slightly terrified and lonely at all times. There always seems to be someone out to get them, even in the sanctuary of the set. It's yet another reason why you'd better love the work and be able to do it to the wall.

If the director is any good, then he will have seen all these little tricks before and will help you out. So there's no need to be overly afraid. But do be aware.

Frame Sizes

And now a little note on acting for frame sizes. You will want your performance in the master to be slightly different from your performance in the close up.

You can think of a *long shot* (which includes your feet) as someone talking to you from across the room. Say you're at a party and someone across the room says, "Hey Ashley, didn't I see you in that Johnny Depp movie?" You would naturally raise your voice just a little bit so he could hear you, and you'd magnify your gestures and facial expressions a bit so he could read them over there by the fireplace. "Oh, my God, you saw that? How did I look?"

Right?

Well, that's your long shot performance. It's not theatrical by any means; it is natural but slightly magnified so it can be understood from 15 feet away.

Similarly, you can think of the *medium shot* (waist up) as a normal conversation with someone standing in front of you. You wouldn't shout at them, would you? In fact, you could whisper things to them without any problem. No need to overdo gestures or pull faces to get them to understand what you're saying. It's just very normal conversation for the benefit of the two of you. You wouldn't be broadcasting the talk to the rest of the room; on the contrary you would probably keep it down to prevent eavesdropping. That's your medium shot performance.

Think of the *close up* as someone lying in bed next to you having pillow talk. Everything is very small and very quiet and very intimate and mostly happens in your eyes because your lover knows what you're thinking before you say it. That's your close up performance.

Think of the *extreme close up* as a conversation with yourself. Everything happens inside your head and heart, and you don't need to express it to anyone. In fact, you're probably trying your hardest to hide it. That's your extreme close up performance. Don't worry that the camera can't see it. It can. You just need to be, to exist there in the frame, and the camera will see what you're thinking.

If you want a demonstration, then ask a theater actor friend of yours to do a scene from a play as he would on stage. Shoot him in a close up. Rewind. Laugh your head off. You will see a buffoon shouting at you and pulling faces like a clown. Of course, he is not a clown; he is an actor doing a totally appropriate performance for theater. It is just totally *inappropriate* for film. If you go and do your film performance on stage—which I have unfortunately done—then it's the same thing in reverse: you will vanish on stage.

Then repeat the exercise, but this time ask him to do nothing. No acting at all. Just say the words. Literally try to do absolutely nothing. Depending on the actor this could be difficult or impossible; it's hard for many film actors to do. But if he can do it, then play it back and watch again. What you'll see is the kind of performance you see all the time on screen.

In my classes I will occasionally put a student in a close up and ask him to just think something. It's surprising how often the class can see what it is, even when it's totally out of the blue like this, with no story context whatsoever.

You know I'm a big fan of Michael Caine. In his show on film acting for the BBC, he tells this story: Jack Lemmon was one of the most famous film actors of his day but he came from the stage. On one of his early projects he was working with director George Cukor. Jack did a take. George called cut and said, "Jack, smaller." Next take: same thing. Smaller! Finally, Jack gets impatient and says, "Jeez, George, if I do any less I'll be doing nothing." George nods and says, "Now you've got it.'

The camera seeks the close up, the audience craves the close up, it's the close up that sells you and gives you your career, so if in doubt, do everything in pillow talk. You will lure the camera in. At least get very, very comfortable with the pillow talk performance. It is your bread and butter and future fortune.

These various performances would be a lot easier to do if the camera was where it was supposed to be when you did them, i.e. right in your face for the pillow talk. You would naturally make everything more intimate. The trouble is, it isn't. The camera can have you in a close up from across the street and in a long shot from five feet away. So, find out what size shot you're in—just ask—and then do the appropriate performance. I have seen very experienced film actors ask the camera crew what lens they're using, which tells them what shot size they are in.

Of course, there are exceptions to every rule. Some directors hate it when you ask such questions. *They* want you to be raw and raging and completely unaware of the filmmaking process. *They* think *they'll* get a better performance out of you. *They* just want you to act and leave everything else up to them. Fine. Do that. But you had better hope that he's a good director, because otherwise you can come off looking really bad when you are invisible in the long shot and shouting at the audience in the close up.

Working with Directors

I've said elsewhere that directors are like a box of chocolates: you never know what you're going to get. Some have literally no idea what they're doing; some you can trust with your life. Some are very savvy and work differently depending on the actor in question. Some wouldn't know how to talk to you even if they did want to say something. Some are terrified of you. Others hate you just for being beautiful and talented because deep down they really want to be beautiful and talented. Some of them are legendary movie stars, like Kevin Costner and Clint Eastwood. Then you get your writers, your former DOPs, your producers, your talented youngsters, your nephews of producers, your theater directors, your drug addicted former greats, your geniuses, your idiots, your screamers, your charmers, your communicators, your players, and your wannabes. Whatever you can imagine, that guy or gal has been a director and will be again.

This is why the BFSs are so careful about which directors they work with.

Don't like it? Too bad. He's got the job. He's the boss. You need to do your job. Ignore him, shout back at him, calmly argue your case, befriend him, tolerate him, whatever. Figure it out. I can't really help you. The actor/director relationship has been both a rocky road and a beautiful friendship throughout movie history. That's the biz. If you find one you really connect with, then you are artistically and economically blessed.

Examples:

John Ford with John Wayne.

Martin Scorsese with Robert De Niro.

Sidney Pollack with Robert Redford.

If you are incredibly lucky, then you'll befriend two! Stephen Spielberg and George Lucas with Harrison Ford. Nice going, Harrison.

On my most recent gig, the director was a prince of a guy. We laughed, we joked around, we collaborated, and we had lunch together. I realized after the fact how many subtle things he was doing to help me out, from blocking scenes a certain way, to changing my lines so they'd suit me better, to lighting me in certain ways, to the little bits of direction he'd give me. Most of all, he gave me confidence to do my best work. A dream. I can only hope to work with him again.

Advice: learn how to do your best work regardless of the director, and build a network of directors who like working with you. You might be the next Dark Knight.

Here are a few more general suggestions about working with directors:

Reach Out

Do not wait for him to come to you. You are the *actor*, the bright light, the magical artist who will bring his vision to life. Think of yourself as the prettiest girl at the ball. Everyone is kind of scared of you, so make the first move.

Find a Common Tongue

You two need to communicate somehow, so let this be your first priority. Some of *them* are actors themselves and know exactly what you're going through; others are simply terrified of you and your black magic. Try to find the common ground and a way to work together. If you find none, then at least you know you are on your own and can make plans.

Check Your Ego at the Door

After opening official relations, this is the single best thing you can do. If you don't want to hear from him at all, then go ahead and be an egomaniac. No one will talk to you. Ever. If you want to be a working actor, then make it about the story and the filmmaking process. Let him know you are on board, that you cannot be offended by anything, that you are open to discussion, direction, collaboration and getting the job done, and that you have easy confidence and complete control over your craft.

Manage Expectations

It's always a good idea to get a sense of each other's expectations. When I'm directing, I like to have a little expectations talk early on in the process. Actors visibly relax. I relax too when I hear what they have in mind, if anything. It gives us a starting point and a way to work. Not all directors are as forthcoming, so come forth yourself and find out what he's expecting. He might say, "Your audition was great." Now you know he expects to see what he saw. He might say, "I love it when actors are anarchists. Crazy, wild beasts!"

Then you know that.

Either way, you can manage those expectations.

Talk Story

Directors don't want to hear about your process. They couldn't care less, unless it becomes clear that hearing about it is the only way to get the movie made. Then you'll get a reluctant ear. Otherwise, it's pretty much in the same category as hearing about the plumber's process. Don't really care. Just fix the sink.

On the other hand, they are very interested in story. Talk about that all you want.

If I'm directing, and I hear my actress say something like, "We want heartbreak here, right? She's swearing at him, but what she's really saying is 'I love you,' so it's her confession really, which will res-onate when she says the exact same line at the wedding later in the movie, right? So, we want to break the audience's heart here?" then I just want to hug her for all time and put her in every film I ever do. She gets it. She's confirming it with me, and we are on the same page. We have a chance to discuss it and take it even deeper. I can go set up my shots with an easy mind, and she can go do her process with confidence, and we can meet in the middle of the scene. Thank God.

Be Ahead of the Game

In my experience, one of the main problems that slows down a shoot is having to stop everything to tell the actors what's going on. To do their job for them. This drives me nuts. We work our butts off to set up the shot—to set up the whole project—and the actor saunters up and says, "What are we doing?" He's not asking about the set-up; he's asking me to explain the story and the scene and the sub-text and everything else so he can then do his next crappy performance without doing any work at all.

On one of my films, we spent seven hours, *seven hours*, trying to get the leading man to understand and play a key scene so it would advance the story. He couldn't get it. So we tried to get him to just do it. Literally do the stuff the script called for in some kind of order so we could save the movie. Not a complicated scene: a little kitchen romance scene, eat, give her a ring, and say the words. He'd had the script for a month. Never once in those 30 days did he mention that he didn't get the scene and couldn't play it. We had no time nor money for reshoots. If we didn't get it, then we were toast. We tried and tried and tried. We flattered him, we explained it to him, we asked what we could do for him, we explained the importance of the scene, we got the leading lady to talk to him, and we lost our tempers in his general direction. Nothing. He didn't get it and couldn't do it. We tried shooting it in little chunks. Couldn't do it. He wasn't drunk or stoned or trying to sabotage us. It was like all the wires in his head were suddenly disconnected, and he didn't care. He never 'manned-up,' and tried to help or offer suggestions or do anything. He was like a crash-test dummy. Everyone on set was inwardly shaking his or her heads. I had to strenuously restrain myself from killing him, because he was killing my movie dead before my eyes. I hated all actors at that moment, and I'm sure there's still a little residual hatred even now. Eventually, we just ran out of time. We turned around on the leading lady, shot her stuff—all perfect—in 60 minutes, and went home. The movie was never released.

Don't be that guy.

The End of the Day

After you've mastered all this, after you have completed all the coverage, after you have shot your last shot of your first day, you will hear something like this: "Well, that's a *picture wrap* for you."

You will be momentarily stunned. Then you will realize that you are done. *Wrapped* for the picture. In other words, there is nothing more for you to do on this movie. You're done. Then you will continue to be stunned because it suddenly seems to have been a dream. You will wonder if you were there at all.

If it's a very polite set, then *they* make an announcement: "Everybody? That's a picture wrap for Ashley, our waitress." Everyone will pause from his or her labors to give you a limp round of applause. It's going to be limp because people are busy and sweaty and the whole thing is kind of awkward and no one ever applauds for them. You will give a little wave and a smile. They will turn back to their jobs.

Try now to sneak in a little thank you to the director and Johnny and everyone else you can think of before they are too far gone into the next thing, and before the AD hustles you off to the trailer to get out of your wardrobe. For now, you are no longer a glorious actor, the queen of all you survey. You are a girl who is taking up space in a trailer that they need for the next guy. So quickly do your rounds, say thanks, shake hands, kiss babies, but make it fast. As you know, *they* are busy.

When done, you will be traveled to your trailer.

Grant will often wait for you to change out of your wardrobe, and then possibly invite you to have your make-up removed, and then ask you to sign out. You see, every extra second costs them money, so they will be eager to officially end your day by having you sign out on your union paperwork. Usually they will ask you to do that in their trailer so they can keep all their paperwork in one place and because someone will already be in your trailer cleaning it up. If it is still early in the day, then there will be another actor in there in a few minutes. If it's at the end of day, then they just want to go home.

And that's it.

Have a nice day.

That's it?

That's it. Have a nice day.

And you will smile fakely, and head out to your car. Still kind of stunned, you will pull away. You will wave at the guy in the traffic vest. You will turn onto a main road. Someone will cut you off. Never fails. You will yell at him, "Hey! Watch it! Do you know who I am?"

He will give you a rude hand gesture.

You will realize you're back in the real world.

You will drive home.

You will take out the garbage.

You will recall the early pages of this book in which I said you had better love the work because the rest of it is a pain in the ass. You will know that I was right. You will accept it. You will be happy you helped the film, you booked a job, you made some money, you built your resume, you got some experience, you met Johnny Depp and you played waitress for a day. You gave yourself a chance to do it all again sometime. Maybe to do it as a full-time job one of these days.

If you are smart—and you are—then you will now promote yourself to the world based on your recent success. You will report back to your agent, and your friends, and your associates in the biz. You will make sure all your Internet pages are up to date: your own site, your agent's site, Facebook, Twitter, IMDB, and all your casting sites. You will update your resume. You will look for ways to get the word out that you are experienced, employable, and have worked with Johnny Depp. If you asked Johnny for a photo, and he consented, and you didn't get fired, then you will post that everywhere you can think of. You will keep training and working your business.

Nine months later: you get a call from a friend saying, "Oh my God, your movie is out!" And you will get a ticket like everybody else, and you will go. (No, you are not going to get an invitation to the premiere in Los Angeles.) You will buy a ticket, you will go, you will be amazed and weirded-out by seeing yourself flash by saying "Would you like cream with that?" to Johnny Depp. Your friend will elbow you in the ribs.

You will feel proud but awkward. People will ask you questions. They will all be about Johnny Depp. You will answer that he was nice, and great to work with, and he puts his pants on one leg at a time, and it was hard work but a lot of fun. The conversation will turn to something else.

Walking to your car you will feel terribly regular.

Soon it will all be forgotten.

A week later, your agent will call saying, "Hi. I have an audition for you tomorrow for a low-budget movie called *Zombie Breasts of Death*. You'd be reading for another waitress, but this one kills two zombies and then gets impaled on a fencepost. A nice step up! Okay?"

And you sigh.

And you wonder.

And you laugh and you shake your head.

And you say, "What time is my audition?"

.

APPENDIX

50 STUPID STUNTS IN
THE AUDITION ROOM

1. **You sent your *Regrets*.** After going to all the trouble to get a casting director to invite you in for an audition, you decided to go to Disneyland instead, asking your agent to apologize on your behalf. I suppose you think you're being helpful. Well, no. It would have been helpful to save everyone the trouble in the first place. Do it too many times and you'll quit getting invitations and have to start looking for a new agent or a new career.

2. You **Didn't Show Up**. It's bad to send your regrets, but it's just plain criminal not to show up when you are expected. Now you look flakey and unreliable, your agent looks bad, the casting director is disgruntled and potentially embarrassed, and the actor who could have taken your place hates your guts. By forgetting that the first rule of show business is to show up, you made it worse for everyone. Lucky for you there's lots of openings in the food service industry.

3. You were **Late**. At least you showed up. If you're smart, then you'll make a simple apology ('Traffic!') hope they'll still see you, try not to let it affect your focus, and start working right away to rebuild your reputation as a reliable actor. Start with an extra-brilliant audition, and don't do it again.

4. You went **Green in the Greenroom**. You let the sight of the other actors psych you out, and they did everything possible to frazzle your nerves, undermine your confidence, and disperse your focus. You prepared for failure. Maybe next time think about doing it the other way around.

5. You **Second-Guessed Yourself**. You totally lost confidence in your preparation and yourself and sabotaged yourself by changing your mind at the last minute. So you came in confused and doubtful. Good luck. Next time, have a little faith in yourself, make a strong choice, and give *them* some confidence.

6. You **Doubted Yourself**. You forgot that you are enough. You always have been. You always will be. You are a child of God, entirely unique. You have no competition, unless you doubt yourself and try to be like someone else.

7. You made a **Horrible Entrance**. Forgetting that *they* make up *their* minds about you in the first two seconds, you gave *them* every reason not to like you: mostly by being self-involved and scared to death. Next time, try a little confidence. Maybe a smile? Some enthusiasm for the project and your craft?

8. You **Unloaded**. You walked in lugging everything you own: a large bag, a briefcase, a purse, your coat, your scarf, a poodle, and your son Max. It took five minutes to unload everything before you hit your mark. Sorry, time's up. Especially since it's going to take you another five to re-load. Leave it in the car or the green room.

9. You were **Unprepared**. You didn't learn your lines, you didn't bother to rehearse the scene, you didn't bother to read the script, you neglected to relax and focus, you forgot your headshot, and your dog ate your resume. Yeah, that'll work.

10. You came in with **Attitude**. You strutted around like the Queen of Sheba at the mall, asked the casting director if she would like to neck later, and told the producer his last picture was lame-o. Funny you didn't get that part. You must have been too good.

11. You **Slimed** everybody. You insisted on shaking everybody's hand even if *they* didn't want to, or you even proceeded to hug and kiss and fawn over everybody in the room, offend *them* with your bad breath, chat about your life, leave your perfume on *their* clothes, and ask when *they're* going to hire you. How about win-

ning *them* over with your talent and skill instead of your creepy social skills?

12. You came in with a million **Excuses**. You have excuses for everything. You just got the script 20 minutes ago, your blouse was at the dry cleaners, your brain isn't working today, you got lost trying to find the place, you were in the hospital last night with laryngitis, you drank too much coffee, and you're just not feeling good lately. Then you thought it would be a good idea to plead for the part and beg for special treatment. From now on, if you're there, you have no excuses. Get it?

13. You did a **Crappy Slate.** Well, first you said, "What's a slate?" And then you mangled your name and looked scared out of your mind. Sure, they gotta love that.

14. You **Faked** your headshot and resume. Yep, you thought it'd be smart to run your headshot through Photoshop a little bit, making you look like Claudia Schiffer when in fact you more closely resemble Danny DeVito. I guess you thought *they* wouldn't notice. Then you cleverly padded your resume by claiming you'd done five seasons of live television in the Australian Outback and understudied for Angelina Jolie on that movie she did. Sure, you'll get away with that.

15. You were **Nervous**. You came in all shaky, and strange, and couldn't really talk at all, and not to mention you couldn't hear at all, got dry mouth, nearly passed out, and when the camera rolled you totally freaked and took off like a jail-break instead of a) admitting it, b) seeing it as excitement instead of fear, or c) using it as ammo in your performance.

16. You decided it was all about the **Wardrobe**. You went out and rented a police uniform and a dog for the audition forgetting that what *they* want are actors, not wardrobe assistants, models, or sniveling hopefuls. On the other hand, some of you erred in the reverse. You decided that clothes shouldn't matter at all, so you wore cut-off jeans, tattoos, a Metallica T-shirt and a nose ring to your audition for that Washington lawyer guy. I wonder why you didn't get the part.

17. You didn't **Take Over the Room**. You came in like a puppy and let *them* push you around and tell you want to do. Any time

they have to direct you in any way, *they* lose confidence in you. Professionals don't need to be directed, or maybe you forgot.

18. You **Let Them Freak You Out**. Yeah, *they* are strangers who are judging you. So what? That's the biz you wanted to get into. Selling yourself often means being unsuccessful. Deal with it by realizing that *they* do want to hire you, *they* do want you to be good, and *they* do want to help you if *they* can. And get on with it.

19. You **Didn't Make the Scene Audition Friendly.** You came in, examined the dead body in the corner where no one could see you, French-kissed the air, and then ran out of the room to get the police. Where nobody could see you. Just keep running until you figure a way to play it where *they* can see you, where it's about the scene and not your stupid distractions. Make the scene work for an audition. It's not the movie.

20. You weren't **Technically Correct**. You missed your mark, screwed up your eye lines, spoke too loud and too fast, blinked your brains out, entered at the wrong time, and flipped through your sides looking for your lines. Notice: you need to be able to act for the camera, which means technique matters.

21. You **Offended the Nose**. You smokers thought it would be smart to have five in a row before your audition and come in smelling like a tar cloud. Some of you spilled the cologne, some of you haven't showered for a week, and still others need a mint in the worst way. Apparently, you thought offending *them* right out of the gate would work wonders. How about just be clean and fragrance-free and make it about the performance rather than the aroma?

22. You didn't **Apply Your Brand**. You forgot that you walk around broadcasting a message whether you like it or not, and that message is kind of important. It's the number one reason why *they* called you in in the first place. And then you left it at home? How about having the courage to bring yourself to it next time?

23. You went a little heavy on the **Chemical Courage**. If *they* don't sniff you out in the room, then *they* will definitely see that you smoked or drank your cares away when *they* project it on a big screen later. This job takes guts. Get some or get out.

24. You **Asked To Do It Again**. *They* are looking for reasons not to cast you, so the longer you are in the room, and the more times

you do it, the more ammo you give *them* with which to shoot you down. You probably closed the deal and then unclosed it by your lame lack of confidence. Even if your performance was 20 percent better, then *they* are now 80 percent more convinced that you are weirdly unsure of yourself. You lose. It's showbiz, baby; shoot both barrels and get off stage.

25. You **Did a Cliché.** Apparently, you think commonplace, old, and banal is what makes a star. Good luck.

26. You **Tried to Think Your Way Through It**. Apparently, you think real people rehearse all their scenes and then direct themselves as they go along. Odd. By the way, *they* can see you do it. Next time, get out of your own way; just try to get what you want and let the scene take care of itself.

27. You weren't **Ready For Anything**. You had it all worked out in your head, and then you freaked out when it didn't fit into the audition room. You can't plan spontaneous action, dude. Roll with the surf. Have an intent, and make it fit the room, the circumstances, and whatever bullcrap *they* hand you.

28. You **Made it about the Props.** You brought a ferret for your audition for that veterinarian guy. How charming. What a great way to get *them* to focus on anything but you. Wanna bring in the newspaper? Be prepared for *them* to read the headlines you've put in their face and ignore you. Maybe stop hiding behind stuff? Maybe bring in what you want *them* to hire? As in: you.

29. You didn't **Set The Stage.** If you don't know that you are in a courtroom for this scene, then *they* won't either. You'll look like a dumb actor in an audition room. You've got to know everything about your scene, including what your pen looks like, who's next to you, and where the judge sits. Kind of important. The more you set this stage in your mind and believe it, the more *they'll* believe. Which is kind of the point.

30. You **Raced Through It.** Apparently you think the fastest actor wins. Nope.

31. You **Didn't Have any Fun.** You came in and suffered through the whole experience thinking *they* wouldn't notice. Well, noticing is what *they* do. And suffering is not that attractive as a sales technique. *They* suffer enough on their own; *they* don't need to be reminded.

32. You Brought Out the Boobs. Forgetting that boobs are not an accomplishment, you were falling out of your top. Or maybe you made sure *they* were seeing through your top. You distracted everybody and made t*hem* all feel a bit cheaper. Keep them in the holster, please.

33. You made it all about the **Lines**. Yes, in a stage play we tell the story with dialogue; I understand that. But in a movie, we tell the story with pictures; the dialogue is almost always at odds with those pictures. That's what makes it interesting. But you thought the actor's job was to say the lines, in order, fast as you can, to the end. There, I did it. Or you decided the script was crap and rewrote the whole thing better. The writer has to appreciate your vast talent, right? Next.

34. When the camera turned on, you **Turned off.** You made the huge mistake of making the real-life-you better than the on-camera-you, leaving the impression that you're a special person who can't bring any of it to the screen. You forgot that it's *you* they want, not half-you, or actor-you. You. All of you. And you either had so little faith or let others bully *you* so much, that you left you out of the audition. Dope.

35. You didn't make a **Choice**. You played the scene right 'on the nose' without a hint of sub-text and without applying your brand, hoping somehow to sneak through the audition and get hired by covering none of the bases. By not making a specific choice about the underlying truth of the scene, you displayed no courage, took no risk, and did no intelligent actor homework at all. What you did do was the same as the last ten people through the door: the obvious and the bland. Good luck.

36. You **Twitched.** When the camera rolled, you moved around like a jumping bean, blinked incessantly, walked in and out of frame, did weird things with your mouth, and stuck your finger in your ear for some reason. Just stand and deliver. Anything more means your work isn't tight enough.

37. You **Looked at the Camera**. The camera does not exist in the courtroom, so why are you looking at it? Answer: because you are a terrified amateur. Re-read this entire book.

38. You **Overacted**. The camera sees everything in extreme close up: all your attempts to be funny, to project, to throw your per-

formance to the back of the room, to indicate or 'telegraph' what you are feeling, are all wasted on it. It doesn't want acting; it wants behavior—real, quiet, and believable behavior. It's like lying to the cops.

39. You didn't deliver **Vocally.** Forgetting that your voice is half your image, you came in looking like Steve McQueen but sounding like Daffy Duck. You spoke too fast, or too loud, or you mumbled meekly, or smeared your enunciations like a tongueless cur, or announced your lines like a game show host. Please! Get real and believable.

40. You didn't **Connect**. You played the scene like a robot, forgetting that acting is about connecting with another person and having a real-life, believable, conflicted, emotional exchange. That's why there's a reader in the room. You act with that person, not at them. Get it?

41. You didn't **Adjust**. When the director asked you to make a change, or 'adjustment,' in your performance, you agreed, you even had a brainy talk about why that was such a good idea, and then you went ahead and did it exactly the same way a second time. By doing so, you showed that you are either bizarrely defiant, thickheaded, a crummy journeyman actor, or otherwise completely intractable. Moments later your headshot hit the trash bin and your career hit the skids. You must be flexible in your performance and able to make changes moment by moment. Go back to class until you can do it.

42. You **Apologized**. Even worse than making a million excuses, you thought it would be a good idea to simply apologize in advance for how crappy you are, how wrong, inexperienced and unimportant you are, as well as how stupid *they* were for calling you in at all. If you were a very idiotic apologizer, then you waited until after you did a perfectly good audition and then apologized, making you look like a total loser, and making the auditors feel like losers for liking what you did in the first place. Never apologize. Ever.

43. You **Picked Up the Energy in the Room.** Sure, you're an actor, so mimicking people and picking up their energy is what you do. Just don't do it in the room. The auditors are usually hot, cranky, impatient, frazzled, and often downright freaked out. Sometimes

the producer and director hate each other with a palpable odor. Leave *them* to *their* torture and do what you came to do. In spite of *them*. Unless of course you want your love scene to have a nice, smelly, freaked out overtone. Focus like a pole-vaulter in the green room, and don't pick up the crappy vibes.

44. You **Let the Reader Throw You**. You never know what you're going to get. Might be an actor; might be a janitor. If you're really unlucky, then it'll be the casting director who will try to even the playing field by rattling off the lines in a meek mutter. Generally speaking, your reader will suck, forcing you to create the entire thing on your own. Guess what? You're probably going to have to do that anyway on the set. So be ready for anything in the room. By the way, if you luck out and get a talented reader who tries to steer you in a particular direction, then odds are good you should go.

45. You did a **Crappy Accent**. If *they* don't ask, then don't do. Simple. If *they* do ask, then make it perfect. Also simple. Sadly, the American Idol rule applies here: most people who think they can do accents can't. If, in fact, you can, then you'll prosper. If you can't, then you'll feel a swift kick around your ass area. Your audition must be done in either a perfect Standard American accent—the accent of the Movies—or a perfect version of the requested accent. When in doubt, it's Standard American. Nothing else will do. If you can't do Standard American, then take classes until you can. Don't assume you can. Even Americans have to learn Standard American.

46. You **Repeated Yourself.** You did a good strong scene, got a chance to do it again, and then repeated your actions and blocking exactly for the second take, making us think it was a device and not an impulse. Each take should be a completely new event.

47. You **Stopped.** You got 90 percent of the way through your three-minute scene, forgot one word, and stopped. You actually stopped and said, "Sorry, can I do it again?" Well, actually, no. You can't. Even if *they* say, "sure, go ahead," you can't. *They* don't have time, you ruined *their* take, you branded yourself an amateur, you showed that you have zero ability to stay in a scene, let alone save a scene with a little improvisation. You offended your audience, you judged yourself, you violated set protocol, and you

made all it about you... shall I go on? Because you should. At the cost of your life, get through to the end and wait for cut. Pay close attention: real people do not say, "Sorry, can we stop?"

48. You **Offended People**. You thought it wise to interrupt and contradict the director, for example, in front of everyone else in the room, which later caused the casting director to apologize and lose her job, which later became an angry phone call to your agent, which later resulted in you looking for work at a tuna packing plant. Everyone appreciates professional give-and-take. No one likes a no-class jerk.

49. You totally forgot that **Everything Counts.** You spent the previous evening in a bar, loudly complaining about a certain casting director, not knowing you were complaining to her hairdresser or that the bartender was actually her brother-in-law. You got drunk, started a fight, and tried to pick up several married women, and then rolled into the audition smelling like a brewery. You eventually did a great audition, but for some reason you didn't get the part. Damn casting directors.

50. You made a horrible **Exit.** Yes, you did everything right all along and then fell over a chair gloating on the way out. Congrats, you just erased all the good you'd done. Try again some other time.

APPENDIX

50 STUPID STUNTS ON SET

1. **You were *late*.** You forgot that early is on time, and on time is late. Oh, and late is looking for another job.
2. **You were *hung over or 'medicated'*.** Everybody knows, and will start thinking about how to work around you, or without you.
3. **You brought a *friend*.** Did your friend get cast, too? No? Oh, so you just wanted to show off? Have someone hold your hand? When you knew it wasn't allowed? How great.
4. **You didn't *read the call sheet*.** It tells you everything about your day, like for example, when and where and with whom you're shooting your big scene. So you can be ready. So, maybe you'd better look at it?
5. **You didn't *check your script for changes*.** The script may have changed overnight. You may have a whole new scene. There's a copy of it on the table in your trailer. Keep up, please.
6. **You *changed your hair or makeup* in your trailer.** Yeah, don't do that, you dummy. They're going to notice, change it back, and report to the producer.
7. **You were a *rude jerk*.** Right off the bat you made sure nobody liked you. That's got to be helpful, right?
8. **You were a *bad-mouther*.** It doesn't matter who you're bad-mouthing, or why. Bad-mouthing is a boomerang that comes back to knock you out of the business.

9. **You brought a *camera*.** Most sets forbid cameras. So, don't bring one, and don't get sneaky with your cell phone either.

10. **You *were a fan*.** You asked the star for an autograph and a selfie, then asked a million questions about her personal life. She's got to love that, and not have you fired. Right? If you want to be a fan, you will end up where the fans are: outside looking in.

11. **You just wanted to *run lines*.** Although some are willing, most screen actors have their own, private, method of preparing, and would rather not run lines before the shoot. Especially the stars. Take a hint.

12. **You went *off the grid*.** The assistant directors need to know where you are at all times in case you are needed. If you want to disappear so badly, why not just stay gone, and let somebody else do the job?

13. **You were *unprepared*.** This is number one on the list of capital offences. Do your homework, and be ready. No excuses.

14. **You got *nervous*.** The second capital offence, and the most difficult for many to deal with. Deal with it. Find a way.

15. **You were an *egomaniac*.** The third capital offence. I won't give you any advice, because you won't listen anyway. Good luck in food service.

16. **You *stopped a take*.** No matter what, save the take wherever possible. Pick up your lines, call for a line, make it up, or look at a script. It's what the pros do; why don't you do it too?

17. **You were *difficult*.** Filmmaking is all about collaboration. You didn't collaborate. See the problem?

18. **You *complained*.** Oh, everybody loves it when vain, coddled, over-paid, beautiful children sit in their luxury trailers and whine.

19. **You *spilled beet juice on your wardrobe*.** Be careful eating and drinking, please? Your space suit took four days to make.

20. **You were a *creepy pick up artist*.** I hope that's all I need to say about that.

21. **You weren't *ready when they were*.** Um, you're getting paid to be ready when *they* are. That's filmmaking. And, no, it doesn't matter that we've been here for 14 hours already.

22. **You didn't *learn anybody's name*.** Everyone on set will know

your name to help you feel welcomed and valued. You have a convenient list of their names in your hand. Hmmm.

23. **You were a *monkey wrench*.** You ruined somebody else's take by not fitting into the flow of the shoot, and knowing set etiquette. Keep your eyes open, stay out of the way and learn how it all works.

24. **You started *directing the movie yourself*.** In fact, you started doing everybody's job but your own. I guess you don't really want to be an actor after all?

25. **You didn't *hit your marks*.** What's the matter with you? Everybody on set needs you to hit your marks so *they* can do their jobs. Plus, you're going to look better.

26. **You forgot to *be the guy*.** Remember to use all your talent and skill to not 'act'. Get your mind behind the scene, explore it, react, and be the guy.

27. **You kept asking to *do it again*.** Just a reminder that you are not the director. Plus, we don't have time. And it's expensive. And your lack of confidence is contagious. And you're being difficult. And the editor is going to build your performance in post-production, so every take doesn't have to be perfect. Thanks.

28. **You started *coaching the other actors*.** Yeah, other actors hate this just as much as you would. It's not your job. Don't be a jerk. Don't interfere with their process. Don't offend anybody. Work with what you get.

29. **You couldn't *adjust*.** You could only do the scene the way you practiced, and couldn't make changes as required. Wow. So, where did you park?

30. **You *shot all your bullets in the rehearsal*.** Be careful to save it for the take. Manage your energy so you can deliver when the cameras roll.

31. **You *blinked and blinked*.** Blinking on camera makes you look weak. It is very distracting from the story. Each blink is chance for the audience to disengage with you. Actors blink when they can't remember their lines. And a few other things. Keep your eyes open like all good screen actors do. Okay? And maybe slow down as well?

32. **You did the *wrong performance for the frame*.** You did your

pillow-talk performance in the long shot, and yelled at the camera in the close up. Oops.

33. **You botched your *continuity*.** Continuity is your job. Plan it and lock it in, so the editor can cut your scene together and keep you in the movie.

34. **You *couldn't do it to the wall*.** You will frequently be asked to act for the camera without your scene partner present. Practice by doing scenes to a sticky note on your wall at home. Feel free to draw two little eyes on it to help your reality.

35. **You couldn't *match the master*.** Your performance in this close-up needs to match the master shot from last week. Your job, again.

36. **You *upstaged the other actors*.** You are one of those jerks who try to upstage and derail your fellow actors to get more screen time for yourself. How was your last day on set?

37. **You tried to *pull focus*.** You stood in the background trying everything to get the audience to look at you instead of at the main action in the scene. I don't think the director will notice.

38. **You couldn't *ride the horse*.** You are one of those dumb actors who lie about your skills, like your ability to ride a horse. If you're lucky, *they'll* just 're-cast' you. Meaning, you're fired. If you're unlucky, *they'll* let the horse bite you first.

39. **You started *gripping*.** You offered to help move things, or set up lights, or carry the camera so you wouldn't come across as a snobby actress. Well, somebody already has that job, and they do it better than you. Plus, you could get sweaty, tired, dirty, distracted and injured. Focus on your job, please.

40. **You didn't get the *accent*.** There is an accent of the movies in general, and perhaps an accent for this one in particular. Master it long before you get on set, so you'll have enough brain power for everything else.

41. **You tried to *brave the cold weather*.** It's fine to be a hero in the movie, but don't try to be one on the set. *They* need you alive and well for the rest of the shoot. Let *them* look after you.

42. **You *let yourself get tired*.** Managing your energy is a big part of your job. You need to be ready for anything at all times.

43. **You *took it personally*.** Plumbers, lawyers and baristas don't

take it personally when they make mistakes, or when people complain. They get on with the job. Why don't you do that?

44. **You didn't reach out and *find a way to work with the director.*** Directors are thought to be gods, but most of them are actually people who would like to have a good working relationship with you. And they would really love it if you helped out.

45. **You forgot *this whole thing is about story.*** Your number one responsibility is to tell the story. Let that be your guide for the day.

46. **You forgot to *use your brand and put some special sauce on top.*** But feel free to use what sells you, too.

47. **You forgot all *the people and things that are helping you.*** Calm down. Everyone and everything is there to help you. You are standing on a lot of shoulders. It's going to be okay.

48. **You *gained five pounds.*** You started nervous-eating, and ate yourself out of the wardrobe.

49. **You made a *terrible exit.*** On the way out, you thought it would be a good idea to tell the producers how to do a better job. And that the script needs work.

50. **You *stole the shirt.*** Some actors think it's fun to steal things out of their trailer when they leave, like bits of wardrobe. That's just so loveable! We're thinking of ways to hire you again right now!

Well, there you go. I've given you everything I can think of to help instruct and inspire you as you navigate this crazy but wonderful biz.

For updates and even more information, visit me at www.peterskagen.com.

I wish you all the best.

See you in the Movies.

Peter Skagen has an MA in screenwriting, and over 35 years experience as a professional actor, director, producer, screenwriter, and coach. He is currently in Beijing producing a movie.
Learn on-line at www.peterskagen.com

Photo by Raymond Yu

Printed in Great Britain
by Amazon